Christian Soc.
Involvement

Not Only Dreamers

Not Only Dreamers

The Story of
Martin Luther King, Sr.
and Martin Luther King, Jr.

David R. Collins

With a Chronology of the Lives and Times of Martin
Luther King, Sr. and Martin Luther King, Jr. developed
by Barbara Armentrout and Sterling Stuckey and The
Peace Museum, Chicago, Illinois

BRETHREN PRESS
Elgin, Illinois

Not Only Dreamers
The Story of Martin Luther King, Sr. and
Martin Luther King, Jr.

Copyright © 1986 by David R. Collins
BRETHREN PRESS, 1451 Dundee Avenue, Elgin, IL 60120

Cover design by Ken Stanley
Chronological timeline editor, Barbara Armentrout

Scripture quotations are from the King James Version (KJV) of the Holy Bible.
Negro spirituals have been stylized according to *Songs of Zion*, Abingdon Press, 1981.
The Chronological timeline is adapted from The Peace Museum, Chicago, Illinois, exhibit "Dr. Martin Luther King Jr.— Peacemaker" (January-April 1984), Barbara Armentrout and Sterling Stuckey, curators. Used with permission.

Library of Congress Cataloging-in-Publication Data

Collins, David R.
    Not only dreamers.

    1. Afro-Americans—Biography. 2. Baptists—United States—Clergy—Biography. 3. King, Martin Luther, 1899-   . 4. King, Martin Luther. I. Title.
E185.96.C65   1986   323.4'092'2 [B]   85-22440
ISBN 0-87178-612-5

Printed in the United States of America

This book is dedicated to the memory of Mary Brecht Collins and Raymond A. Collins who shared their love, their faith . . . and their dreams.

Preface

Christmas, 1967.

As the holidays once again pulled the members of the King family together for traditional observances, Martin Luther King Jr. could not hide his troubled feelings. Faces of the poor and homeless Vietnamese people haunted him, as America continued to be embroiled in this overseas conflict. Because of increased defense spending in Vietnam, programs to help the poor at home had been severely slashed. There was constant bickering among his own staff members, some wanting to move more slowly and others wanting to pick up the pace of activity. As he did so often, M. L. shared his problems with his father.

"Sometimes I feel like we only have God on our side," the younger King commented.

Daddy King nodded, then smiled. "It could always be worse, boy," the old man answered. "Just think if God was against us."

As father and son, Martin Luther King Sr. and Martin Luther King Jr. shared an unusual bond of devotion and understanding. They argued ideas and convictions, explored new attitudes, and offered each other strength.

Not that either man was without flaw. Few men could be as stubborn and domineering as Daddy King. He lacked intellectual depth, patience, and often noted he could be taken to court for his crimes against the English language. As for Martin Luther King Jr., his temper was widely known and frequently displayed. He yielded to temptation of both the flesh and spirit. He could be arrogant and brash, moody and brooding.

But the contributions of Martin Luther King Sr. and Martin Luther King Jr. offer inspiration and direction to every Christian. Few individuals suffered greater personal insult and loss than these two men. Yet both men stuck rigidly to a code of nonviolence and forgiveness. Daddy King, who lost a son and a wife to assassins' bullets, had little use for those who stood in judgment of the men convicted of the killings.

"I don't hate James Earl Ray or Marcus Chenault," he declared. "There is not time for hate, and no reason either. Nothing that a man does takes him lower than when he allows himself to fall so low as to hate anyone."

It is hoped the reader will want to know more about each of these men after *Not Only Dreamers* is read. For a more personal and thorough account of the life of Martin Luther King Sr., the volume *Daddy King* (1980) is highly recommended. King, Sr. provides an autobiographical look at his life with the help of writer Clayton Riley. For a definitive biography of Martin Luther King Jr., *Let the Trumpet Sound*, by Stephen B. Oates (1982) is superb. Both of these titles were most useful in piecing together the story contained in this book. Important information was also gathered from past issues of the *Atlanta Constitution* newspaper, as well as other sources. A select list of source material is included in the Bibliography of this volume.

The author is extremely grateful to all those who read the manuscript and made helpful suggestions. A special word of thanks goes to The Peace Museum, Chicago, Illinois, for their permission to use and adapt an exhibit timeline for M. L. King, Jr. Likewise, I am particularly happy that this book is being brought out by the Brethren Press, a religious publisher with a strong commitment to the nonviolent struggle for peace and social justice.

But as one extends thanks and gratitude, he is reminded that without Martin Luther King Sr. and Martin Luther King Jr., there would be no book at all. *Not Only Dreamers* is the story of two peaceful men with extraordinary courage. It is the story of a father and son whose faith in God and compassion for their fellow men directed their lives. It is not only the black race who has benefited from the contribution of these two men. It is all people, everywhere. The Kings managed to hold a mirror to individual conscience and the soul of a nation. They revealed the blemishes, then offered cures for the afflictions. *Not Only Dreamers* is a story of triumph and tragedy, of joy and sadness.

But most of all, it is a story of love.

David R. Collins
Moline, Illinois

1

"Hey, Lord, you in there?"

Slowly the eight-year-old boy craned his head in every direction, carefully inspecting the inside of the big dead oak. A brisk autumn breeze danced through the woods near Stockbridge, Georgia. The year was 1907, and Martin Luther King, known to many of the folks in the area as Michael, was spending a typical Friday afternoon exploring.

"Lord, I know you is in there. You is everywhere." The boy's voice took on a melodious sound, a cheerful vibrant tone. "Lord, Lord, I'm a-lookin' for you. I'm a-lookin' for you, to say how'd ya do . . ."

Stepping back, the boy continued his song as he scrambled and scampered among the fallen twigs and branches along the countless paths. A streamer of sunlight filtered through the lacy treetops and the boy knew it was time to head for home. Emerging from the woods to the dusty road, young Martin Luther King stopped suddenly.

"Hey, nigger boy!"

The yell came from one of six men sitting along the road about twenty yards away. Millworkers, displaying hefty whiskey jugs, enjoyed a Friday drinking spree after work. Two of the men leaned heavily against each other. One of the men rose, started singing loudly, then toppled over. The scene brought a round of raucous laughter from the entire group. Only young Martin stood stone-faced, not knowing whether to continue past the men or to return into the security of the woods behind him.

The decision was unnecessary, for the attention of the men shifted to another solitary black man coming down the road. A few Negroes were employed by the mills in town. Since blacks were willing to do any jobs for considerably less money, whites around Stockbridge seldom took issue with the practice. But whiskey had robbed the men of their usual thinking.

"Hey, nigger. You work at the mill, don't you?" one of the men called out.

Slowing his step, the black man merely nodded. Despite the content and tone of the white man's question, the lone traveler tried to force a friendly smile.

"What are you laughin' at, nigger? Laughin' cause you got a job a white man should have? You gettin' money a white man should get, nigger. How 'bout you givin' us that money?"

Sensing that there was nothing he could say or do to satisfy the band of men, the black man hurried his steps. One of the white millworkers grabbed at his back pocket. "Got no damn right takin' white man's money, nigger. You just better be givin' us all the money you got."

Without turning, the black man yelled, "That money's for my kids. Don't belong to nobody but them and me."

Martin's eyes widened as he watched the men leap on the lone figure. The black was strong and well built. He tossed two men aside, then headed down the road again. Enraged, the attackers all converged on the target. One man stepped to the side of the road and pulled off a tree branch. He cracked it against the black man's head. Like bloodthirsty lions around a dazed antelope, the men tore at the black man. He fell to the ground, becoming a powerless victim of the heavy boots with which the men kicked him repeatedly.

Martin, too terrified to move, could not make a sound either. The man's anguished cry for help drifted into the late afternoon air. On and on the beating continued until the men themselves could barely stand. With a final burst of strength, they lifted the man and carried him past the spot where Martin was standing. They seemed not to notice him, so intent were they on tying the body to the tree with a belt.

And then they were gone. Laughing and swinging their jugs of whiskey, they went stumbling on down the road. In the space of minutes, a life had been snuffed out, ruthlessly and without purpose.

Martin trembled as he felt himself breathing heavily. How long he had held his breath in shock and disbelief he did not know. Now, as his lips opened, a silent scream poured out. He took a final look at the dead stranger, his torn, twisted body hanging against the tree in the autumn air.

Then the boy turned and ran. He hurried home to the rundown sharecropper's house where he lived with his father and mother, and sisters and brothers.

The eight-year-old boy did not tell anyone what he had seen that day. He knew words would not carry the ugliness and hate he felt. He hated the white man for feeling superior and taking advantage of blacks. "I must protect myself," he told himself. He decided that he would build a wall of armor in his mind, a wall no white man could ever penetrate. And although he felt strange asking, he begged the Lord to help build that wall.

It was not the first wall that young Martin Luther King constructed when he was a boy growing up near Stockbridge, Georgia. Raised among poor farming people, often plagued with debts of the pocketbook and drabness of the human spirit, Martin struggled to find hope and beauty in his day-to-day life. From each of his parents, the boy borrowed a collection of unique features.

His father, James Albert King, grew up tough and hard, as wiry as he was strong. As a young man, he'd landed a job working with a quarry crew outside Stockbridge. But an accident at work one day ripped off part of his right hand. There were no such things as company insurance benefits or workingman's compensation. James found himself out of quarry work, tossed into the work force of sharecropper farmers.

As a quarry worker, James King had felt he had a chance to get ahead. It was possible to make far more money excavating in the giant rock pits than any sharecropper could make caring for another man's farmland. James King plunged into a state of gloom and depression. His present life was dismal, his future looked worse.

Enter Delia Lindsay.

The daughter of hard-working farming parents, Delia gave fresh hope and optimism to James King. "God will provide," was a creed she shared and lived by. Married in Stockbridge, the young couple began sharecropping cotton on a nearby farm.

Soon Mr. and Mrs. King welcomed a daughter, whom they named Woodie. Their first son arrived on December 19, 1899. Naming the first male born in the family caused lively family discussion. Mama King insisted the infant be called Michael, in honor of the strong and powerful archangel in the Bible. Papa King was just as insistent that the boy be named Martin Luther, in recognition of two of his brothers. Papa did not want to cause major family turmoil and agreed to call their new son Mike, although Mama still stuck firmly to Michael.

The third King child. Lucius, lived only a few days. He was followed by two girls, Lenora and Cleo, born about a year apart. Three more boys joined the ever-growing King household. They were named James, Henry and Joel. The family circle was completed with the birth of two daughters, Lucille and Ruby.

To feed and clothe his family, James King toiled in the

fields from sunrise to sundown. He was a proud man, willing to match the work he did with any man. Often his wife worked beside him, gradually joined by their daughters and sons once their hands grew big enough to pick the cotton and pull the weeds. Mama frequently went into Stockbridge during the wintertime to wash and iron for the wealthier whites of the town.

Sharecropping another man's land offered little personal satisfaction to a man like James King. What caused even more discontent in the family homestead were those times when men tried to cheat an honest farmer. White traders knew they carried the advantage in dealing with blacks. The black sharecropper could put up little argument when greedy, dishonest tradesmen cut prices on goods bargained for and contracts agreed upon. In truth, the white businessman who did not try to take advantage of the black farmer was considered a fool.

"They treat us like dumb animals," Papa King would declare angrily, his fierce tone causing his children to cower in the shadows of the homestead. "Like dirt beneath their feet!"

In the midst of such outbursts, Mama King would begin to hum a song she had heard at the last revival meeting, hoping the soft music would cool her husband's blazing temper. Sometimes her method worked. But as time went on, Papa King took more and more comfort from a whiskey bottle. It was a brief and empty escape. Mama urged him to plant his faith with the Lord rather than in the soil.

"James," she would say, "no matter where you are or what you've done, the Lord stands ready to take your hand. He's here with us, love. Turn to him."

But Papa King could never bring himself to share his wife's faith. He felt like a thing, a useless object on the earth. In the spring, he planted seeds in soil. In the fall, he harvested the crops. He loved their children, yet longed to give them more. He felt trapped and alone.

Although Delia Lindsay King shared many of her husband's frustrations, she would not let herself fall victim to the same doubt and depression. No matter how bad things were, they could always be worse. She faced family hardships head-on, unflinching and steadfast. God will provide. More than a prayer, it was a code to live by each and every day.

Church services, revival meetings, prayer gatherings—all offered an avenue of joy and thanksgiving that Mama King introduced to her children. Especially young Michael. From his first visit, the boy fell in love with the rousing gospel singing and chants. His youthful voice joined those around him, all declaring their trust in the Lord and their faith in God.

> Up on the mountain, my Lord spoke,
> Out of his mouth came fire and smoke,
> All around me looks so shine,
> Asked my Lord if all was mine.
> Ev'ry time I feel the Spirit
> Moving in my heart I will pray,
> Ev'ry time I feel the Spirit
> Moving in my heart, I will pray . . .

"Listen to that little Mike King, just a bellowin' his lungs out!" people would say.

"The Lord's sure to hear that voice of his, all right. Never did hear the like of such carryin' on. I'll betcha the Lord is smilin' right now, listenin' to that angel child."

In truth, young Michael King understood little of the eloquent testimony and scripture shared by the traveling evangelists who passed through the countryside holding revivals and taking over church pulpits. It was the music that caught the heart and soul of the boy, causing his spirit to lift itself in glory to the Lord's Holy Name.

Papa took little pleasure in watching his first son heading to local revivals, weddings, prayer meetings and baptisms. But neither did he voice open objection. Perhaps he knew his complaints would do little good, for if there was anything Mama believed in deeply, it was the importance of knowing God's wisdom and strength.

Of all the preachers who traveled across the Georgia countryside, those who pleased young Michael King the most were those who could combine talents of speech and song. Few of the black country folk around Stockbridge had ever learned to read, therefore they would sit mesmerized by Country Circuit ministers (called C.C. Riders since they often traveled by horseback) who stood holding the Holy Bible and reciting page after page. Appreciative congregations considered themselves doubly blessed if the preacher could also lead a few rounds of spirituals and gospel singing.

No set of eyes and ears gave closer attention to the visiting evangelist than those of Michael King's. He sat hypnotized by the motions of the speaker, studying each gesture and movement. The rhythm and cadence of each emotive voice sank deeply into the boy's mind, ready to be imitated in the days and weeks that followed the visit.

While he was concentrating solely on the speaker in the pulpit, Michael carefully observed the faces of the people around him. Tired, weary countenances looked fresh and cheerful. Eyes seemed filled with new sparkle and life. Lips, formerly rigid and taut, swept upward in smile.

Not that the only message carried by the preachers was of happiness and cheer. Hardly. Often, the rafters of the churches rattled with threats of "the Lord's ways of dealing with sinners," the punishment to be suffered by "all those servants of the Devil" who stood in the gathering.

But the message was always one of hope, an awareness that God loved everyone, was willing to accept the most unworthy of sinners who was willing to repent, and that a world of eternal peace was waiting after this life was done. It was this world of hope that Michael dreamed of constantly. It helped provide shelter against the hardships he encountered growing up poor and black.

The hardships were many and cruel. Once Michael grew big enough to plow, he was given charge of the mule on the family farm. Each morning before heading to school, he curried the animal, leaving him with a scent of mule. Classmates at the all black Stockbridge school taunted him often.

"You sure can smell that Michael King a-comin'," can't you?" friends would laugh.

"Not for more than a mile or so," another voice would offer.

The insults hurt. But Mike clenched his fists, trying to conquer the anger he felt building inside him. Too often he had seen his Papa in a rage, hurling ugly words at his Mama, sometimes breaking furniture and ripping clothing. Finally, teased once too often, Mike stopped, turned, and glared back at his attacker.

"I may smell like a mule," the furious boy hissed, "but at least I don't *think* like a mule!"

Another rebuff came at the hands of one of the white families Mama King worked for in Stockbridge. Approaching the imposing red brick home, Mike saw the children of the household playing in the front yard. Invited to join in their games, he happily accepted. He was even more delighted when they asked him to stay for lunch.

"Glad to," he sang out. "And I'm much obliged to be invited."

But as Michael scampered up the front porch stairs leading into the house, he was met by the stern, cold face of the mistress of the house. Surprised her children had extended such an invitation for lunch, the woman felt obligated to provide food. She ordered Michael to the back door. Head lowered, the boy obeyed. After several minutes of waiting, Michael looked up to find a sandwich being handed out of the half-open door. Inside, he could see his mother working, ironing the clothes of the white family. Grabbing the sandwich, the boy scurried down the back steps and began running for home. He heaved the sandwich into the wind. Someday, he promised himself, someday he would have a grand brick house as fine as any brick house in all the world.

As he dreamed of the house he would someday have for himself, Michael King added still another brick to that wall of armor in his mind. Each hurt, each rejection, added one more brick. It was a wall of hate, of determination, of fear and frustration.

One white boy, Jay, took a special liking to Michael. Together they shared the life known only to two special friends growing up.

"Let's see who can climb this tree the fastest," Jay would challenge.

"You'll lose!"

"Prove it."

Like human squirrels the boys would scale the tree. It did not really matter who won the race. The fun lay in the challenge. Who could run the fastest? Who could jump the farthest? Who could skip stones the best? Sharing. Caring. Knowing even when there was nothing to do, you had a friend to do it with.

Then the day came, as so often those kind of days came in Michael's life. The two boys balanced themselves on the railroad linings that ran through Stockbridge. One would slip off, then the other. Laughter. Another challenge hurled. Try again. Tripping, stumbling, more laughter.

Gazing up at the sound of men's voices, the two boys smiled at the men killing a few minutes time at the town depot. Michael saw one of the men nudge Jay's father. His voice carried clearly in the still air of the afternoon.

"Who's the kid with Jay?"

Mike glanced at his friend. Each boy seemed to brace himself for the answer, hoping against hope that it would not be cruel.

Jay's father grinned, chewing on the remains of a tobacco reed. "Just one of my niggers," the man answered.

With the words, something inside Michael withered and died. No matter how many adventures he could share with his friend, how many times they could laugh and cry together, there would always be a difference. Black. White. Different. Why couldn't Jay's father just have said, "That's Michael King, just a boy Jay knows." Would that have been so hard to do? Jay had a name, and people called him that name. Papa King always called Jay by his name when he spoke. Michael King. Or Mike. Anything, but "one of my niggers."

And another brick of rejection and rage was laid upon the wall.

By the time he was twelve, Michael King was certain of one thing—he would never become a sharecropper. The boy hated farming, the following of a yearly calendar that dictated a person's life and financial fortune. Papa King sensed his son's feelings, indeed, he shared most of them. But like many fathers of that time and place, he secretly hoped Michael would remain on the land they worked. To bolster the boy's interest, Papa King took young Michael with him to call on the landlord for the yearly settling of accounts. Carefully the boy listened as the two men spoke of the figures recorded in the ledger books before them. According to the white landlord, the debits and credits balanced. What James King had spent was covered by the prices paid for the harvested cotton.

Michael shook his head. He knew something was wrong with the accounting. Suddenly he had the answer. He looked up at the two men.

"Look here," Michael exclaimed. "Yes, the profits from the harvested cotton do match the debts. But now there is the cotton seed. That should bring money free and clear."

True enough. Neither of the men had remembered

the cotton seed which was worth almost $1000 in clear money. But the surprise registered on the face of the white landlord quickly turned to disgust. Who was this young black boy coming in and talking so? This business was between adults, grown men.

"Who are you to be meddlin' in our affairs?" the landlord snarled, raising his foot to give Michael a kick. "You got no business here."

Michael shot a quick look at his father. Surely Papa King would not allow himself to be swindled like this. Stand up for yourself, Mike heard himself screaming inside. Stand up for me.

"There ain't no cause for gettin' upset," Papa King mumbled. "There's no need for anyone to take care of my boy here. I'll take care of him."

Tears welled in Michael's eyes. A pain shot through his stomach as the humiliation of the moment mingled with anger and disappointment. Words choked in his throat. As he left the landlord's home, he walked silently beside his father. Each step the boy took he promised himself again that he would do whatever he could to avoid this existence that allowed whites to treat blacks any way they wished.

The next morning the landlord came to the King shack and ordered James King and his family off the land. "Don't need no sass from niggers!" the white landlord declared. "And make sure you leave the mule here too."

Another brick was laid on young Michael's wall of confusion and resentment.

While Michael continued to accumulate resentment against those he felt treated his family unfairly, Mama King worked equally hard to crumble his wall of hate into dust. A tireless worker, she always found a moment, the right moment to hug her children close, listen to their troubles and wipe away their tears.

Neighbors and friends too shared in Mama King's love and kindness. Despite their own humble surround-

12

ings, Mama was constantly finding a way to offer what was needed when local folks were in distress.

In one such case, a neighbor's cow was dying. Knowing the need for milk in the home, Mama filled a bucket of milk from the King homestead, tossed a handsome piece of butter on top, and directed Michael to take it to the neighbors.

The day was hot and humid. As boys are apt to do on such excursions, Michael dawdled near the town sawmill. The sounds and sight of the strong oxen lugging huge logs from the nearby woods fascinated the boy. He was wiping the sweat off his face, when a voice from behind interrupted his thoughts.

"Boy, get a bucket of water from the stream for my work crew."

Michael turned, recognizing the speaker as the owner of the mill. "Sorry, sir, I'm doing an errand for my Mama. I just stopped here to catch my breath. Now I'll be moseyin' along."

Clearly, Michael's reply angered the millowner. Without warning, the man grabbed the boy's shirt and jerked him forward. Old and overworn, the shirt ripped to pieces. Struggling to free himself, Michael backed away. The millowner swung one foot forward, smashing against the bucket and spilling the contents on the ground. Bewildered, Michael fell to his knees and tried to scoop the butter into the bucket. This time the millowner aimed his kick at Michael's head. The boot connected on the boy's ear, sending Michael sprawling backward. As he scrambled to his feet, the millowner moved forward and swung his fist into Michael's mouth. Again the boy fell, dizzy and bleary-eyed. The taste of blood soured his mouth. He could hear voices, and when his eyes finally cleared, he saw men holding the millowner.

"Get away from here, boy," someone whispered, giving Mike a shove. "Go home."

Another voice spoke the same advice. His head aching, but refusing to cry, Michael stumbled away. He dashed toward home, hoping and praying he could sneak inside and clean himself up before anyone saw him.

But Mama King and Michael's sisters were busily washing a full iron tub full of clothes over a fire in the front yard. The girls were too frightened and surprised to speak when they saw their brother. They backed away. Mama King, dropping the washing she was holding, advanced and faced her oldest son directly.

"Michael," she demanded, "who did this to you?"

Gazing down at his feet, the boy did not speak. He could not. Would his mother spank him for not completing his errand? The boy trembled, despite the summer heat and sunshine.

"Michael?" Mama King repeated. "Who did this?"

This time the tears were there. The words came too. As the boy poured out the story, his mother gripped his wrist and led him back over the path he had just come. The sight of the mill and a crowd gathered in front of it made Michael jerk back. But if he had any thought his mother would stop from the mission on which she had set out, he could not have been more mistaken. Her jaw was set, her eyes cold and glaring. As the pair approached, the sound of the millowner's voice could be heard above the mumbling of the surrounding people.

". . . and then I showed that smart ass little nigger just who was boss around here!"

Men stepped out of the way as Mama pulled Michael forward. She did not stop until she faced the millowner head-on.

"Did you do this to my child?" Mama King asked, her tone low and steady.

The millowner glanced around. No one spoke. "Woman!" he finally bellowed. "Have you lost your mind? Get the hell outta here before I—"

Mama stood firm. "Did you do this to my child?"

"Yeah. What about it? You got somethin' to say about it?"

For the first time mama released the captive grip she had on Michael's wrist. At the same time, she lunged forward, aiming her shoulder right into the millowner's stomach. He toppled back against the millshed, struggling to keep his balance. As the crowd backed away, Michael's eyes widened in disbelief. In desperation, the millowner jumped forward and tried to get a hold on the woman in front of him. But years of heavy labor as a field worker and housekeeper had provided Mama King with unusual power and strength. Sidestepping the millowner, she tripped him and he fell to the ground. Before he could even think of getting up, she pounced on top of the man and began pounding his head. One of his helpers attempted to assist, but Mama landed a fist on his jaw that sent him stumbling backward. By the time the woman stood up, the millowner's face was battered and beaten.

Mama King faced the crowd. "You can kill me if you want to," the woman shouted, "but if you dare harm any of my children, you'll answer for it."

Slowly the millowner struggled to his feet, his balled hand rubbing away blood that was pouring from his nose. Mama King tensed, ready to battle again if that was what was needed.

"Get off my land!" the millowner ordered. "You come back here again and we'll see who answers. Git!"

Michael was certain someone would probably shoot both of them as Mama and he walked away. But Mama King knew better. There were too many witnesses to exactly what had happened. Ordinarily, whites killing blacks in Georgia would have little to fear. But this was no ordinary situation. With good reason, a mother had revenged her son in a fair fight. It was to the millowner's advantage to have the entire event erased from the memory of all who saw it happen.

"Don't tell your Papa about this," Mama warned Michael. "If he asks, just tell him you fell down and hurt yourself."

It was almost the only time Michael had heard his mother suggest lying. But the boy knew the reason why. If James King heard a white man had hit his son, the angry father might grab a whiskey bottle in one hand and a rifle in another and go off to settle the account.

Michael did *not* tell his father, but James King found out anyway. Mama's fears were justified. With rifle in hand, the angry sharecropper headed to the mill. Thankfully, the millowner was gone.

When others learned of James King's plans, they jumped on their horses and headed for the King cabin. Sending the children to hide, Mama faced the armed mob in the front yard. She persuaded the men that Papa King was not at home and she did not know where he was. As far as she was concerned, the matter was settled, all accounts paid in full.

For months no one saw Papa King. Mama King did her best running the farm. Try as they could, the King children could not keep the farm running smoothly. They had the spirit and energy, but they lacked experience. The cotton crop was a failure; the vegetables were picked too late. It was winter before Papa King reappeared. When he did, he was angry and bitter about the developments on the farm. It did not matter at all that he had been absent when the work needed doing. All he could see was that it had been a poor harvest and much of the farm needed repair.

Despite the financial drains placed on the King family, Papa King always seemed to find the necessary funds for drinking. His drunken flings became a daily ritual, causing a never-ending string of quarrels inside the cabin.

"I'm goin' to throw the whole damn lot of you out!" the wild Papa King would threaten Mama and the children. "You're a pack of thieves, stealin' and squanderin' everything I've got."

"Now, just soothe yourself some," Mama would coax softly. "You'll be feeling better tomorrow and we can all talk civil."

But that tomorrow never seemed to come. Papa never felt better. Even when he wasn't drunk, he walked around in a dazed stupor, forgetting things he wanted to do and carelessly breaking tools.

As the oldest in the family, Woodie King did her best to keep some order in the homestead. But Michael knew his elder sister was waiting for just the right opportunity to break away and go out on her own. More and more, he yearned to do the same.

Somehow, Michael knew the way he would take to travel away from the sharecropper's farm in Georgia. It would be the Lord himself. At each revival meeting and gathering of church folks called to worship, the boy sensed a special calling to the Savior. Hope rumbled through the boy's chest as he belted out the songs of faith and love.

> De gospel train's a-comin', I hear it jus' at han', I hear de car wheels rumblin', and rollin' thro' de lan'. Git on board, little children, git on board, little children, git on board, little children, dere's room for many a mo'.

The gospel train. What better way to cast away the shackles of sharecropping and go into the world, a world wide and bright with the Lord's promise? Michael studied the Bible with fresh fervor. He memorized chapter and verse, psalms and parables. With intuitive sense, the boy knew when to pause, when to pound, when to praise and when to shake a cautioning finger.

"Someday you'll be standing behind your own pulpit in your own church," Mama King would say.

Michael smiled. "Maybe," he answered. "If the Lord sees fit to put me there."

Mama nodded. "Well, the Lord helps them who help themselves," the woman murmured. "And you're sure enough doing all *you* can."

There was no doubt of that. It was no easy task handling all his assigned chores and trying to go to school too. Feeding the pigs and chickens, carrying in firewood and water, helping fix breakfast—everything had to be done before heading to the old damp shack set aside for the education of Stockbridge black children. The preacher's wife, Mrs. Low, taught all the boys and girls who attended. There were no books or writing materials, not a chalkboard in sight. Yet somehow the children learned, by rote memorization and oral sharing. Michael took a special interest in numbers and figures. His mind caught fire with adding and multiplying, subtracting and dividing.

But the real fire within Michael was his love for the Lord. He looked forward to every moment he could spend in Floyd's Chapel. No one sang with more gusto and spirit than Michael King. No one knew the Scriptures better and spoke with more sincerity about the beauty of faith than Michael King. Now if only he could convince the deacons of the church to give him a trial sermon. He had already taken and retaken the tests covering the Bible that every serious student was given. But a trial sermon was required before anyone could become a fully licensed, or authorized, reputable preacher.

"The deacons probably just think you're too young," Mama King told her impatient son.

Michael shook his head. Other boys of his own age had already earned their licenses to preach. No, there had to be another reason they were putting him off. One time they claimed it was because Reverend Low was going to be gone. Another time, there was talk of bad weather. Then they alibied that they couldn't get a full deacon board together to make a decision. Excuses, excuses. Deep inside, Michael was certain he knew the real reason for their actions. They were jealous. Here they were, all deacons of the church, and not one of them could read. But Michael could. He had listened to every word Mrs. Low said in the black school. He knew every letter in the alphabet and knew thousands of words as well. He was proud of knowing how to read and write, but he knew talent could sometimes bring on jealousy.

Finally, the deacons could no longer say no. Others in the congregation, long aware of Michael's love for Jesus and the church, applied pressure to help the boy get his chance to preach.

As the morning came for young Michael to speak before the congregation, the boy was understandably nervous. Papa King gave him no encouragement.

"Damn showoff," the older man snarled, the whiskey smell strong on his breath. "You're a fool pig, you is. Thinkin' you is special 'cause you can pray and spout off Bible rubbish. I say you're a damn fool, an ignorant cuss, and don't be tellin' anybody whose son you is."

Michael tried to shut out his words, yet they kept repeating themselves in the boy's mind. Thankfully, Mama King came along and held her son close.

"You speak words to the Lord, boy," the woman said. "And anytime you want to leave this place, you do it. You have your life to live, Michael, and if you have to go from here, you go and don't look back."

"But what about you, Mama? And all—"

Gently the woman touched her son's lips with her finger. She smiled. "The Lord will provide," she whispered. "The Lord will provide . . ."

Provide He did, at least as far as Michael getting his preacher's license. In December, 1914, just past his fifteenth birthday, a confident Michael King took the pulpit in Floyd's Chapel in Stockbridge, Georgia, and delivered his first sermon with the board of deacons looking on. Suitably impressed with the presentation, they granted the license. One deacon approached Michael personally.

"You sure do know how to praise the Lord," the man declared. "I've heard men twice your age and they couldn't share a holy service the way you did. You probably won't be stayin' around these parts too long, but let me know where you'll be preachin' cause I'll come give a listen anytime."

Michael thanked the man, grateful for every kind word. And that night, as the boy lay on his bed begging for sleep to come, he wondered what the future held. Whatever it was, Michael could hardly wait to get on with it.

Yet earlier that same year, another event had given Michael reason to pause. Thinking about it sank him into terror and depression. It was a memory the boy would carry with him for the rest of his life.

2

Seeing Papa King drunk was hardly an unusual occurrence around the family cabin. In truth, sometimes Michael, Woodie and the older children had to strain to remember him without his eyes half closed and his mouth hung open. No matter how hard Mama would scrub at his clothing, no matter what kind of strong soap she used, the stench of whiskey lingered. Whenever it seemed to be in danger of leaving, Papa would spill some more on while swinging a bottle around. Despite the frequence of such occasions, Mama still tried to protect the younger children from witnessing their father when he was so totally ravaged with, as she called it, "the Devil's brew."

Late one spring afternoon, Mama King glanced out a front window of the cabin. The sight was all too familiar, that of Papa King wobbling down the road and stumbling up the path leading to the front door. The concern showed on her face and in her voice as she turned to Michael.

"Why don't you take the little ones outside for a spell? It's still early and I've just started supper. Hurry along."

Quickly Michael followed the suggestion, rounding up Ruby, Lucille and James and leading them past their father into the fresh air outside. The older man just stared, a dazed unseeing look, as his sons and daughters carefully edged around his staggering frame. Sensing he had best return indoors, Michael came back through the front door. He found his father opening a newspaper he clutched under one arm. Inside it was a fish.

"I want this fish for supper, Delia," Papa King said, his words slurred. "You cook it right now."

Humming to herself as she stirred a pot on the stove, Mama King looked over at the fish. "James Albert," she answered softly, "I already started supper for the children."

Papa stepped forward, leaning his face near his wife's. "Woman, I told you I want this fish for supper. You cook this fish—now!"

At first Mama King did not speak. She simply kept stirring the contents of the pot on the wood stove. Then, her face set in firmness, she looked at Papa. "I am cooking supper, James Albert!"

There was nothing that was going to change her mind and Papa King knew it. But something snapped inside and he slapped her hard across the face.

It was not the first time Michael had seen his father hit his mother. But this time was going to be the last. The boy leaped behind his father, grabbing the older man's arm just as he lifted it to strike Mama King again. Whirling Papa around, Michael stared in the man's face.

"Don't you hit her again, Papa!" Michael yelled. "I ain't gon' let you hit my mama again—ever."

Papa's frame staggered back and forth, his eyes trying to focus. He squinted, zeroing in on the figure standing before him. "You ain't gon' what?" he blurted, trying to shake his head clear. "I'll knock you into next week, boy!"

Lashing out with his free hand, Papa King knocked Michael away. Yet the boy managed to grab the man's other hand and pulled him farther away from Mama King. Papa and Michael banged against the table and off the walls. Years of working the Georgia soil had hardened the muscles on both of them and the cabin shook with the commotion. Mama stood beside the stove, her eyes wide with fear and concern. Grabbing Papa around the neck, Michael glanced frantically up at his mother.

"Git outside, Mama!" the boy ordered.

Mama King did not move. Perhaps she was too frightened or too bewildered and amazed. Whatever the case, she stood still as stone.

Pressing his full weight on the drunken man, Michael managed to drop Papa King to the floor. Rolling the man over, the boy straddled him quickly, gazing down at the flashing eyes and mouth venting rage.

"I'll kill you, damn you!" Papa King shouted. "I'll kill you!"

Squirming and twisting, Papa King fought to free himself. But Michael had no whiskey inside him to slow his movements. Papa King telegraphed his every motion, and Michael was ready to counter. Gradually, the older man's efforts to break away grew weaker and weaker. He finally lay still, his eyes closed.

For several minutes Michael did not move. He needed to be sure his father wasn't just trying to fool him. Once convinced, Michael stood up and walked a few steps away. Slowly, ever so slowly, Papa King opened his eyes. He glared at Michael. "If you stay in here, I'll kill you."

No longer was the whiskey talking. The words sounded true and even. Michael gazed over at his mother. Mama King motioned for the boy to go outside. Her head nodded, telling Michael she would be safe and that it was best if she were alone with her husband for a time. Michael stepped to the front door and slipped outside.

The fresh air felt good on his face. There was little that could be done, however, to stop the hurt inside, or the anger, confusion and frustration. The boy walked to the woods where he so often felt secure and peaceful. On this night, the security and peacefulness were gone. Never had Michael felt so low, so sick inside. What kind of a husband strikes his own wife? What kind of son fights with his father this way? "I'll kill you," his father had said. Over and over Michael heard the words. "I'll kill you."

Dusk came. Still Michael walked along the edge of the woods as anger mingled with shame. He tried to fight off the bitter feelings he carried toward his father. Yet the boy knew if ever the situation happened again, he would do the same thing.

"Oh, God, help me," Michael whispered into the empty, solemn night. The boy suddenly realized that his anger and resentment had so clouded his mind, he had forgotten the One who was always listening, who was always there. As clearly as he knew how, Michael spoke to his Master, sharing all of his anguish and hurt. Hours later, when Mama King came to tell Michael his papa was sleeping, the boy was still praying.

Early the next morning, Papa King came out of the house. Slowly he crossed the road to the woods. When he met up with Michael, neither of them spoke for several minutes. Finally, Papa King broke the silence.

"You're all right, boy," the man said. "You're all right. But I never want you goin' up against me like that again. You hear me, boy?"

"Yes, sir," Michael answered, his head lowered.

"And I tell you here and now, boy, that I won't never hit your Mama again. Y'understand?"

Michael nodded. "Yes, sir," he replied softly.

With that, Papa King lightly shoved Michael's shoulder, almost a final sealing bond of affection.

And the boy knew his father meant to keep his word. He would never hit Mama again. Michael was sure of it.

Despite his father's pledge, and as convinced as Michael was that Papa King would honor his word, the entire incident weighed heavily on the boy's mind. Sweating and trembling, Michael would wake up suddenly in the middle of the night. It wasn't so much the relationship with his father that troubled the boy. For the time being anyway, that was settled. They had an understanding. No, it was the relationship with the Lord that bothered Michael. Could the Lord ever forgive a child who would strike out at his own father? "Honor thy Father and thy Mother." This was the fourth commandment of God. Was it "honor" to strike your own father, to shove him to the ground, to take advantage of someone whose thoughts were muddled by the Devil's brew? Was this the person who had climbed into a chapel pulpit, proclaiming the glory and goodness of the Father of everyone? What hypocrisy! What dishonesty! Surely the Lord had little use for such a sinner.

One night, when the nightmare came again, Michael could stand the pain no longer. He had to run away, to leave the scene of his pitiful actions. Silently the boy stole out of the house while everyone slept. He had no thought where he was going. All he knew was that he had to get away. His steps took him into Stockbridge, to the railway depot where a freight train was stopped. He hoisted himself into a boxcar, not knowing the train's destination. Had he known, it would have made no difference. Michael had no desire to go to anyplace in particular; he only wanted to go away from home.

Slowly the train chugged out of the Stockbridge depot. From his place in the boxcar, Michael watched the land slip quickly by. Leaving. Yes, he was actually leaving home. He remembered his teacher, Mrs. Low, speaking of the vast world beyond Stockbridge. Cities like Macon and Atlanta. States like Alabama, Florida, Virginia. Countries across the sea. The clickety-click of the rails sang its own song. Going. On the move. Farewell, Stockbridge. What of Mama? ". . . and if you have to go from here, you go and don't look back." Her words echoed in Michael's mind. She would be all right, the boy was sure. A grin crossed his face as he remembered the way Mama had laid out that millowner. Yes, she would be fine. But Michael promised himself to get in touch with her as soon as he could. She would understand his going. She would explain it to his brothers and sisters. Of course, Mama would miss him at first . . . but the Lord would provide. She would console herself with that. She always did.

Shortly before dawn, the freight train carrying a confused boy from Stockbridge rolled into Atlanta's Southern Railroad Yards. After scrambling out of the boxcar, Michael strolled around the area. Despite the hour, men busily loaded and unloaded freight, shouting to one another as they worked. Suddenly a tall fellow wearing a badge on his shirt approached Michael.

"You looking for work, nigger?" the stranger said.

The boy was taken off guard. Awkwardly, Michael glanced over his shoulder to see if the official might be talking to someone else. No, there was no one else there. The heavy farm labor had piled muscle upon muscle, molding Michael into a young man who could pass for eighteen, even twenty years old. As the new Atlanta arrival plunged his hands into empty pockets, he swallowed deeply.

"Yessir, I'm lookin' for work," the boy answered, lowering his voice a notch to sound older. "You got a job for me?"

"Cleanup work, if you want it."

"Yessir, I'll take it."

By six o'clock that morning, Michael King was swinging a broom and loading trash into a wheelbarrow. A good feeling stirred within him. The first day in Atlanta and he already had a job. Not only did the railway yards provide employment, they provided a place to stay. There was always an empty boxcar to curl into, or the toolshed offered a roof over one's head too. At the end of his first week in Atlanta, Michael filed through the pay call line and proudly collected twelve dollars. Over and over he counted the money, enjoying the feel of each bill in his hand.

Before long, Michael was doing much more than cleanup work for the railroad. The boy liked making money, and he was willing to try anything for a little "extree" cash, as railworkers called it. Firing engines with coal was easy labor for the young black boy from Stockbridge who had passed his childhood years performing burdensome chores on a sharecropper's farm. Although firing coal in a steam engine failed to challenge Michael's strength, the work carried built-in danger. Hot coals could pop out and burn severely, and men had even been tossed from trains as they spun around corners. But Michael was willing to take the risks.

As well as pulling in the "extree money" doing any job asked of him, Michael learned when to talk and when to keep his mouth shut. Since he slept in the yards, he arrived early for work each morning and he was always willing to stay late as well. His foreman and co-workers respected Michael for that. They liked the way he listened too, not like "other niggers who knew too little and talked too much."

Whenever one of the regular firemen got sick or did not show up for work, Michael was tapped for extra duty. He never refused, even when it meant going out at night after a twelve-hour work day. No matter how his muscles ached, how sore his whole body felt, he'd take on more work.

"Must be savin' up that money for somethin' special, huh, boy?"

Michael nodded. How often he dreamed of walking into the cabin back at Stockbridge and tossing a few hundred dollar bills in front of his Mama and Papa. Wouldn't their eyes pop right out of their heads in disbelief? Then Michael would just smile and say, "It ain't that much. I'll be bringin' home some more soon."

Only one thing bothered the boy. It wasn't that his arms sometimes felt like they would fall off as he shoveled coal into the stoves. It wasn't that his legs felt like they would buckle right under him. No, it was the shouts of the trainmen.

"Nigger! Toss that coal, boy! Don't matter you get dirty! Black on black don't show at all. Swing that shovel, nigger!"

Yes, those words stung. They stung worse than any bits of blazing coal chunks that leaped from the furnaces and sizzled on the flesh. Yet, Michael did not say anything. He simply nodded and smiled, a thin little smile that would rile no one and satisfied everyone.

On the train runs to Macon, Michael always stared out toward the hillsides where he and his brothers had climbed and played. For a moment, he set his shovel down and under the engineer's watchful eye, pulled on the train whistle. Just the sound of it made Michael feel nearer home, knowing that Mama or Papa might be hearing the engine's *toot toot . . . toot ta toot.*

One morning, as the train lumbered back to Atlanta from Macon, Michael gazed out at the hill crest coming up. His eyes widened. There, racing down the hill, were two very familiar faces. It was his brothers, James Jr. and Henry. They waved a big red cloth between them, their faces completely splashed in wide, toothy smiles. Michael pulled on the train whistle, the tooting sounds rolling across the countryside. He could not stop the tears that hurried to his eyes. His brothers looked so happy, so thrilled to see him. Home. Mama. Yes, even Papa. Michael missed them all.

"Something wrong, nigger boy?" the engineer asked.

Wiping his face with his sleeve, Michael just shook his head. "Got some coal dust in my eyes, that's all. I'm all right."

The sight of his two brothers stayed with Michael for

days. He pledged himself that he would pay a visit home as soon as he could. But before he had time to return to the family at Stockbridge, in a sense, the family came to him—in the form of Mama King. She boarded a train to Atlanta, a train Michael was coaling, and traveled right into the Atlanta railway yards. Not wasting a minute, the determined woman marched right into the boss's office.

"You got a boy workin' here, Michael King, and he's got no business working here. He's only fourteen!"

The yard boss, a tough and hearty fellow named Bailey, was shocked. Like most workers around the yard, he had thought Michael was about twenty. When the boy appeared in the office, he was too surprised to speak.

"This boy is but fourteen and he's done workin' here," Mama repeated. "I've been worried sick over him. Look at him, barely able to stand up from workin' so hard. Come, Michael, you're finished here."

"He's got money coming," Mr. Bailey offered. "Couple hundred dollars, I'm athinkin'. What should I do with the pay he's earned?"

Mama turned, casting a glowering look at the yard boss. "Do whatever you want with it," she answered. "We don't want a penny of it!"

It was settled. Mama King pushed her son ahead of her through the yards, ignoring the snickers of the workers who had accepted Michael as one of them, little knowing he was so young. As for Michael himself, he felt foolish and hurt. He did not challenge Mama—never would he do that. Mothers were to be honored, respected. It would have done little good anyway. When Mama made up her mind about something, nothing would dissuade her.

"We could have some awful nice things with the money they owe me," Michael finally offered. "Maybe some dresses for the girls, something' nice for you—"

Mama's nostrils flared. "Nothin' I want would have me let anybody take advantage of a child of mine," she announced. "Not for any amount of money."

That was the end of the matter. The events of that day in the Atlanta rail yards were never mentioned again. Sometimes the boy wondered why Mama had told him when he felt like going that he should go, and then had come after him and brought him back. But inside he understood that she was not ready to let go of him yet. And her love would never let him do anything that might hurt him. Surely, the thought of him shoveling coals into a blazing hot furnace as a train whipped around turns and over rails was not something Mama could live with for a minute.

Once back in the Stockbridge cabin, Michael wasted no time pouting for things that could not be. His preacher's license was granted that winter and there was no reason the talents for singing and speaking in the Lord's behalf should not be put to use.

"I'll not object to you travelin' in behalf of the Savior," Mama King told Michael. "Just you be comin' home now and then when you're nearby."

Traveling preachers were common in the rural sections of the South. Sometimes one would take over the pulpit of the local church for just one service or two. Other times, a preacher might visit a place for quite some time, offering services for any group of people who asked him to stay. Cash for such services was seldom paid. More often, a pig, horse or mule would be given to the preacher. He might then head to another spot where he could trade the livestock for a new suit or some food.

Michael turned to traveling and preaching, wanting no part of sharecropper farming. Church folks in the area spread the word about the young boy preacher from Stockbridge. Before long, Michael had more invitations to come and preach than he could honor. Whenever he shared his rousing message of love and faith to the Lord, he combined it with loud and cheerful singing.

It's me, it's me, it's me, O Lord
Standin' in the need of prayer.
It's me, it's me, it's me, O Lord,
Standin' in the need of prayer.
Not my brother, nor my sister,
But it's me, O Lord,
Standin' in the need of prayer,
Not my brother, nor my sister, But it's me,
    O Lord
Standin' in the need of prayer.

Age mellowed Michael's voice, making the notes rich and powerful. There were no off tones, no mixed beats. Each word of joy and glory resounded true and firm. The boy bellowed out the powerful news of the Good Book as everyone could hear clearly. Truly, Michael King had found his calling. He belonged in the Lord's service, he was convinced of that.

On a visit to Atlanta in 1916, Michael attended a church supper. Through a friend of his from Stockbridge, the traveling preacher was introduced to a young woman named Bertha Chaney. Unlike many Methodists of the time, Bertha did not withdraw her warm friendly manner when she learned that Michael was of the Baptist faith. Her father, a Methodist minister, openly expressed his displeasure at Bertha having anything to do with Michael, while Bertha's mother chose to ignore the entire situation. But Bertha could not hide her feelings. She loved the young man from Stockbridge. Carefully she taught him how to take care of his money by keeping it in a bank, a practice he had never acquired. She talked to him about books that she read and magazine articles. Her laugh came quickly when she was with him, but Michael knew he did not share the same strong feelings toward her. There was no question that Bertha was fun to be with, had a fine sense of humor and was quite attractive. A guest sermon helped Michael make an important decision.

Bertha's father, Reverend Wilson Chaney, invited Michael to speak to a gathering of Methodists at a church retreat. Eager to please the older church leader, the boy quickly accepted. He chose his text carefully, and when he headed into the wooded clearing where the crowd was gathered, Michael felt comfortable and relaxed. Within minutes, his feelings changed drastically. Desperately, he sought to share the agony of Jesus, "totin' " the heavy wooden cross to Calvary.

"Cain'tcha feel that ole heavy wood, that weight on his shoulder and the pain jabbin' in his heart?" Michael cried out. "Ain'tcha with him, our Beloved Savior, stumblin' and fallen in the ole dirt and dust?"

It was clear the people in the crowd were totally unmoved. No, they were far from the dusty road of Calvary. They were cool and bored, standing in the refreshing brush arbor as they watched a young country preacher make a fool out of himself. So Michael thought at least. Even as he spoke, he sensed his own lack of vocabulary, his country clothing, his hillbilly mannerisms. These were refined city folk. No matter how the boy tried to get his audience to share his feelings and thoughts, he felt inferior, too far away from the folks around him in spirit. Why, he wondered, why couldn't these people open their doors of thinking and let him in. Methodists. Baptists. Did such labels really matter when the Lord's final walk to Calvary was being described?

"And when he died, when our blessed Savior died, he opened the doors of Heaven to us all," Michael shouted, his eyes pleading for understanding. "Joy and jubilation, we was saved. We was saved."

"Amen," the people in the country churches used to cry out. A loud "Amen" would shake the walls and the rafters. But not at this gathering. Here Michael felt alone, outside of the crowd completely.

Later, when Bertha tried to cheer him up, Michael knew what he must do. He made it clear that he sincerely valued her friendship, but if there was any chance she wanted anything more from him, it was not there. No, it was not just the difference in religion, it was much more. That sermon had only served to make so many other things more clear—that the two of them were worlds apart.

"You have so much to offer another fella," Michael acknowledged. "But not me. I'm much obliged for all you showed me and I sure hope you'll be wantin' to be good friends. I'm just thinkin' you might be hopin' for somethin' more to come of us bein' together, and I just know that ain't goin' to happen."

Bertha felt angry and hurt. With tears in her eyes and sobs in her throat, she ordered him out of her house. Michael nodded and left. As he descended the front steps, the disappointed girl called out to him.

"Mike King, you've got a lot to learn!"

Not turning back, the boy from Stockbridge simply nodded. "That much is true," he thought to himself. "That much is true."

Bertha Chaney's words still ringing in his ears, Michael knew that whatever he had to learn, it was doubtful that it would be found living at home. This time, however, there was no sneaking off in the middle of the night. What young Michael had seen of Atlanta he had liked, and that was to be his destination. Mama King put up no argument this time. Michael was eighteen now and had grown up a lot traveling the countryside as a visiting preacher. But telling Papa King was more difficult. Stockbridge and the farm were all the older man really knew of the world. It provided food, a house, a speck of land. What more did a man need?

Michael King knew *he* needed more. One morning, the boy caught up with his father at the far end of the cotton acres. Quickly he blurted out his plans. There was so much more the boy wanted to say—how he did love his father and hoped that he would understand and perhaps even forgive him, but that this was the way things had to be. The words did not come, however, and when Papa King simply turned and ordered the mule forward into the fresh planting ground, Michael stood silently. The figure of his father grew smaller in the distance, moving farther and farther away. It was strange, having come to tell Papa he was leaving the farm and then to watch Papa leave him, strange and lonely.

3

Atlanta, 1918

It did not take Michael King long to realize that although he had lived in this city three years before, he was still a stranger. After all, he had slept in the railway yards, eaten in the railway yards and worked in the railway yards. Upon his return to Atlanta, he vowed that he was going to become a part of the entire city, mingling and sharing with people. He rejected the thought of returning to the railway yards, as he was sure there would be workers who would remember that fateful day when his mother came and escorted him away.

Jobs were plentiful. America was at war, fighting the German military machine across the sea, and young Atlanta white men had eagerly enlisted in the armed forces. American military and government leaders seemed to care little about organizing the blacks to volunteer. What Negro soldiers were involved in the conflict were kept completely segregated.

After finding a room in an all-black residential boarding house, Michael quickly got a job working at an auto tire shop. The growth of the auto industry had skyrocketed, and any business connected with the production of automobiles or its parts was always hiring workers. Easily the fastest and hardest worker in the shop, Michael asked for a raise after a month's employment.

"Pretty uppity for a nigger, ain't you?" his boss asked, sneering.

"Too uppity to work in a place like this," Michael snapped back, surprised at his own words but equally determined to stand by them. "I'll take the wages you owe me and go."

For the first time Michael King asserted himself when being called "nigger." The label did not bother him so much when it was used simply as a word. What really made him angry was when someone used it as a degradation, an insult. Then it bothered him—a lot. Walking out of the tire shop gave Michael a good feeling inside. He left the place with no regrets.

The same day he quit his job at the auto tire shop, Michael hired on loading bales of cotton. It was heavy labor, testing every muscle of his stout frame. The job paid less than working at the tire shop too, but Michael's supervisor was considerate and fair. That made a big difference. Every worker was expected to do the same task and each worker was paid the same. There were no special assignments, no shirkers and loafers. Fair enough, Michael thought.

After several months of bale loading, Michael heard about a job driving a truck. The pay was better and the thought of learning to operate such a vehicle was also attractive. Michael got the job, and soon he was driving a truck through the streets of Atlanta, delivering and picking up barber chairs.

One afternoon as Michael came strolling out of his boarding house, he got the surprise of his life. Rolling up in front of the building, seated in a Model T Ford, were Mama and Papa King. Jumping down from the vehicle, Mama was smiling. She hugged her son in a viselike grip. Over her shoulder, Michael looked up at Papa. The older man just nodded, but somehow in that nod, Michael sensed respect and love.

"Well, do you like it?" Mama exclaimed, leading Michael by the hand around the automobile. "You jest better, son 'cause we sold a mighty fine cow to buy this contraption for you."

Michael's eyes widened. "This is mine? You bought this for me?"

"If yer not likin' it, we can take it back soon enough," Papa King grumbled.

"No, no," Michael babbled, shaking his head. "I like it fine. I . . . I just don't know what to say."

Mama smiled again. "You said you like it and that's all you have to say. Now, when you get done workin' today we want you to take us for a drive around this big city."

"Glad to, Mama. And much obliged." Michael looked up at his father and nodded. "Much obliged to you too, Papa."

Papa just nodded, not changing his expression.

Not long afterward, a second piece of good fortune came Michael's direction. Several families from Stockbridge had moved to the East Point of Atlanta. Many of these people remembered the young boy who could quote the scriptures and praise the Lord far better than seasoned preachers. Since they were building a church, they were looking for someone to be their preacher. Hopefully, they extended an invitation to Michael. It did not take him long to accept the offer.

But the experience preaching before Reverend Chaney's Methodists still troubled Michael. He was sure of his love for the Lord and for God. He knew how to relate the Bible. He knew more hymns than most preachers, and could sing them through to every last verse. But Michael still felt uneasy. He had listened to Reverend Chaney, and like most Methodist ministers, Chaney was college educated and formally trained. Maybe that was it. One person might be spiritually reached through their emotions. Yet another might be reached by the mind, the intellect. If a preacher could use both an emotional and an intellectual approach, both types of people could be reached. For as important a task as saving souls for eternal glory, should not a preacher try to do all he can? Michael decided to go back to school with such a purpose in mind.

It was no easy task. The state did not provide free education for blacks beyond the eighth grade. There was not a high school in Atlanta that had any black students. The libraries in the city were restricted to whites too. But Michael would not be dissuaded. He enrolled at Bryant Preparatory School—and was placed in the fifth grade, attending night classes.

It did not take Michael long to realize there was much he had to learn. At first, he held deep resentment for Mrs. Low at the Stockbridge School back home. After all, had she not made him think he was a good student? But gradually, as Mike began to understand the obstacles Mrs. Low faced without books and with so many students, his resentment disappeared. It was replaced by a determination to master all the knowledge available in as little time possible.

Parts of speech, numbers, maps, historical events and famous people—there seemed no limit to all there was to know. So many words Michael was using, especially when he wanted to arouse emotions during a sermon, were labeled "slang" or "substandard." No wonder the Methodists had turned up their noses when he spoke. Deep in his heart, though, he felt the road to the Lord should never be cluttered with right words or wrong words. It was what lay within the soul that was truly important.

Michael felt a certain satisfaction with his life. The work as a truck driver paid all his bills. The night classes he attended at Bryant School were helping him become more educated. The weekends he devoted to church activities at East Point. Yes, it was a good life, a full schedule.

All the reading he was doing took a toll on Michael's eyes. A classmate suggested to him that he look into getting glasses. One afternoon, during his lunch hour, Michael walked into a shop with a large eye on its sign in downtown Atlanta. The proprietor came running out from behind a curtain. His face was flushed and angry.

"What you want here, nigger? You got no business here." The man's English was heavy with a foreign accent and halting.

"I just came in for some specs," Michael answered. "Can't I get some specs here? I got money to pay for them."

The shopkeeper was obviously amazed. "No nigger ever came here wanting specs . . . before," he blustered.

Michael shook his head. "We got eyes," he said. "Sometimes our eyes go bad too."

"What you want with glasses?"

"I'm learnin' in school. I'm takin' night classes tryin' to get my di— diploma. Ya need an education to get ahead in this world. I'm gettin' one. I got a job drivin' a barber supply truck. Get paid every week, and I'll pay you every week when I get paid."

The shopkeeper seemed to settle down a bit as Michael spoke. Apparently the sight of a Negro in his place of business was a bit alarming, to say the least. But once Michael finished, the proprietor agreed to check Michael's eyes. Then he told him to return in a few days.

When Michael came back, the shopkeeper was smiling. He handed Michael a small, rectangular box. He opened the box carefully and pulled out a pair of round metal-rimmed glasses. He slipped the spectacles over his ears, looked all around the shop, and smiled broadly.

"You take them," the shopkeeper ordered. "You read good with them and get your diploma."

For still another moment, Michael gazed around, taking in the details that previously had been blurred and fuzzy. Then, reaching into his pocket, he said, "How much do I owe for these?"

The proprietor shook his head. "No, nothing. I new to this country, come here from Germany soon after war ended. I do not like how some people are treated here. Your people. But nothing can I do to change that. It is the way things are. I must act as everyone else acts . . ."

Michael knew what the man meant. Still, a person should not work without pay. "I want to give you some money," Michael offered.

Nervously, the shopkeeper glanced aside to where a white woman and white girl were just entering the business. Both the newcomers wore quizzical expressions, obviously surprised at seeing a black man present. Suddenly the shopkeeper turned back to Michael.

"I have nothing you want in here, nigger," the man snapped curtly. "You had better get out . . . before I call police!"

How quickly the man had changed, a whole new person leaping inside his flesh and showing his worst side. But Michael understood. What if the woman thought the proprietor was trading regularly with blacks? What if the little girl would become frightened with a Negro standing so close by? Everyone has to do what he thinks he must do. A man in business must try to please his customers. What a sad existence. Black is black and white is white, yet both cry often in the night.

Whatever the case, Michael was grateful for the new glasses. His teacher at Bryant, who was also the school's principal, was a man named Charles Clayton. "Those spectacles make you look like a real scholar," Mr. Clayton teased. Michael did not care so much what he looked like in the new glasses; he was just glad he could see better.

Mr. Clayton introduced Michael to much more than the wonders and rigors of acquiring academic knowledge and skills. The astute instructor challenged his students to reach out into the world and change anything that needed changing. One such arena was the electoral process of choosing government leaders. Although the federal laws guaranteed the right to register and vote, local governmental units in the South made the process difficult for blacks. There were special rules and restrictions aimed at preventing any Negro from entering a voting booth.

"You have to keep your right to vote by using it," Clayton told the students. "Votes can bring change and improvements. Lord knows we need some of that here in Georgia, in fact, right here in Atlanta."

Michael listened closely to his instructor. Everything seemed right and sensible. As soon as Michael turned twenty-one, he headed down to the City Hall to register to vote. A guard looked surprised when Michael told him why he was there.

"Well, you take that elevator over there," the man directed, pointing his finger to a spot under the sign clearly labeled COLORED. Michael followed the directions only to discover the elevator was not running. Several yards away, he noticed a staircase also marked COLORED. But when he got closer, he found a smaller sign which read WHITES ONLY.

"Well, they sure don't make it easy," Michael mumbled to himself. Hoping that the elevator problem was only temporary, he decided to wait. After half an hour, it was obvious that the elevator was totally out of commission. The elevator labeled WHITES went up and down, taking men and women up and bringing them down. Those who preferred, took the staircase. There was absolutely no way a black person could register to vote without breaking the building rules that enforced strict "Jim Crow" segregation. Shaking his head in disappointment and frustration, Michael left his spot by the elevator. The building guard chuckled as the black man passed him.

Michael returned the next day. And the next. In fact, for a whole week, he came back. It was always the same. The elevator for blacks stood empty and unmoving. Young white school children came excitedly into the City Hall, gazing and gawking at the offices and halls that housed their local governing units. Teachers spoke of "services provided by the city" and "rights and freedoms guaranteed citizens of Atlanta."

As twenty-one year old Michael King stood watching and listening, he wondered about those rights and freedoms. For a moment, he stood at the same level with the people waiting for the elevator. Then, while he remained in his same position, the whites glided upward, out of sight and reach.

"It's not just the elevator," Michael told Mr. Clayton. "It's so many other things too. The black man just stands still and watches the white man get ahead."

Mr. Clayton shook his head. "And often the white man stands on the black man's shoulders to get where he's going, Michael."

Getting to the voter's registration office was just the first hurdle for blacks in the South. Once there, he would often be charged a poll tax. Poll taxes could be assessed not only on the individual wanting to vote, but for all of his ancestors who had lived in the area, whether they had voted or not. Often, this involved quite a sum of money, more than many Negroes could afford. Those who could pay then had to take a test to show if they were educated enough to vote.

Michael King was determined to jump every hurdle. By the time the city hall elevator for blacks was fixed, he had carefully studied the United States Constitution, national and state laws, American history—and he was ready to answer any questions anyone might ask him.

The registration process took several months. Again and again Michael had to return, each time with a payment or information. The City Hall guard simply shook his head.

"Must be pretty important to you," he told Michael.

"Sure is," the determined youth answered.

Finally, Michael King walked out of the Atlanta City Hall with a voter's registration card. He flashed it proudly in front of the guard's face and met the open fresh air with a happy smile.

But Michael lost his smile not long afterwards. He had arrived at his regular night classes when Mr. Clayton asked him to come into his private office. When Michael did, he was surprised to find his father sitting in a chair. No, he was not really sitting in the chair, he was sprawled in it, his red eyes and hanging lower lip reflecting the condition Michael had witnessed so many times before.

Papa King wasted no time telling Michael why he had come to Atlanta. The farm was falling apart. Michael's younger brothers and sisters could not help as much as was needed.

"You're comin' home with me," Papa declared, not asking but telling. "I'm your Papa and you'll do what I say."

Michael's head pounded. His throat felt scratchy and dry. Nervously he glanced at Mr. Clayton, hoping to receive some support. The principal's gaze was downward. No, this was not his problem.

"But Papa," Michael said, "I've sent you and Mama money. I'm helpin' Woodie Clara. You know she lost her job at the yarn factory when there was a fire. I'm going' to school, tryin' to better myself—"

"Nothin' to say more. You're comin' home, boy. Now."

Michael stared at his hands, twisting his fingers together and then pulling them loose. His face felt hot, and body seemed to ooze with a cold, clammy sweat.

"I—I can't do it, Pa."

"You got to, I'm saying'. You got to. I can't do it myself. I'm doin' all I can, but it ain't enough. You come home with me now."

Finally, Mr. Clayton leaned forward. "Mr. King, your son is getting an education here. He wants to learn, and his future depends on all that he can learn. Let us keep teaching him. Don't ask him to go back."

No one spoke for a long time. In the distance, sounds of the outside world filtered into the office.

"Honor thy Father and Mother" pounded over and over in Michael's head. Was this the right thing to do? Was it wrong to seek to better oneself, to find a life free and unchained to the past?

Suddenly Papa King was on his feet, lurching toward the door. He swung around, his eyes almost shooting sparks of anger and rage. Take this life, he seemed to shout, and I'll never bother you again. But never call me father . . .

Papa King staggered out of the office, his steps echoing in the hallway. From the window in Mr. Clayton's office, Michael watched the lone figure cross the street and head on down to the bus station. He was going back to Stockbridge, to the farm, to the past.

"God, give me your strength and power," Michael whispered, knowing that from now on when he went home again, it would never be quite the same. Two worlds. Two such different worlds

Tears ran down Michael's cheeks.

4

It was done. The break was complete and sharp. But for Michael King, that meeting in Mr. Clayton's office haunted him for weeks. At night he would wake up sweating, his mind cluttered with nightmare visions of his father standing all alone among the long rows of cotton and corn, his arms reaching out in silence for the son who would not come back.

"You do not look well," Mrs. Laster murmured. A kindly widow who ran the boardinghouse at the end of Auburn Avenue where Michael lived, Mrs. Laster took a gentle but not intruding interest in the lives of the young men who lived in her big wooden house. At times Michael felt an urge to share openly with the old woman, yet something held him back. Finally, the landlady offered a soft comment that triggered a quick response in Michael's thoughts.

"When one door closes, you simply open another," Mrs. Lester whispered one morning at breakfast.

As Michael drove through the city of Atlanta that day, picking up broken barber chairs and delivering those that had been repaired, the landlady's words re-echoed in his mind.

And with those words was still another voice. Distant. Indistinct. But present nonetheless. By the end of the long work day, Michael knew which door he was going to open wide and full. He would turn to the Savior through his own preaching in the pulpit. With all the uncertainties of life, there were always the strength and security of God, the Father and the Blessed Lord.

It was not as if Michael had ever torn himself away from his role of preacher. The people of East Point in Atlanta could testify to that. When Michael King climbed into the pulpit to share the Word of God with the assembled congregation, folks listened—and listened well.

> We travel the road of life, yes we do. And there is a path here and a path there. One may be dark and on one we see sunlight. For one path, we can see the end and another we see only to the horizon. But as we travel, we never are alone. On the darkest or brightest or shortest or longest path, the Lord is walking right beside us, ready to take our hand, ready to give us strength, ready to hear our moans and groans. Oh, yes, He is there, every inch of the way . . .

"Amen!" the people would shout out "Amen! Amen! Amen!"

Michael would continue, relishing in the fervor of the moment, the joy of knowing he was bringing a flock closer to God. With their hearts beating, their heads nodding, their spirits swept up in hope and love, Michael took them into prayerful song!

> All I want, all I want, all I want is a little
>   more faith in Jesus.
> Whenever we meet you here we say,
> A little more faith in Jesus.
> Pray what's the order of the day?
> A little more faith in Jesus.

With each hymn and every sermon, Michael's commitment to the Lord grew stronger. His name and reputation spread beyond the pulpit at East Point. Folks scattered throughout the black community in Atlanta began to speak regularly of "that inspired, young preacher, Michael King." The people of College Park invited Michael to be their minister. He accepted eagerly the opportunity to preach there as well.

It was not as if he were alone in his desire to build his personal relationship with the Lord and find a greater congregation among the folks of Atlanta. At times, it seemed as though the city was full of young preachers trying to sermonize themselves into the hearts of the people and into church pulpits. Michael grabbed every chance he could to attend revival meetings, camp conclaves, baptisms, funerals. The tires on the old Model T wore thin, jerking and jostling over the roads of Georgia, occasionally heading into Florida or Alabama for a special Baptist gathering.

Of all the distinguished ministers living and preaching in Atlanta, few were more respected than Reverend Adam Daniel Williams of the Ebenezer Baptist Church. "The Reverend Williams speaks like he is the personal messenger of the Lord himself!" some folks said. "Moses, himself, couldn't deliver the Good Word with as much force and power," claimed others.

When Michael got word that the Reverend Williams was to deliver the major speech at the Atlanta Missionary Baptist Association's convention, he and three friends jumped into his Model T and headed to nearby Jonesboro for the gathering.

Unfortunately, Reverend Williams failed to appear. Having traveled to Cleveland to investigate a possible pastorate there for himself, he was held up by a disabled train. Announcement of the news caused a wave of disappointed moans to crisscross the assembled crowd. A local young preacher tried to fill in for the absent churchman, but the size of the group caused the volunteer to fumble and mumble his words. Only when he spoke of the Reverend Williams' family did Michael King take special interest.

"It is a family built on love and sharing, truly an example for all good Christians to imitate. Though the Reverend Williams shares his goodness with all of us, surely the goodness he brings into his family has made them the wonderful people they are."

One by one, the young preacher described the members of the Williams household. When he spoke of Alberta Williams, a daughter of the kindly churchman, his voice carried a poignant tone of admiration.

"If there's an angel on the earth, it has to be Alberta Williams. Poised, gentle, an accomplished musician, scholarly . . ."

Michael listened to every word. And on the way back to Atlanta that night, he made an announcement to his friends.

"I think I'm goin' to marry that Alberta Williams."

For a split second, there was dead silence. Then, three voices erupted into simultaneous laughter and yelping. "King! King! You're crazy, King!"

Michael stared straight ahead.

"King, do you even know this 'angel of the Lord'?" one of his friends asked, imitating the preacher who had so described Miss Alberta Williams.

"No, I don't yet, but I plan to mighty soon."

Again the laughter broke the silence of the moonlit Georgia countryside. but as Michael King lay awake that night in his roominghouse bed, 1 Corinthians 9:24 kept racing through his mind, fighting away sleep: "So run, that ye may obtain." Turning his pillow over to enjoy the coolness of the other side, Michael smiled to himself. "Run beside me, Lord, to make sure I keep on the proper path," he whispered into the darkness.

In every sense, the first time Michael actually saw Alberta Williams was totally by accident—hers. A broken ankle had brought her home from studying at Spelman Seminary (College) on the other side of town. Once having discovered that the Williams family home rested comfortably along Auburn Avenue—and that it was quite easy to walk to classes at Bryant School by way of the same Auburn Avenue, Michael King did precisely that. Although they did not speak, the young man's first impression of the distinguished minister's daughter was that the substitute preacher at the Baptist convention had hardly exaggerated. Alberta Williams appeared to be an "angel," even on crutches!

Michael became more convinced than ever that he was on the proper path and the Lord was running beside him when his sister Woodie announced she was moving one night. She had been living with one of Mama King's cousins, but a new job offer made Woodie want to relocate.

"It's a lovely family, Michael, not far from your boardinghouse. One of the daughters is away, attending Spelman Seminary and living in a dormitory on the campus. It's a Reverend Williams, Reverend Adam Williams."

Michael almost spit up the coffee he had been sipping. It couldn't be! His sister living at the Williams house! "Praise the Lord!" he declared.

"Beg pardon?" Woodie asked.

"Nothing," Michael offered quickly. "Let us just say I hope I'll be able to come and visit you there."

"Of course, Michael. Of course."

But Woodie's living at the Williams house of Auburn Avenue did nothing to promote Michael's opportunities to meet Miss Williams. Dedicated to her studies at Spelman, she seldom came home. When she did, she was caught up in a frenzy of family activities or church events. She, herself, had organized the choir in her father's church and maintained close contact with its members.

Weary of trying to get acquainted through his sister, Michael decided to attempt a more direct introduction. Slowly he trudged the route to and from his classes at Bryant every night. Slowly and ever more slowly. His gaze fell straight ahead, obviously a man who knew where he was going and determined to get there. Yet, the side glances toward the Williams porch revealed the passerby to be something different. Weeks drifted quickly along with no sign of Alberta. Both her father and mother appeared on the porch, sharing quiet conversation or stealing a breath of fresh air, but no Alberta.

Then it happened. She was there, sitting on the porch, appearing to simply enjoy the light breeze or an autumn sunset. Without hesitation, Michael walked by, nodding and smiling. No response. Once past, he turned around and retraced his steps. This time he waved, hoping to just catch her eye so that she might introduce conversation. Once the door was opened—

But there was no reaction to the wave. Surely she saw him, Michael thought to himself. She was only a few steps away, she on the porch and he on the sidewalk. Was it a girlish game? Or was her father watching from a parlor window? Whatever the case, Michael was not going to let this opportunity slide by again. His throat dry, his stomach curiously churning and his feet feeling suddenly weighted by heavy stones, he marched up to the porch.

A book rested in the young lady's lap. Michael felt relieved. She had not been ignoring him. She had been engrossed in her reading. But now, when she still did not look up, Michael felt a clammy sweat coat his body. Nervously, he coughed.

Looking up, Alberta Williams studied Michael a moment, then smiled. Once more, Michael remembered the young preacher's words about her graciousness and warmth. It was there, all right, in abundance.

"Hello," Alberta said. "You're Reverend King, aren't you? Woodie has talked about you. I'm glad we're finally getting to meet."

How smoothly her words flowed, like a song. When Michael started to reply, he felt the dry throat, the lump in his chest, the somersaulting stomach.

"I understand you are quite a preacher," Alberta offered.

"Well, right now, I'se preachin' in two churches." Michael bit his lip, wishing he could stop sounding like some country bumpkin. Here he was, finally getting to talk with this young college girl, and he was tripping over every word that he uttered.

Despite his own uneasiness, Michael sensed that Alberta Williams did not care that he sounded fresh from the country. Her eyes met his directly, and she was listening to what he was saying rather than how poorly he was expressing himself.

In a short while, Alberta excused herself and entered the house. Michael felt good inside, delighted that he had climbed the first rung on the ladder. He headed home, skipping classes for the first time since he had started them. He wanted to think about every word that had been exchanged. He was certain this was just the beginning. Alberta Williams. Mrs. Martin Luther King. Yes, it was just a matter of time.

Once again, the Lord seemed to be running along the path. Woodie had a friend named India Nelson. India also happened to be Alberta's closest friend. When Michael learned that students at Spelman Seminary could entertain guests on Sunday afternoon, he graciously offered to drive India over to visit Alberta "Any Sunday you feel like going visiting."

"Why, you are so very kind, Mr. King," the grateful Miss Nelson declared.

"My pleasure," Michael replied.

Visits to Spelman Seminary on Sundays required considerable preparation. Michael would put his best set of trousers between flat wooden boards, then lay the boards under his mattress on Saturday night. A spoonful of lard borrowed from Mrs. Laster, combined with a glass of ice water coupled with some dynamic arm motion, provided a shiny luster to a pair of old shoes. Choosing a dress shirt was only a minor problem since Michael had only one which had to be carefully laundered on the scrub board, the collar doused with a bit of starch and neatly placed under Mrs. Lester's iron for pressing. Michael left little doubt about his seriousness in seeing Alberta Williams. But wanting to make certain that there were no misunderstandings, he declared that he was interested in something much more than friendship.

"I hope you'd be thinking of us as courting," he told Alberta one night. "You're a mighty fine woman, and I'm willin' to work to make myself worthy of you."

Alberta could not hide her surprise. There was no doubt that she enjoyed Michael's company. But courtship? Marriage? For years her future had been revolving around teaching, a classroom, music.

For the first time in their relationship, Alberta fumbled with words. "I'm not sure what my parents will say."

"First of all, you should think about it," said Michael. "I believe two people like us could have a wonderful life together."

Once he had expressed his intentions openly, Michael felt no more need to hide his feelings. He felt good strolling up to the front door at the Williams house and calling on Alberta. Together, they laughed about his initial attempts to get her attention.

"Why, it's just like the book Tom Sawyer," Alberta giggled. "Except, you did no acrobatics on a fence like Tom did."

"You don't have a fence," Michael exclaimed, promising himself that he would read the book to which Alberta referred.

One night, as Michael and Alberta sat visiting on the front porch, Reverend Williams joined them. Politely but firmly, he expressed the desire to speak with Michael alone. Alberta excused herself to go inside to prepare lemonade.

"I sense you have some serious intentions which involve my daughter," Reverend Williams began.

"And they are honorable, sir," Michael answered. "I am hoping to convince Alberta to be my wife."

"Her mother and I do not want Alberta's education interrupted, young man. We have no rooms in this house for broken hearts."

Michael nodded. "I have no wish to break any."

By the time Alberta returned with the lemonade, talk of marriage and the future filled the air. Upset that it was her life being discussed and she was not in the discussion, Alberta retreated into the house. Soon Mrs. Williams could be heard trying to calm her daughter down. Then Woodie's voice joined in the conversation, followed by yet another friend's—all of whom stayed inside. "Like hens in a hen house," Reverend Williams chuckled.

A few minutes later, Woodie came out and went to Michael and hugged him. After a few more neighbors stopped by, Reverend Williams pulled Michael from the gathering and the two men headed down Auburn Avenue.

"This town is changing, King," Reverend Williams announced. "The South is changing. We got black people owning businesses, teaching, sending their kids to college. Whether the white man is ready or not, the South here is changing."

"Yes, sir."

"Lots of things happening here. But this isn't the right time for you and Alberta to be getting married. You want to be a quality preacher, then establish your ministry—now. Alberta wants to be a teacher. Let her reach that goal—now."

The two men continued walking. Finally, Michael felt he had to share his feelings openly.

"You know, what you say is true, Reverend Williams. But I feel mighty strong about Alberta. I'm inclined to think she feels pretty much the same way about me. I don't think that's going to change."

Reverend Williams stood still. "I'm not talking about your feelings. I'm talking about time. If your feelings are love, they'll not be changing in time. But just get yourself established, a place in the world. Then that love will serve you even better."

There was much wisdom in what Reverend Williams was saying. Michael promised to think everything over, and the two men returned to the house on Auburn Avenue.

In the months that followed, Michael saw Alberta every weekend. They discovered they had more and more in common. Baptist social life allowed no dancing, smoking, or drinking. It had never been a part of Michael's life in the country or of Alberta's life in the city. Gradually, Michael managed to convince Reverend Williams that picture shows were not filled with sin either, and the movies became a regular weekend activity. Picnics in the summer offered special fun, while winter outings included sharing good meals and conversation with friends.

Reverend Williams took a personal interest in Michael's preaching. In addition to splitting his preaching duties between two Atlanta churches, Michael helped out as often as he could at Ebenezer Baptist. It was the least he felt he could do for the assistance Reverend Williams provided with sermons and Bible study.

Once Alberta had finished her studies at Spelman, she was even more determined than ever to teach. But the Atlanta Board of Education refused to hire married women as teachers.

"If you really want to test your relationship," Reverend Williams suggested to Michael, "let her continue her studies just a bit longer. Before you came along, she'd planned to go off to Hampton Institute after she finished at the seminary. Let her try it."

Michael looked down at the floor. With Alberta away studying at Hampton in Virginia, he knew they would seldom see each other. Oh, they could write letters, but what good was that? It was being together, sharing the fun of doing absolutely nothing, laughing at the littlest things, learning—

"Perhaps we might remember Ecclesiastes 7:8 here, son. 'The patient in spirit is better than the proud in spirit.' Those are wise words."

Michael gazed up, looking Reverend Williams directly in the eyes. "I might be able to battle your own arguments, sir, but when you start hitting me over the head with Scripture, you sure do have me beat."

So it was that Alberta went off to study for a year and a half. The letters flowed back and forth regularly, though Michael immersed himself in religious studies in an effort to become the most polished minister he could be. He counted the days before his love would be returning. When she did, he headed for the railroad station with a bouquet of roses in his hand. Rain pelted the depot. Jumping out of his car and attempting to cradle the flowers from getting drenched, Michael leaped up the steps to the waiting area. "Coloreds wait down there, boy," a white railway employee directed. "This is a White Only area."

Michael flinched a minute, then recovered his composure. Nothing was going to ruin this day. Alberta was coming home.

Thunder rumbled across the sky. Michael glanced upward, smiling a moment. My, that Lord could certainly make a lot of noise when he wanted to. Man puts together these giant locomotives that whistle, blare and blast, yet the Good Lord can drown out any manmade noise he wants, anytime he wants. Yes, sir, Michael thought, that is one powerful God up there—or wherever he is.

And then, Alberta was there. Standing on a platform a hundred yards away. Like a galloping horse, Michael hurried to her, enveloping her in his arms and hugging her close.

"Aw, here you are home!" he shouted. "My little bunch of goodness is right here back with me again. I love you. Love you. Love you more than anything, you little bunch of goodness."

Alberta laughed. "What's this bunch of goodness business?"

Michael pulled the woman close. "Well, that's what you are to me. I'll shorten it if you want and just call you Bunch!"

"I rather like that," Alberta whispered. "Bunch of goodness. Bunch. Yes, I do like that, King."

The following Sunday morning Reverend Williams officially announced the engagement of his daughter Alberta to Mr. Martin Luther King, presently of Atlanta, formerly of Stockbridge. As the happy couple stood outside the church after services, members of the congregation paused to offer their congratulations and good wishes. One tired old woman gently leaned over to murmur into Michael's ear.

"I imagine you'll be taking over the church when the old man goes," she said.

Michael had never entertained such thoughts. He could not conceal his surprise at the remark.

But Reverend Williams, standing nearby, had also heard the old woman's comment. The minister rested a steadying hand upon her arm.

"An hour ago, I announced I was giving away my daughter to this young man, Mrs. Billings. Now would you have me give away my pulpit to him as well?"

The old woman raised her hand to her lips in a girlish giggle. Michael smiled, glanced at Reverend Williams, and laughed.

"The Lord works in mysterious ways, but we must be careful never to rush him," Michael offered.

Reverend Williams nodded his approval.

Christmas of 1923 was the most joyful Michael had ever experienced. As he spoke to the people in his churches, his voice reflected the inner happiness he felt. Never before had he felt so much love for the little baby Jesus, for just as God had sent his own beloved son into this world, this same God had sent Michael's own beloved Bunch, the love of his life. Yes, Michael King was totally in love.

And yet, as it so often happens, when one reaches the pinnacle of joy, he can be brought to the depths of sadness. That is exactly what happened in the spring of 1924 to twenty-five-year-old Michael King.

5

Atlanta basked in the glow of a rich April sunlight. As he slouched in the driver's seat of his car in front of the bus depot, Michael closed his eyes, remembering the words of one of his favorite spirituals from childhood.

> Oh, Peter, go ring them bells,
> Peter, go ring them bells,
> Peter, go ring them bells,
> I heard from heaven today.

Sometimes Michael felt a twinge of guilt, feeling as good as he did, engaged to the most wonderful girl in the world with more and more people coming to his churches to hear him preach, adding a few more dollars every week to a savings account at the bank . . .

> Oh, Peter, go ring them bells,
> Peter, go ring them bells,
> Peter, go ring them bells,
> I heard from heaven today.

The sound of a bus horn broke Michael's thoughts. Quickly he scrambled out of his car, eager to welcome his brothers Henry and James who had come to spend the weekend. But when he saw their sad, tired faces, Michael immediately knew something was wrong.

"It's Mama, Mike," Henry admitted. "She's awful

sick. Said we shouldn't be worryin' you with her troubles, but—"

"You care if we just head on back to Stockbridge right now?" Michael queried.

James forced a smile. "We was hopin' you might want to do just that."

Never before had Michael driven his car so fast. Now and then Henry and James exchanged nervous glances, but they were not about to slow down their older brother.

As Michael drove, he prayed. Mama. How badly he wanted to share the good life with Mama. She had seen so little. Work and struggle was all she had known. If only she could get to know Bunch, beautiful, kind Bunch. In so many ways, they were alike. Always caring for others. Wanting to please. Michael made a promise to get home to Stockbridge more. There would be happy times again. Maybe Henry and James were making more of this than they should . . .

But once Michael saw Mama sitting in her favorite stuffed chair, the Bible resting in her lap, he knew his brothers were not just telling stories. Beneath her chin, a huge tumor had grown. She could not even turn or lift her head. Yet her eyes sparkled when she saw Michael.

For an hour they talked before she began to doze off. "Darn fool medicine the doctor sold me just seems to make me sleep all the time," Mama murmured.

"I'll be here when you wake up, Mama," Michael whispered, pulling a blanket a bit higher around her thin frame.

Learning from his brothers that the doctor who had sold Mama the medicine was just a quack passing through town, Michael knew what he had to do. One of his friends at the boardinghouse had a cousin who practiced medicine in Atlanta. Michael was determined that Mama should have a real examination.

Back to Atlanta Michael drove, the wheels of his car barely touching the ground. The winter weather had played havoc with the old country roads, but Michael did not seem to notice. Mama was sick and needed help. Within two hours, he had picked up the doctor and was heading back to Stockbridge.

Waiting outside the cabin while the doctor examined his mother, Michael prayed. He prayed harder than he had ever prayed for anything. Surely if God were merciful, truly merciful, Mama would be spared . . .

But the doctor's report held no such hope. "There's nothing anyone can do for her," the medical man said as the two of them walked around the cabin together. "Just keep her comfortable. She has a while yet, a few months perhaps."

A few months. The words rang in Michael's ears. Where was this merciful God? Why? Why did Mama have to be taken?

And yet later, as Michael helped his mother into bed, a new thought came to him. She was suffering much pain. She was in agony. To have her live on like this would be showing no mercy. It was selfish to hope for that. A merciful God, a truly merciful God would take her home.

"Forgive me for doubting you," Michael whispered into the night breezes as he walked alone. "What fools we are to doubt you." Michael returned to the family home to be with his mother during her final months. The pain grew deeper and longer as time passed. But somehow Mama King always displayed a light smile as she listened to "her young preacher boy" recite Scripture. And sometimes, especially when Michael would read her favorite Psalms, a tiny voice within the sick old woman would hum, just as Michael had remembered years ago.

At nights, as he fought for sleep to come, Michael tried to avoid cursing the whites who had brought so much pain, so much hurt to his family, and on all blacks. He thought about how hard Mama had worked for the wealthy white families in Stockbridge. He remembered the day she had gone to the mill, angry because the owner had hurt her son.

But when he shared his feelings with Mama, the dying woman only shook her head. "Don't hate, Michael. Hatred makes nothin' but more hatred." Her voice was weak, yet her hand lay firmly over Michael's.

One morning her breathing became heavier, more difficult. Shortly before noon, Delia Lindsay King slipped into a final sleep.

Mama King's death left Michael feeling empty. But the awareness that her suffering was done and his firm conviction that the good Lord was only showing mercy and love when he took her home to him offered considerable comfort.

Sadly enough, Papa King felt no such comfort. He was devastated. Whereas Michael gathered strength from his Christian faith, Papa turned once more to whiskey. At the funeral services, he wept uncontrollably, holding himself accountable for Mama's suffering while he could do nothing to help. At the graveside, Papa's grief grew even worse. Michael clutched the older man, trying desperately to find the right words to soothe.

"I can't live without her, boy!" Papa wept. "What can I do now?"

Closely Michael leaned toward his father's ear. "Remember what she always told us, Papa. 'God will provide.' And he will, Papa. We must believe that he will."

Despite the fact that he had been living in Atlanta for six years, Michael still considered Stockbridge home. But it was a home of the past, of his childhood. With Mama gone, the King homestead seemed so empty, so barren. Within the same year, tragedy struck once again. Michael's sister Ruby suffered a ruptured appendix and died. Once more, the shadows of grief hung over the family. Michael did his best to bring his loved ones comfort, but he knew he had to get back to Atlanta before he physically collapsed. Remaining in Stockbridge would only hold him back.

"Back home, I just feel like a nigger," Michael confided to Bunch one evening as they sat on the Williams' front porch. "I know I'm just as black here in Atlanta as I am at home, but somehow I feel better about myself here."

"It might be because you're getting an education here in Atlanta," Bunch offered. "You feel like you're moving ahead in that respect."

"Could be. But I got so much further I want to go. And I just get so angry cause it seems like whatever you do, whites are standin' in the way, trying to stop us from gettin' anywhere. And those who aren't standin' right in the way are just standin' behind the curtains in their front rooms, watchin' what's happenin' and not doin' a thing to stop it—"

"King, you're raising your voice . . ." Bunch lay a warm hand over the young man's clenched fist, carefully prying it open and slipping her own inside. "Remember what your Mama told you."

Nodding, Michael looked down at his feet. "I know, I know. But someday I'm goin' to make a few whites sorry for what they done to my Mama and all of us. Someday . . ."

Bunch continued to maintain a steadying influence. When Michael finished his studies at Bryant School, she encouraged him to continue his formal education. Reverend Williams encouraged the plan too, suggesting that he investigate the class schedule at Morehouse College, a Baptist sponsored school in Atlanta. Having attended the college himself, Reverend Williams was familiar with the institution.

More than a bit unsure of himself, Michael visited the Morehouse campus in the fall of 1926. When he presented himself at the registrar's office, the man behind the desk looked dubious about Michael's chances. Lloyd O. Lewis hardly looked old enough to be a registrar, but he spoke with authority.

"Frankly, Mr. King, I think you would be wasting our time and I think you would be wasting yours as well." Mr. Lewis shook his head as he gazed once again at the past school records Michael had brought along. "Clearly you have tried to better yourself. That is fine. But in looking over your records and talking with you, I just don't think you belong here."

"Can't I take some tests? Maybe that would show you different."

Mr. Lewis rubbed his chin. "Yes, I suppose we could do that. But I don't want you to get your hopes up."

Michael nodded. "I just want a chance."

A series of exams were given. Mr. Lewis administered and graded them himself. When he finished, he was even more pessimistic about Michael's chances.

"You just don't have the background for college work," Mr. Lewis explained. "We speak of the best spoken language as being 'the King's English.' No insult intended, but they certainly aren't speaking about your language usage. And your test results just don't convince me you could handle the work."

Inside, Michael seethed. It was hard enough battling obstacles tossed in his way by whites. But when other blacks tried to stop his goals, it was unbearable.

"Let me try," Michael demanded. "I'll work hard. There ain't anything I can't learn."

"Sorry," Mr. Lewis said, closing Michael's folder. "It's nothing personal. You just don't have the background. Be satisfied with how far you've come."

The words stung Michael. He was not about to give up. Yet, when the registrar will not let you into the college you want to attend, what do you do? An angry, frustrated Michael King stormed out of the office.

When he shared his disappointment with Bunch, she merely shook her head. "You said you had a terrible time getting to know me at first," the woman laughed. "But you stuck with it. There has to be a way here. If you want to be a truly fine preacher, you had best get all the education you can."

With new spirit and determination, Michael returned to the registrar's office. Once more, he talked with Mr. Lewis, begging for an opportunity to prove what he could do.

"Give me just one term," Michael begged. "If the work is too hard or I'm failing, I'll drop out and never bother you again. I just want a chance."

Lloyd Lewis was not impressed. He simply sat in his chair, woefully shaking his head from side to side. "You would just be wasting your time and our time. I've looked at your test scores. You can't do the required work at Morehouse. You just don't have the stuff, Mr. King."

It was hopeless to argue and Michael knew it. Mr. Lewis had made up his mind and there was no changing it. Feeling battered and defeated, Michael trudged out of the office.

For an hour the downhearted young man wandered about the campus. He heard students laughing, watched them hurrying to class, listened to their conversations. Why not me? he wondered. I could do it. I know I could.

Michael walked through the front doors of Morehouse Administration Building. Barely giving the secretary a glance, he proceeded directly into the office of the president of the college. From behind a large ornate desk, a man looked up. President John Hope made no attempt to hide his anger at the unannounced intrusion. But Michael met the older man's stare head-on.

"Sir, I am Reverend Michael King. I took tests to come to this school, and I know my scores weren't too good. Still, I want more education, and I want to come here to Morehouse."

"Have you spoken to Mr. Lewis, our registrar?"

Michael almost laughed out loud. "Indeed I have. He has tested me and said I don't belong here. But he don't know what I can do if I put my mind to it. I've been taking classes at Bryant Preparatory School. I've been making up about two years worth of schooling a year. I don't want to stop now . . ."

The more Michael spoke, the less interested the college president looked. The situation appeared hopeless. Finally, Michael got up, thanked President Hope for his time, and left the building. No sooner had he reached the front steps when President Hope's secretary summoned him back into the office. There, John Hope handed Michael a letter. It was addressed to Mr. Lewis.

The sight of Michael obviously did not please the registrar. The contents of the letter pleased him even less.

"It seems you may begin classes at Morehouse Monday morning," Mr. Lewis said, tossing the letter on his desk in disgust. "Don't ask me why, but you can."

Resisting the temptation to burst out "Praise the Lord!", Michael simply nodded and backed out the door. All the way home he thought about President Hope's willingness to take a chance. Michael promised that he would not let the college leader down.

Fighting as he did to get into Morehouse also helped push Michael forward in another way. Bunch felt totally convinced that he was truly serious about his future. A student at Morehouse College—a practicing preacher in churches in Atlanta's East Point and College Park—yes, Michael King had proved himself to be a capable, responsible young man.

"I think we've been engaged long enough," Bunch announced one evening. "Perhaps we should select a wedding date."

No news could have made Michael happier. He proudly notified his family in Stockbridge. He took special delight in telling his friends who had once laughed at his intention to marry Miss Alberta Williams.

"When I say I'm goin' to do somethin', I mean just that!" Michael laughed.

The marriage ceremony was held Thanksgiving Day, November 25, 1926. The sanctuary of Ebenezer Baptist Church was filled to overflowing with members of the King and Williams families.

"I'll do my best to make you happy," Michael promised Bunch as he pulled her away from the well-wishers.

Bunch smiled. "I will do the same, my love."

6

Moving into the big Williams family home on Auburn Avenue after the marriage did not bother Michael. It was common among the Negro community in many areas of the South to share living accommodations with relatives. The upstairs floor was spacious and comfortable. Reverend and Mrs. Williams were accustomed to having members of their family live with them. They welcomed Bunch and Michael.

What did trouble Michael were the rumors that he had married into the Williams family for social prestige or to take over the pulpit of Ebenezer Baptist Church. Such situations did take place, especially within Baptist circles, and Michael wanted to make certain no one suspected him of such evil motives. Even when Reverend Williams encouraged his new son-in-law to join full-time in the work at Ebenezer, Michael refused. He turned a deaf ear to Bunch's coaxing too.

"I have two congregations of my own to tend," he declared. "I feel needed there, at East Point and College Park. Your father understands. His people at Ebenezer need him."

Bunch, never one to give up easily, suggested, "He could use your help too."

Michael shook his head. "Not now, love. Someday, maybe. But not now."

Living in the Williams house gave Michael a new picture of ministry as a profession. Ever since he had received his license as a preacher, he had looked at ministry as a part-time job, a responsibility to be juggled with going to classes and earning a living. For the most part, his preaching duties fell heavily on Saturday and Sunday.

But firsthand observation of Reverend Adam Daniel Williams revealed that ministry was much more. It was a full-time calling. Saturday might well be the day set aside for writing a sermon and Sunday the day for delivering it publicly, but effective ministry found its way into every day. Members of the congregation visited the Williams house often, sometimes for discussion of a minor domestic problem, other times for counseling about major family conflicts.

"A good minister is a good listener," Reverend Williams often reminded Michael. "Often, if people are allowed to share their feelings, the good Lord will suddenly slip in and point the way. You may give your best direction by keeping your mouth closed."

"That's not easy for a preacher like me," Michael admitted.

"Not for any of us, I'm thinking. Yet it's true nonetheless. Anyone who professes to have all the answers probably knows much less than they think."

Michael learned from his father-in-law. The older man also carried his ministry far beyond the limits of Ebenezer Baptist Church. Reverend Williams emphasized the need for social as well as spiritual involvement.

"Yes, a minister's job is to feed the soul, to make it fresh and pure in the eyes of God," the preacher declared. "But we can not ignore the needs of the body as well. No one can hear me speak of the road to heaven if their empty stomach is drowning out the sound of my voice."

Reverend Williams made sense to Michael. It all seemed to fall into place. If a person hoped to attain the joy and richness of life hereafter, the life lived on earth must follow the Lord's example.

Michael was impressed with the way Reverend Williams functioned within the Atlanta community. Many black ministers were content to take orders from whites, whether it be in the realm of religious faith or existence in the day-to-day life. Not Pastor Williams. He saw black people as human beings, equal to the whites, no more or no less in the eyes of God. Just as blacks were expected to assume responsibility for their actions, they were also entitled to the rights accorded to whites. Not all blacks agreed with Reverend Williams. Many black leaders would do anything to avoid confrontation with whites. These leaders carried the message to their followers, both in church and in the general community.

"It did not take us a day to get in the position we are in," Reverend Williams said often. "It will certainly take us longer than a day to get out."

Through his living with and talking to Reverend Williams on a daily basis, Michael learned a great deal about the successful management of a church. Of course, at the core was leading the congregation in humble worship of God and his beloved Son, Jesus Christ.

There was much more to managing a church, though, than worship. Whereas Michael had trained himself well in a study of Holy Scripture, prayer, and song, he lacked an awareness of how a church was organized or program administered. With Reverend Williams as a patient mentor, Michael began establishing youth activities within his own two churches. Church councils were set up, choirs were formed, volunteers were recruited to fulfill church chores. Regular calls were made to the sick and shut-in.

"And keep careful records of your money, Michael," Reverend Williams suggested. "People work hard to make it and they want it spent wisely."

Michael nodded. "You seem to know so much about everything. I only wish I'd have had your background."

"Just about the same as yours, son," the older man laughed. "Just a country preacher from Greene County.

Packed up and came to Atlanta on my thirtieth birthday. Got me a little church in nearby Kennesaw while I worked full-time in a machine shop. No, I didn't have any advantages as you might be thinking. Had a Pa with a gift for words and a good heart. But other than that, I just listened to the Lord for direction."

Michael made his own silent promise to "listen to the Lord for direction." Surely it was a generous Lord who had brought him a loving wife in Bunch, and a good home with the Williams family. The more Michael saw and learned of his father-in-law, the more he respected him. Reverend Williams was not one to speak often of himself, citing Proverbs 15:33 "before honour is humility" as his reason. Michael pieced together a fairly complete background of the man through Bunch and others who knew him.

True, Adam Daniel Williams had come to Atlanta as a man of thirty in 1892, but he wasted no time in emerging as an eloquent spokesman for the black community. It was not eloquence in the usual sense of the word, for like Michael, Reverend Williams often displayed a difficulty with the English language. Growing up black in rural Georgia seldom provided a firm command of language rules. But Williams spoke with feeling and power. What he lacked in the fundamentals of grammar and vocabulary, he made up for in intensity and fervor. From the moment he took over the pulpit of Ebenezer Baptist Church in 1894, the congregation grew steadily. When Atlanta suffered a race riot in 1906, it was Reverend Williams who quickly organized the Atlanta Civic League, an organization that met with white civil leaders to relax racial tensions. He was also an early member of the National Association for the Advancement of Colored People. When the editor of a white newspaper labeled Atlanta blacks "dirty and ignorant," many were outraged. Some wanted to burn the building housing the newspaper down. Reverend Williams did not.

"Violence begets violence," he told one angry mob. Rather than an aggressive physical attack, Reverend Williams designed a boycott which closed the newspaper down in a matter of weeks.

Reverend Williams took a keen interest in the lives of the young blacks of Atlanta. He welcomed eager newly ordained ministers into his office, pouring out advice for hours. He led a Negro citizens committee that persuaded Atlanta's educational leaders to build Booker T. Washington High School, the city's one and only secondary school for blacks.

To Michael, Reverend Adam Daniel Williams represented the ideal black man of the times, recognizing problems of his race and working actively for solutions. He was a man worthy of imitation. For hours, the two men sat in the garden behind the house on Auburn Street and exchanged thoughts and ideas.

"I have been doubly blessed by the Lord," Michael told Bunch one night. "First of all, he brought you to me. Secondly, he brought your father to me. Sometimes I think my heart and mind will burst with all you both give me."

Bunch lowered her head. "Would you mind being 'triply' blessed?" she asked softly.

Michael shook his head, confused. "What do you—" The words caught in his throat as he suddenly realized what Bunch was saying. A baby! She was—they were going to have a baby. Michael pulled his wife close to him, hugging her firmly but gently. "I surely don't deserve all this goodness in my life. I sure don't."

Born in September of 1927, the baby girl was named Willie Christine. It was not an easy birth and Bunch's recovery was very slow. The baby, too, became ill, running high temperatures and obviously in much pain. Day after day, Michael divided every minute between his wife and infant daughter. "Give me the strength, Lord," he prayed often. Somehow the strength was always there. Whether coaxing Bunch to sip a few more spoonsful of broth or carrying Willie Christine in his arms, Michael offered a cheerful face and happy spirit.

Finally, Bunch began to regain her strength. But the baby still cried constantly, frequently shaking in violent spasms. One night, as Michael tried to catch a short nap on the front porch, he suddenly jumped up. Willie Christine was not crying. There was no sound at all coming from her room. Hurrying inside, Michael raced to the infant's bedside. There she lay, her eyes wide open and her face displaying a wide smile. Lifting the child into his arms, Michael felt the coolness of her skin. The fever was gone. Hallejujah! The fever was gone.

The joy Michael felt at having his wife and baby healthy again was taken into the pulpit. His preaching told of a great and wonderful Lord, a loving Savior, a God worthy of all sacrifice. "Amen!" the people answered. "Amen! Amen! Amen!" With renewed spirit, Michael led the singing:

> I spoke last night to Jesus
> I spoke to him awhile,
> He listened to me closely
> 'Cause I am Jesus' child.

Having an infant in the twelve-room Williams home brought a closeness to the family. At times, Bunch worried that the baby was getting too much attention. But she could hardly complain to her husband. Michael was the chief offender. Although he was busy with classes at Morehouse, trying to balance the duties at two Atlanta churches and helping with responsibilities in the family home, he still managed to find time to shower attention on tiny Willie Christine.

If he had hoped for any special consideration at Morehouse College, Michael hoped in vain. There was an unspoken rule that Morehouse men did not quit; there could be no thought of dropping out. With the struggle Michael had faced getting in, that idea seldom crossed his mind. But there were days of serious doubt whether or not he could get through. English proved a major hurdle with the instructor, Miss Constance Crocker, determined to make every one of her students reach definite standards before she passed them. She flunked Michael during his first term. Undaunted, he tried again—with the same result. Finally, on his third attempt, he managed to squeeze by with a "D".

"I do believe Joshua had an easier time fightin' the battle of Jerico than I'm havin' at Morehouse College," Michael joked to Reverend Williams.

The older man nodded. "Ah, but the sounds of those trumpets make mighty fine music! Keep up the battle, son."

When Bunch told Michael she was once again expecting a baby, he took the news with mixed emotion. The birth of Willie Christine had been difficult for Bunch. The doctors could not promise this birth would be any easier. Still, Bunch wanted to have more children, and Michael found it impossible to deny his beloved any of her wishes.

On January 15, 1929, a son was born to Michael and Alberta King. The pregnancy had taken its toll on Bunch, and the birth drained what little strength she had left. The family sequestered itself in prayer. Slowly but steadily the woman rallied.

"When you've got all the folks prayin' for you that we had," Michael told his wife, "you know God is going to listen."

Since the folks of Atlanta had always known Michael King as Michael, it was decided to call the new infant Michael Jr. Papa King still maintained his own son was

Martin, named after one of Papa's brothers and Luther, after still another brother. However, since there was no birth certificate stating such facts, most accepted Mike Sr. and Mike Jr.

On July 30, 1930, the third and final member of the King family made his appearance. Named Alfred Daniel, the new baby was immediately nicknamed "A.D."

With increased intensity, Michael threw himself into completing his studies at Morehouse. Four years of stubborn determination got him through. It was a triumphant moment in June of 1930 when Michael received his bachelor's degree in theology. At the age of thirty, he was almost ten years older than most of the other graduates. He won no awards for scholarship, but he felt the inner satisfaction that comes from knowing a task with many obstacles had been completed.

If the three young babies brought cheer and happiness to the Williams house on Auburn Street, it was greatly needed as a new decade opened. The bitter Depression, which closed banks and left people without jobs, swept into Atlanta like a human tidal wave of agony and despair. Churches which had constantly climbed in attendance through the 1920's suddenly dropped sharply. Many people felt confused and disillusioned. Had God turned away from them? Some thought so, and they reflected their sorrow and their mood by staying away from services.

Still the preacher at East Point, to help the family's financial situation Michael decided to accept an invitation to take over the pulpit of the Traveler's Rest Baptist Church. It was not a rich congregation, but one in which the people contributed food to help pay the preacher when needed. Michael felt a personal calling to serve this congregation, although he knew the Williams family would welcome his addition to the running of Ebenezer Baptist. He was still concerned that people might think he was taking advantage of family connections.

As Michael worked desperately to meet the needs of his congregations, he could not help but marvel at the energy and devotion of his father-in-law. What money came into Ebenezer Baptist was carefully dispensed among the most needy families. Reverend Williams maintained a week-to-week check on every member of his two hundred person congregation. He visited the most destitute homes himself, taking food and clothing. Children were carefully supervised while their fathers and mothers worked at whatever jobs they could find. Special prayer services were held, group conversations promoted to share problems and concerns.

"Our pockets may be empty, but our hearts are full," Reverend Williams told those who gathered.

But sadly enough, the good minister's heart was as tired as it was full. As Reverend Williams played with his three-year-old granddaughter one spring morning in 1931, the respected church leader suddenly collapsed on the floor. Quickly the girl ran into the kitchen to tell her mother and grandmother, "Grandpa fell asleep on the living room floor."

Michael took the death of his father-in-law and good friend deeply. Still immersed in his own shock and grief, he was called to take over the pastorate of Ebenezer Baptist Church. The decision weighed heavily on him. Surely he would be compared to Reverend Williams, and Michael King knew that those were shoes he could never hope to fill. There was Bunch to think of too."

"Don't accept the pastorate at Ebenezer," she told her husband. "You'll never be in Daddy's shadow if you stay at Traveler's Rest. I'm my own person too. I can be the First Lady at Traveler's Rest. That will never happen at Ebenezer."

It was a convincing argument. Michael tried to seclude himself while he pondered his decision. But ultimately, he knew it was not his decision to make anyway.

"God, show me the way," Michael prayed. "Let me know what direction you will have me take. Whatever choice you make, I shall abide by it, as always."

A humble Michael King waited for his answer.

7

In the autumn of 1931 Michael King assumed the pastorate of Ebenezer Baptist Church in Atlanta. In his mind, he had felt the call from God to make this selection. Not able to completely hide her disappointment, Bunch nonetheless vowed her complete devotion and support. For some of the church deacons who would have preferred a more experienced, older minister, it took only the appearance of Mrs. Williams in the pulpit, declaring her loving respect and trust in Michael, to lay their fears to rest.

Within weeks, Michael had cause to wonder if that respect and trust had been wisely placed. He arrived at the church one morning to find the front doors padlocked. From the marshals present, Michael learned that the church had been seized for non-payment of debts.

A visit to Atlanta Federal Savings Bank revealed that the realty company which had the mortgage of Ebenezer Baptist had gone broke. The bank simply seized all the realty company holdings.

"But we have to have our church open," Michael insisted. "These times are bad enough for our people. They need us. We need them."

"There's an outstanding balance of $1100," one of the bank officials said.

"We can raise it. Let us try."

A payment schedule was carefully charted. A note was written to be met in five years.

When Michael took the agreement to the church deacons, some balked at the idea of telling the congregation. After all, most families were struggling with money problems of their own. Sixty-five percent of Atlanta's black community were on public relief rolls. Did they want to hear about more financial difficulties in church on Sunday?

"Are we not forgetting Luke 6:20?" Michael asked. 'Blessed be ye poor; for yours is the kingdom of God.' The people are the church. Let us share everything with them. Would God have us keep secrets? People come together during hardship and suffering. I believe our people will."

Michael's instincts were right. Like a giant family, the people of Ebenezer Baptist Church unified. Fathers and mothers scrimped together what nickles and dimes they could, proudly depositing them in church collection plates. The five year note was paid off in three.

Michael was deeply moved by the unselfish spirit of his congregation. He had further reason for thanksgiving when Papa King came to spend his final years with Michael's brothers and sisters in Atlanta. Not only that, but the weary old man stopped drinking, became a churchgoer and took a keen interest in the Bible.

One problem still troubled Papa King. He knew Michael had never had a birth certificate. Few people did who were born at the turn of the century in rural Southern communities. As his life was ending, Papa became more and more adamant about getting Michael officially to declare himself Martin Luther King. It seemed a modest request in light of Papa King's own personal reformations, so Michael completed the necessary documents. Papa died in 1933, knowing his oldest son was Martin Luther King, Sr. Glad that he had satisfied his father's dying wish, Michael then took legal action to have his own elder son, whose name was listed as Michael King, Jr. on his birth certificate, officially become Martin Luther King, Jr. To family friends and family members, they were still called Mike and M. L.

Grateful that he had been able to heal many of the wounds with Papa King before he died, Michael vowed never to let such painful hurts happen in his own family. "Too many years were wasted between Papa and me," he told Bunch. "I'm not going to let that happen again."

Whenever he could free himself from the activities at Ebenezer Baptist, Michael spent time with his children. The open field in back of the King house was perfect for playing baseball and flying kites. M. L. displayed a strong throwing arm in his early years.

"Watch me Daddy King," M. L. shouted. "I can throw farther and faster than anyone."

The boast was a bit exaggerated, but a proud Daddy King applauded his son's efforts. Chris, M. L. and A. D. each took to calling their father "Daddy," while Bunch was referred to as "Mother Dear" by the three youngsters.

Daddy King insisted on hearing his children recite Scripture after evening meals in the dining room. He chuckled as they mispronounced names, then offered correction and encouraged them to continue.

Grandmother Williams was the family's favorite storyteller. With M. L., Chris and A. D. on the floor at her feet, she kept their eyes open wide and their hearts skipping fast with the adventures of King David, Daniel and all the rest. They begged for more, but scampered quickly to bed when Daddy King gave the order.

By the time M. L. officially joined the church at the age of five, people were already commenting how similar he was to his father. It was no accident. As Daddy King spoke in the pulpit at Ebenezer Baptist, he was ever conscious of the wide eyes of his older son watching. Afterwards, M. L. would imitate his father, bringing family members to happy tears with his small arms flailing and mispronounced words tumbling from his mouth. Whenever he got the chance, and the opportunities came often as word spread, the boy would burst into a chorus of "I

Want to be More Like Jesus." His youthful voice with its blues overtone brought tears to the eyes of listeners as they rocked and swayed to the music. M. L. loved to sing, but did not understand what people got so excited about. Daddy kept a close eye on the boy, not wanting him to get "puffed up and proud."

Coming from a background where every penny had to be counted and carefully spent, Daddy King hoped to instill the same frugality within his own children. Often he prayed, "God, grant that my children will not have to come the way I did." Not only did he pray for God's help with his family, Daddy budgeted every cent for their welfare. He would not tolerate wastefulness. Plates were scraped clean at mealtime and clothes were worn threadbare.

"He that spareth his rod hateth his son: but he that loveth him chasteneth him betimes." Proverbs 13:24 provided Daddy King with the standard for discipline among his children. A strap was his "rod" and punishment for misbehavior was swift. He took the task of disciplining his children seriously, and both his wife and Grandmother Williams wanted no part of it. Early enough, it became clear that M. L. was Grandmother Williams' favorite, and she retreated to her room whenever the boy was destined for a strapping. Like most children, Chris and A. D. cried loudly during such ordeals, perhaps hoping for a swat or two less out of pity. Not M. L. The tears would roll down his cheeks, but the boy endured his strappings silently.

M. L. loved having books around. Even before he could read a word, he was drawn to books. He stacked them up like other children stack blocks. "When I grow up, I'm going to get me some big words," the boy boasted. "Just wait and see."

Eager to give their precocious son direction on his educational route, his parents enrolled M. L. in grade school a year early. When he came home early one afternoon, Daddy King demanded an explanation.

"Couldn't you do the work? Was it too hard for you?"

M. L. shook his head. "No, I could do the work fine. But I was the only one there who was five years old. Everybody else was six. I guess I shouldn't have bragged that I was five."

Daddy King nodded. "Knowing when to talk is just as important as knowing what to say."

When M. L. did enter school the next year, he learned an even more painful lesson. His favorite playmate, a boy who lived across the street, was also scheduled to start school. The two friends talked about all the fun they would have at school together. But when the schoolbells sounded in September of 1935, M. L. was sent to the all black Younge Street Elementary School where Christine attended. His friend headed to the nearby white school. Why? M. L. wanted to know. His friend's mother answered in a straight matter-of-fact manner: "You're colored, M. L., and we are white."

M. L. was totally bewildered. It was his first face-to-face encounter with discrimination. Not only would he not be going to the same school as his friend, but the mother went on to say, "I really don't think you should come over here to play anymore, M. L."

When M. L. shared the day's happenings at the dinner table that evening, Daddy King's eyes flashed with anger. His initial inclination was to jump up, head across the street, and tell the so-called white Christian neighbors just what he thought. But one look at Bunch and another at Grandmother Williams, and Daddy knew that was not the answer.

"Well, M. L., what happened to you today is just a part of the race problem we got," Daddy explained.

"What's that?" the puzzled boy asked, his face showing his confusion.

"Well, you just listen, M. L. You too, Chrissie and

A. D. This is how things is and you might as well know right now . . ."

Deliberately and carefully, Daddy King told how the first black men were captured in Africa, then brought to America to be sold as slaves. "They was thought of as property, things, not as people," Daddy continued. "Lots of slaves were brought here, to the South, 'cause there were so many farms to raise crops on." The man told about President Abraham Lincoln, the Emancipation Proclamation, how slaves were freed legally, but that whites still tried to act superior and make blacks feel lower than whites.

"Are we lower?" M. L. asked.

This time it was Bunch who spoke. "You are just as good as anybody else, M. L. You are one of God's children, just like everybody else is one of God's children. No person is better or worse than anyone else."

In the days that followed, Daddy King tried to comfort M. L. Losing a best friend was important. Daddy remembered how much it had hurt twenty-five years before when Jay's father had simply called a young Michael "one of my niggers." Then there was the rich white family in Stockbridge who wouldn't let him come through the front door . . . and the mill owner who kicked him . . . yes, there were many stories shared. M. L. listened closely to every word. And the more Daddy spoke of the insults he had suffered, hoping that by hearing them that M. L. would be able to face the real world better, the more shocked the young boy became. Inside of him grew not only an awareness of how mean people could be, but also a hate for white people.

Recalling his own troubled past and mindful of the difficulties facing his own children, Daddy King became more active in his personal battle against segregation. Whether with friends over dinner, from the pulpit at Ebenezer Baptist Church, or at one of the many meetings he attended, Daddy complained long and loud about the unfair treatment given blacks.

"We must live in different neighborhoods than the whites, drink from different water fountains, shop at different stores, use different bathrooms. Yet we do it."

"It's better here in Atlanta than in other places," someone would remark.

"Maybe the whites will see it your way some day, Mike," another would offer.

Such comments only inflamed Daddy's spirit for change even more. Just because Atlanta was "not as bad as other places" did not make segregation right. And why was it necessary for the whites to be ready to make changes? They were not suffering. They did not experience daily insults and hardships. No, if things were going to change, the blacks were going to do it.

When Daddy King spoke of such matters, all three of his children listened. They knew they had better listen— or else. "Respect your elders" was an important rule in the house at 501 Auburn. But although all three listened to Daddy King, M. L. listened best. The sensitive boy worshiped his father, and wanted to be just like him. M. L. did not want to miss anything Daddy had to say. His teachers at Younge Elementary knew everything about words and numbers, coloring and history. Yet they seldom spoke the way Daddy King did. His lessons were in living, and M. L. knew some of those lessons were unfair.

Schoolwork came easily to M. L. He enjoyed sharing what he knew with the members of his family, yet it was not done with arrogance or conceit. There was more of a feeling of self-confidence and pleasure of accomplishment. Often he raced home from school, eager to sing a new song he had learned or recite a poem he had memorized. He would practice it first on Grandmother Williams, assured that she would appreciate his efforts, no matter how rough and unprepared they might be. Once he had attained mastery of his performance, M. L. would be ready to appear before Daddy King. He would be a more rigid taskmaster, not providing praise and compliments unless they had been earned. When they did come, M. L. felt a total satisfaction, a sudden warmth that swept through his entire body.

At school, M. L. made friends readily, often completing his own work and volunteering to assist peers experiencing difficulty at assigned tasks. The "respect-for-elders" code established firmly within the King family transferred easily into the classroom. Among the teachers at Younge Elementary, M. L. earned a reputation as being both academically talented and cooperative with every adult working with him.

At church events, M. L. enjoyed the immediate status that comes from being "the preacher's son." At school, he earned the recognition afforded "the best student in the class." But it was outside of these circles that M. L. suffered the hurt dispensed to all black youths growing up in the South. The color line was everywhere.

"We don't serve ice cream to Negroes over the counter," a waitress would announce. "If you want some ice cream, go over to the side." When the ice cream did come, it was not in a dish like the white people were given. It was in a paper cup.

When he rode a bus, M. L. knew what the bus driver would say before he even opened his mouth. "Colored to the back. Colored to the back."

Downtown theaters were open to Negroes, as long as they entered though a side door and sat in the back balcony. There was a black theater too, but it showed movies ten years old on a dilapidated screen.

So M. L. went to his father often with the question "Why? Why is there one way for whites and one way for us?"

Daddy would often shake his head. "It shouldn't be that way, but that's the way it is. We're workin' to change things son, but it ain't easy. Most folks don't care."

M. L. cared. He cared because his father cared. At

the dinner table when Daddy King talked about the problems of blacks getting jobs in Atlanta, M. L. listened. He listened to Daddy talk about organizing people to march to the City Hall and register to vote. Daddy spoke loudly when he talked. Sometimes he shouted, even pounding the table in excitement. Always Mother Dear remained cool and calm, nodding agreement or asking quiet questions. M. L. did not understand everything being said, but he sensed it was important. If Daddy did something, it had to be important.

Daddy King praised M. L. for being a good listener. "You must learn to work, to play and to think. The first two you can do with others. But it is important that you learn to think by yourself."

M. L. enjoyed being by himself. Often he headed into the backyard, a book clutched in his hand, and found a quiet secluded spot in the shade of the gnarled oak tree. For hours the boy would read, now and then closing the pages and letting thoughts tumble in his mind. How big was God? If everyone laughed at once, how loud would it be? What if all the people in the world were white? Or black? Ideas. Dreams. He liked making up little songs, humming and singing:

> I love you and you love me
> That's the world that it should be
> You love me and I love you
> And we know God loves us too . . .

Yes, the church, the school, the backyard—all offered a special dreamworld, a life of security and safety. And yet, sadly, there was always an event that would turn the dreamworld into a nightmare. Try as he could to protect his children from the ugliness of racial slurs and injustices, Daddy King failed.

M. L. fought for Daddy's individual attention. Always the man was surrounded by other members of the family, church leaders, teachers and other adults. Sharing an afternoon alone with his father delighted M. L. Usually they would go visiting friends or shopping the black business section of Atlanta. As they drove the family car near the center of town one day, M. L. suddenly asked his Daddy to stop the car. As soon as he did, they boy bounded out and raced to the windows of a giant shoe store.

"Can I have those, Daddy?" M. L. asked, pointing at a pair of shoes in the window. "Mama says I'm supposed to get a new pair."

"Right you are, M. L.," Daddy answered.

No sooner had the two customers stepped inside than a clerk appeared. The man sternly ordered them to the back of the store where he would help them in a few minutes.

It was the wrong request to make. Daddy King was in no mood to be ordered around in such a way, not with his young son beside him.

"We're quite comfortable here," Daddy huffed. "If you don't want to sell us any shoes in front of your store, we won't be buying any."

This time it was the clerk's turn to show his indignance. "Negroes are waited on in the rear of the store," he announced firmly. "There are no exceptions to this rule. Stop being so high and mighty and follow the rules like everybody else."

Daddy King clenched his fists. In truth, he wanted to strike out, to soundly thrash the miserable pile of humanity degrading him in front of his son. "Negroes to the back. Negroes to the back." Why was it always "Negroes to the back"?

M. L. stood silent and confused. All he wanted was to get a new pair of shoes. After coaxing his Daddy to bring him to this store, now the boy could see the rage and anger in his father's face. Why? Why?

"Come on, M. L.!" Daddy ordered. "We're leaving."

"But what about the shoes, Daddy?"

Daddy reached for M. L.'s hand. "We'll not be buying anything in this store," he snarled. "Never!"

Back in the car, Daddy King regained his composure. He knew M. L. was frightened at what had happened, not understanding why it was all right to buy shoes in one part of the store and wrong to buy them in another part. How could the color of one's skin have anything to do with such a thing? Some white people were quite dark in skin color. Some Negroes were light. At times, it was impossible to tell the difference. Why should there be a difference? Slowly, carefully, Daddy King tried to explain the whole problem of racial segregation to M. L.

"Tell me again," the boy asked.

Daddy King shook his head. "It's too stupid and cruel to explain even one time. It's just the way things are, and I'm going to fight with everything I have to change it. The color of a person's skin should make no difference in what he can and can't do."

Confusion still coated M. L.'s face. "I'll help you, Daddy," the boy promised, not really understanding what he had heard. But there was a determination and strength in his voice that made his father happy.

Yet neither of them, Daddy King or M. L., realized that a bond had been formed that afternoon. For as long as both men lived, they would each recall the events of that day as a time when a father and son reached inside one another and discovered a common unit of understanding and love.

8

In December of 1939, Hollywood put the city of Atlanta in the headlines. Never before had such fanfare highlighted a movie than with the David Selznick production of "Gone With The Wind." Movie stars, reporters, celebrities of all kinds flooded the city to witness the premiere of a film which turned back the calendar to an era when palacelike plantations dotted the countryside, only to fall in the ruin of Civil War fighting. Lowe's Grand Theater bulged with the opening night crowd, pushing and shoving to see such stars as Clark Gable, Vivien Leigh, Olivia De Havilland and other luminaries.

Amidst the hoopla were the mumblings of a discontented black community. Daddy King and others shook their heads in disgust at the apparent joy of theatergoers reveling in the depiction of blacks occupying only slave roles. The good "niggers" in the movie were portrayed taking orders obediently from whites, almost tripping over themselves to obey their masters. The one bad "nigger" in the show appeared "uppity" and out of place riding with a Yankee carpetbagger in a buckboard.

"The movie costs millions to make," Daddy grumbled among other black leaders. "But no one can measure the amount it costs us on our road to equality. Millions of Americans will again see us only as slaves. We have more work than ever to do."

With renewed vigor, Martin Luther King, Sr. plunged himself into a variety of business and civic activities. Long

active in the local NAACP chapter, he accepted appointment to governing boards of area educational institutions
and the black-owned bank in Atlanta.

"A man must first serve his God, then his family and
then his people," the elder King declared often from his
pulpit. "If possible, a man should serve all three with his
whole heart and spirit."

With each passing year, M. L. understood a little
more what his father was fighting to achieve. The boy
took his own obligations to be achieving good grades and
citizenship marks in school. After completing his sixth
grade year at Younge Elementary, M. L. transferred to
David T. Howard Colored Elementary School operated by
Atlanta University. At Howard, M. L. first experienced
being taught by both black and white teachers. He thrived
in that atmosphere.

But Daddy King's struggle in behalf of the black community was not always safe and smooth. The telephone
rang at all hours of the day and night.

"Damn you, Nigger King!" a voice would shout.
Then silence. In order to spare the other members of the
family any more concern than necessary, Daddy King insisted on being the only one to answer the telephone after
ten o'clock.

The daily mail frequently brought similar obscenities.
Unsigned letters, many obviously the work of Ku Klux
Klan members or sympathizers, filtered into the King
house. Daddy King accepted those messages attacking
him personally with a tough skin, becoming all the more
determined to continue his efforts. But it was the notes
and letters that hinted at harm to his family that troubled
him most.

"You try to act so tough, so mean," Bunch sometimes
teased Daddy King. "But you're as soft and tender inside
as any man in the world."

That same tenderness and softness was clearly reflected in M. L. When the boy listened to the sufferings of

the Lord as told by his father from the Ebenezer pulpit, M. L.'s eyes filled with tears. He sang with feeling, proclaiming his love for God with the loudest "Hallejujahs!" he could muster.

In May of 1941, the true depth of M. L.'s sensitivity was tested. Submerged in a heavy homework assignment, the boy fought desperately to overcome an urge to go to a parade a few blocks away. The parade won. Then, while M. L. stood along the parade route enjoying the marching bands, a family friend brought him frightening news from home.

"It's your Grandma, M. L. They took her to the hospital."

Hurrying home, the worried boy found the house filled. The moment he saw Daddy King's face, M. L. knew. Grandma was dead.

For days M. L. could not eat or sleep. He was convinced the Lord was punishing him for leaving the house and going to the parade. How empty he felt inside, how alone. Nothing could take away the hurt, the pain.

Finally, Daddy King came to his room. The man took his son to him, held him close and gently stroked his back.

"You mustn't blame what happened to your grandmother on anything you've done," Daddy King said softly. "God has his own plan and his own way, and we cannot interfere with the time he chooses to call any of us back to him."

M. L. sniffled a bit. But his eyes did not fill with tears this time. He looked up at his father, remembering all the times Daddy King had stirred the people in the church with talk of "going on home to glory with the Lord." Surely that was where Grandma was at this very moment. And as he stood close to his father, M. L. felt himself humming, then singing softly:

I've got a robe, you've got a robe,
All of God's children got a robe,
When I get to heaven, goin' to put on my
    robe,
Goin' to shout all over God's heaven,
    heaven, heaven
When I get to heaven, goin' to put on my
    robe,
Goin' to shout all over God's heaven.

M. L. stopped, gazing up into his father's face.

"Daddy, do you think Grandma's got a robe up in heaven?" the boy asked.

Daddy smiled. "I'm sure of it, son. She's got a grand robe, I know. And she's probably shouting all over God's heaven right this moment, glad to be with the Lord."

M. L. nodded, snuggling even deeper into his father's warm hug.

Later that year the King family packed their belongings and moved a few blocks away to an impressive yellow brick house on Boulevard. The new residence offered more room to Bunch and the three growing children. But to Daddy King, the move meant even more. It was a dream come true. Never had he forgotten the day in Stockbridge when he was refused admission to Jay's big red brick house. Daddy had tried to buy that very house in 1940, but Stockbridge people—the white folks—did not like the thought of a black sharecropper's son owning one of the town's finest homes. The deal fell through, leaving Daddy still angry and bitter. But the neighbors surrounding the house on Boulevard made the King family feel welcome. They represented the hard-working black community of Atlanta, dedicating themselves to making a better life for their children and future generations.

The move to the house on Boulevard coincided with another move by Daddy King. For years he had involved himself with committees and coalitions that would better the day to day living of blacks. It was a tiring, slow fight, with many leaders suggesting that the road to improved relations with whites was paved with patience. Perhaps it was the shadows of war around the world that caused a mood for fighting and battle. Maybe it was the weariness of moving so slowly, often feeling as if no progress was being achieved. Whatever it was, it caused Daddy King to re-energize his whole attack on the tangled webs of racism and segregation.

"We can only do so much as individuals working within small groups," he told one meeting of the NAACP leaders. "We must be prepared to activate all our people. Yes, there is strength in numbers. As one voice or a committee of voices, we won't get listened to. But if we have the numbers to form a picket line or head a march, we demand attention. We capture headlines. We will only get people to think and change if we use all our people."

But how? From where? Certainly not from the pulpit. For years Daddy King had been ranting and roaring to the congregation of Ebenezer Baptist. Other black ministers had done the same in their churches.

Sadly enough there was no one to take the message to the white congregations of Atlanta. "It's too delicate an issue," one pastor would alibi. "We have so much to do already," claimed another. The worst were those who quoted Scripture. "Remember Ecclesiastes 7:8—The patient in spirit is better than the proud in spirit."

Daddy King had little time for such excuses. "Delicate or not, it is time we followed the teachings of Jesus and all be treated as God's children. Let us set aside that within our churches that isn't so important and give our attention to that which is. As for Ecclesiastes, why don't we listen to 5:9? I believe that says 'The profit of the earth is for all.' "

Realizing there would be little hope for change through the churches, Daddy King turned to another avenue. His memberships on various committees and boards had thrust him deep into the economic structure of the city of Atlanta. It did not take a financial wizard to recognize that as Atlanta went, so went the entire economy of the South. If the walls of racial discrimination were ever to fall, the best place to start was within the powerful business community. But the fight would not be easy. Whites controlled every marketing empire. Blacks seemed willing to live within their own enterprises and were making money. But it was always within their own neighborhoods and within their own realm of influence. No one ventured across racial lines.

Such topics were brought openly to the King dinner table each evening. With growing passion and purpose, Daddy shared his attitudes and feelings. He challenged each of his children to share their own reactions.

Not that Daddy King was willing to accept the thinking of his three offspring. Far from it. As Christine, M. L., and A. D. slid into their teens, they came to a better understanding of their father. To Daddy King's challenges, Christine usually simply nodded and agreed. She found her mother a more reasonable and calmer confidant. She also knew that rebellion and disagreement, displayed most frequently by A. D., merely led directly to a strapping. Despite the thrashings he received, A. D. still did not hesitate to directly confront his father. By the time dessert was served, the dinner table had turned into a vocal battleground between Daddy King and his youngest son.

The middle zone was left for M. L. With a voice growing more deep and full, the boy asked his father questions, countering the answers with remarks showing his clear rational thinking. He felt the sting of his father's strap too, most often when the boy failed to accept angry emotional outbursts.

"Don't you show disrespect for me, boy!" Daddy King would threaten, his voice caked with parental authority. "I don't want to hear another word."

Usually, M. L. restrained himself from another remark. After all, this was his father before him. Yet, there were some times when the boy's independent nature struck out with "If you just want to argue with your lungs, you will always win. I thought you wanted to use your brain too." M. L. paid the price by getting a thrashing, but he refused to show tears.

It was not only at the dinner table that M. L. began to show early signs of rebellion against certain facets of his life. At Sunday School, he was unwilling to accept the embellished stories of instructors who offered their personal Biblical accounts of happenings. He wanted valid evidence, actual proof, of all that was taught. His public denial of the bodily resurrection of Jesus left his fellow Sunday School classmates open-mouthed in shock and his teacher in tears.

"It was confusing to me," M. L. wrote. "I just couldn't see why people needed to exaggerate everything. I just got tired of all the noise connected with worshiping God and loving our Savior. The words of the Bible come across like long ago fairy tales. I resented that. I thought there was a time and a place for quiet prayer and reflection. But sometimes I felt like I was the only one who thought so."

M. L.'s independent spirit reached beyond the confines of home and church. In sports, he was a fierce competitor, often accepting any game as his own personal challenge. Small but wiry, he took shots every time he was passed the basketball, fought to bat every time he could in baseball and insisted on carrying the pigskin in football. His fierce drive to excel sometimes led him into open fighting with opponents. Usually, M. L. could talk himself out of such exhibitions. When he couldn't, he simply exclaimed, "Let's take to the grass." He wanted no part of weapons, always insisting that clubs and knives were for "chickens who didn't know how to use their bodies." M. L. seldom lost in such encounters, being quick thinking and fast enough to make use of his small frame.

Occasionally, Daddy King confronted his eldest son about the fights when a disgruntled parent shared the news of such a squabble. With a vocabulary that dazzled his father and a slowness that annoyed him, M. L. methodically explained the details of the conflict. The explanation was usually satisfying, allowing M. L. to exit singing:

> Joshua fit de battle of Jericho, Jericho,
> Jericho
> Joshua fit de battle of Jericho,
> An' de walls come tumblin' down.

As the minister of an ever-growing congregation, Daddy King felt a security and comfort not every black living in Atlanta could boast, especially when it came into the realm of financial matters. Though neither he nor Bunch was given to luxury tastes, they were both determined that their children enjoy a childhood free from money worries. Nonetheless, Christine, M. L., and A. D. were not to be spoiled. If more money was needed beyond a modest weekly allowance, Daddy King's solution was in the form of two words: "Earn it." M. L. took his father's advice and sold newspapers to earn spending money. He was an industrious junior executive, quickly recognizing that a cheerful smile and "Thank you, sir!" often brought a generous tip.

Such charm spilled into the classroom as well. With sister Christine as a frequent studying partner, M. L. found smooth sailing at Howard School. He compiled an impressive A- average and at the age of thirteen, he entered Booker T. Washington High School. English and history soon became his favorite subjects, although mathematics also came easily to him but he did not find the area exciting. His communication skills in speaking and writing posed a remarkable contrast. While his impressive vocabulary used orally had English teachers reaching for the nearest dictionary, the spelling of words used on paper left the same instructors scratching their heads in disbelief. Even Daddy King, who never did feel at ease using formal English and proved his uneasiness often, could only shake his head in wonder at the countless red marks that came home from school.

From the pages of history books and newspapers, M. L. found two champions of "lost causes" to place on pedestals worthy of imitation. The first was Frederick Douglass, the illegitimate son of a white man and a slave named Harriet Bailey. Born Frederick Augustus Washington Bailey in 1817, he changed his name to Frederick Douglass after escaping from slavery in 1838. Few people opened more eyes to the evils of being a slave than this one man as he gave lecture after lecture. After buying his freedom, Douglass went on to recruit Negro regiments in the Civil War, serve as an advisor to President Lincoln, become a U. S. marshal and an ambassador to Haiti. M. L. was awestruck with the deep racial pride which led Douglass to risk his life again and again for his heartfelt convictions.

Another champion to M. L. was the fascinating Mahatma Gandhi of India. Born only four years after the American Civil War ended, Gandhi had earned a law degree in London only to return to South Africa and his native India to lead protests against the English government. Of particular interest to M. L. was the spiritual discipline and nonviolent manner of resistance offered by Gandhi and their successful results. Economic boycotts, used over and over to bring reforms, seemed to be an important element of Gandhi's strategy. His willingness to endure fasts and imprisonment for his beliefs left an indelible imprint in M. L.'s mind. In later studies, M. L. would explore Gandhi's nonviolent philosophy in more depth.

But there was no need to look all the way to India for example of a successful boycott. In 1941, the blacks of New York's Harlem avoided the borough's buses, causing chaos in the transportation system. Recognizing they could not win in the battle, bus officials cast away all segregation rules. Daddy King heartily approved of the boycotting technique, declaring that "it ought to be tried in the South, even right here in Atlanta." Eagerly M. L. shared his readings about Gandhi at the dinner table, how much the noted Indian leader had achieved through nonviolent protest. Never had Daddy King listened so attentively.

"The boy knows what he's talkin' about," the senior King told Bunch later. "He understands the problems, and he smells the solutions."

Bunch agreed. "But they all have to find their own way. You can't be shaping their future." The woman lay a gentle hand on her husband's. "Christine wants to be a teacher. I think you've accepted that. It's the boys I worry about.

"How's that?"

As usual, Bunch's voice was soft and calm. "You want the boys to be preachers. It's as clear as anything. M. L. and A. D. know it. I know. You know it—"

"Is there somethin' the matter with them bein' preachers?"

A smile curled Bunch's lips. "Oh, Daddy, of course there isn't. I was the daughter of one and I married one. No, you won't find me criticizing anybody being a preacher."

"Then what are you saying, woman?"

"I'm saying you can open a door but you can't force anybody to come in. Nobody knows better than you that we can only offer some directions. It's the good Lord who leads the way. If he wishes, and if they choose, they will become ministers."

For a moment Daddy King sat quietly. He knew

Bunch was right. But he did not like losing an argument—
or even a discussion.

"It ain't wrong for a man to want a good life for his
children. Preachin' the Good Word has been good to me.
I should think it's good enough for my sons."

"It may be," Bunch replied. "But let us not forget that
if you had simply followed your father's wishes, you
would be farming someone else's land outside Stockbridge. That's what he wanted you to do. You wanted
something different. It's hard to know how much a parent
should give to his child. But we have to let them live their
own lives, whatever they choose."

Daddy drew his wife close in a warm embrace. As
usual, she was right. He knew it.

But by golly, he still wanted them to become
preachers!

In December of 1941, the surprise attack by Japanese
bombers at Pearl Harbor plunged America into war.
Across the country, volunteers flooded enlistment centers.
Blacks joining up were kept in segregated units, half of
them overseas and the other half on the home front.

Anticipating efforts to prevent blacks from working
in defense plants across the country, Negro labor leader
A. Philip Randolph demanded that President Franklin
Roosevelt hire blacks as well as whites to man production
lines.

"A black man's hands can work just as fast and as
ably as a white man's hands," Randolph declared. "This is
our war too."

To make his demands even more emphatic, the labor
leader threatened to lead a giant protest march. With a
new war under way, it was not a good time for disunity in
the United States. No one knew this better than the politically astute Roosevelt. Quickly he issued an executive order making racial discrimination illegal in all
governmental agencies and defense plants.

While the older boys in Atlanta's black community

headed off to war, the younger ones were instilled with the idea that they also had a job to do. Hard-working and quick minded, M. L. skipped his freshman year at Booker T. Washington High School and entered the sophomore class in September 1942.

Feeling the pressure more and more to make some declaration of future goals, if only to satisfy his father, M. L. declared his intentions to become a doctor. His feelings about becoming a minister were even more pronounced—it was simply not a socially relevant or intellectually respectable calling. It seemed kinder to proclaim an interest in medicine rather than to explain his personal feelings to Daddy King, so M. L. took the more comfortable way out.

But despite his open declaration of medicine as a career, M. L. showed little interest in science at Washington High School. His attention turned toward oratory. During his final year at the school, he plunged into research for a speech contest sponsored by the Elks Club. For his subject, M. L. selected "The Negro and the Constitution."

Never had M. L. pursued any school project with such depth and intensity. He researched the topic for weeks, carefully analyzing the black man and his relationship to that historic document that guaranteed on paper what had never been achieved in practice. At times the boy felt hatred and anger toward the white race who seemed to cut off many avenues of opportunity for blacks. Housing, employment, use of public places and services— the white man clearly held the upper hand, never allowing the black man equal status. Yet other times, M. L. felt a total disgust and disillusionment toward his own black people for not pushing themselves forward, for allowing themselves to be torn and tossed around like lifeless bags of fodder.

Once the speech was written, all efforts were directed toward its effective presentation. There was little doubt that God had blessed M. L. with one of the richest baritone voices to be found among high school youths. Despite his personal objections to the emotional outbursts from the pulpit at Ebenezer Baptist church, M. L. could not deny that he had grown up aware of the importance of cadence and the emphasis of words and phrases. Like a harp or violin, the voice could be a tuned instrument, practiced and controlled to elicit a variety of reactions. Hour after hour M. L. rehearsed, frequently cornering his mother and father for their listening attention and critical comments.

The work paid off. With his speech teacher, M. L. traveled to Valdosta, Georgia, where he presented "The Negro and the Constitution" before the collected body of black Elks. The members chose him as a prize winner; M. L. could hardly wait to get back and share the news with his family. The high school boy jabbered excitedly nonstop to his teacher as they boarded the bus for the return trip to Atlanta.

Before long, the bus stopped to pick up some additional passengers. The newcomers were whites and there were no empty seats. Glancing over his shoulder, the white bus driver ordered M. L. and his teacher out of their seats.

M. L. did not move. He gazed defiantly forward, the thoughts and ideas of his speech rolling through his head. Every person was entitled to certain rights and freedoms under the Constitution. Wasn't this one of them? Did he and his teacher, because both of them were black, not enjoy those rights and freedoms?

"I guess we better get up," M. L. heard his teacher whisper. "We might make the driver angry."

Still M. L. did not budge. He felt people looking at him with looks of anger and contempt. There were other whispers nearby.

"Hey, niggers," the bus driver yelled. "Get out of them seats. These people want to sit down."

The word "niggers" hit at M. L.'s pride. What a

strange word. As a noun, it was relatively inoffensive. It referred to the color of skin. A label. No, the word itself as a noun was harmless enough. But used as an adjective— an offensive synonym for dirt, slime, scum—that was different. And there was no doubt, no doubt at all, how the bus driver meant his usage.

Suddenly the bus driver left his seat and swaggered back to where M. L. and his teacher sat. Quietly the black woman slowly stood up, lightly tugging at the sleeve of M. L.'s coat. "Come on, Martin," she whispered.

Pushing the woman aside, the sneering bus driver leaned over to a point where his face was but inches from M. L. A stream of heated profanity spewed from the driver's lips. The meaning was clear enough. "Get your black butt out of that seat and let these white folks sit down or—"

Drums beat in M. L.'s head. A cold sweat covered his body. Fists clenched, the boy felt a tremendous urge to strike out at this garbage standing above him. But over the driver's shoulder, M. L. saw the frightened face of his teacher. Her eyes were begging, her teeth biting into her lips in fear.

Slowly, ever so slowly, M. L. lifted his frame from the seat he had occupied. There was applause, obviously from the whites who felt once again they had won another victory. Once more M. L. felt the need to strike out, in words if not with fists. But feeling the trembling hand of his teacher slip inside his, he restrained himself.

For the remainder of the ride home, M.L. and his teacher stood, often fighting to keep their footing as the bus careened along the highway and around the curves. The joy of winning a prize at the speech contest was gone. Rage and humiliation replaced those feelings. He knew that this was a night he would never forget.

9

No matter how hard he tried, M. L. could not erase the bus trip home from Valdosta from his mind. He had wanted to tell his father at once, but the boy knew Daddy King's volatile temper well. That very night the fiery minister might well have taken off to find the insulting bus driver to thrash him within an inch of his life. No, that was not what M. L. wanted.

But there was little question that M. L. had definitely stumbled into a turning point in his life. Certainly he had run into traumatic events encountered by blacks in childhood; the stinging rejection of the friends across the street when he had started to school; the refusal of the shoe clerk to sell him shoes in the front of the store when he was eight. Not to mention the countless trips to the side counters of drug stores to get waited on, the "colored" entrances to theaters, the "Whites Only" drinking fountains. True, the fact that his family enjoyed more financial security than most and traveled in a social circle a step above many others in the black community of Atlanta spared M. L. from some hurt and harm. Still, M. L. had felt the bumps along the road. Often his mother reminded him that he was "as good as anyone else, as good as any white man on this earth." So too read the Good Book, sang the choirs, roared his father from the pulpit in Ebenezer Baptist Church. Yes, over and over the words were spoken. How he had thrilled, from his zealous interest in oratory, to such phrases as "all men are created equal, that they are endowed by their Creator with certain un-alienable rights . . ." and ". . . a government, of the people, by the people and for the people." Words, phrases, documents, speeches. No matter how noble they all sounded, how well intentioned they all were, what good were they in a bus heading from Valdosta to Atlanta carrying blacks and whites?

Although M. L. had listened often to his father at the dinner table as Daddy King complained of the lack of action achieved by blacks in the Atlanta community, the boy now began to hear clearly what the man was saying. Monologue became dialogue. Questions were asked. Answers were suggested and discussed.

Daddy King welcomed the exchange. More often he found himself leaving the table less frustrated, satisfied that a few of his ideas wère taking hold. Seeds were being planted. There was no telling what the harvest might bring in, but the seeds seemed to be falling in good, receptive soil. No rocks. No sand. Just good, clean earth.

Meanwhile, far beyond the boundaries of Atlanta, World War II raged on. Once crowded college campuses continued to bid farewell to students as they traded their books and stylish garb for weapons and service uniforms. The classroom rolls of Morehouse College in Atlanta thinned considerably, and administrators beckoned top quality high school students to take entrance requirements for admission.

Eagerly, M. L. did just that. The entrance tests posed little difficulty when he took them in the spring of 1944. Electing to skip his senior year at Booker T. Washington, M. L. graduated at the age of fifteen after his junior year.

The decision M. L. made to stay at home and attend Morehouse delighted Daddy King. At times he worried at his son's impatience, but for the most part, the senior King was impressed with M. L.'s confidence and certainty. Daddy made little effort to hide his feelings that he could certainly be using a co-pastor at Ebenezer Baptist in the next few years. After all, he wasn't getting any younger and what more graceful transition could be made than to slide in a son who might assist to begin with and eventually take over.

But if he was to remain in Atlanta for his college education, M. L. was determined to get away for the summers. He had no time for wasting though. Summertime was set aside for earning money for college. Mama King had instilled "the King home's three S's" in all three children. What money M. L. could earn during the summer was to "spend, save, and share."

A special work program was offered to students at Morehouse. A huge Connecticut tobacco farm needed summer laborers. Without hesitation, M. L. signed up.

Sending their fifteen-year-old son up north to work the hot and humid tobacco fields of Connecticut caused Daddy and Bunch some degree of concern and much discussion. The boy had never really been away from home. Yet he seemed so ready, so mature. It did not seem fair to stand in his way.

So off M. L. went to Connecticut. Although younger than most of his traveling companions, M. L. worked hard to fit in. No matter how his muscles ached and his body sweated beneath the glaring rays of the summer sun, M. L. did not complain. He wanted no one to say, "Can't you take it, kid?" or "Maybe you better go home to Mommy and Daddy."

Instead, M. L. often took charge. He was the first one to work in the morning and the last one to quit at night. During the daytime hours, sounds of spirituals rolled across the Connecticut countryside:

> Sinner, please don't let this harvest pass,
> Sinner, please don't let this harvest pass,
> Sinner, please don't let this harvest pass,
> An' die, an' lose your soul at last.

Sinner, O see that cruel tree,
Sinner, O see that cruel tree,
Sinner, O see that cruel tree
Where Christ has died for you and me.

Drained of energy at the end of each day, M. L. and his fellow workers had all they could do to grab a bite to eat and collapse into bed. But on weekends, the boys of Atlanta headed into nearby Hartford and other Connecticut towns. Cheerily they strode through the front door of theaters and selected whatever seats they wished in restaurants. A drinking fountain was a drinking fountain, free for use by white and black alike. There were no stairs for one race and another staircase for a different race. Everything was for everyone to use. M. L. felt an exhilarating sense of freedom. The air felt fresh and clean. The Constitution, the Declaration of Independence, the Emancipation Proclamation, The Bible—they had all been read and were being lived. The signs of Jim Crow were gone. Surely, Connecticut was just one rung below heaven itself!

But with the final rays of summer's sun came the return trip to Atlanta. Back to Dixie, the train carried the boys of Morehouse. "Say goodbye to freedom!" the Virginia woodlands whispered as the train snaked southward. M. L. went to the dining car to get a bite to eat. The long summer had dulled his memory. He started to sit down where he wished, but the waiter was quickly at his side and leading him to a table at the rear. Not enough to sit at the back, a curtain was then dropped so that the white passengers would not know of his presence. Gazing from the window, M. L. studied the countryside. A huge hillside of rich black soil swept by, and the boy had a fleeting thought. The blacker the soil, the better it is. What a difference there was with people. He stared at the curtain, that piece of material that hid him from the human beings on the other side. It was as if the curtain had dropped over his own selfhood.

While M. L. experienced the rollercoaster ride of human emotions, Daddy King was picking away at the solid wall of white supremacy that dictated the power structure of Atlanta. At times the battle seemed empty and fruitless. Often Daddy had to hold back his temper at committee meetings when white businessmen referred to "the graciousness for which our city is known." Graciousness, indeed! For whom? For whites, of course. Ah, if but one of these proud white idiots might for a day turn black. Just for a day. What "graciousness" then would there be?

But from the midst of a regime dedicated to maintain the status quo emerged one white leader who seemed to hear Daddy's voice and understand his feelings. William B. Hartsfield was his name, an Atlanta lawyer, one of the few who seemed able and willing to recognize the black community. Beyond that, Hartsfield openly prophesied that the entire South was headed for major changes, a prophecy that stunned some white leaders and horrified others.

Enthusiastically Daddy King shared with M. L. news of the white lawyer whose voice was commanding more and more attention among the leadership circles of Atlanta. Interested as he was, M. L. was caught up in his own world of decision making. Whatever he planned to do with his life, it would be aimed at helping blacks. Where could he do the most good? How could he be most effective? Finally, he made a choice. He would become a lawyer. If the black person was ever to enjoy his rights and freedoms as an American—even as a human being— the world of politics would have to change. Once his decision was made, M. L. began practicing fiery speeches in front of a mirror in his room. Occasionally Daddy would steal a peek, listen a moment, then leave wondering to himself if M. L. could be as impressive before a crowd of people as he was before a pane of shiny glass.

M. L. did not jump quickly into the mainstream of college life at Morehouse. Like a cautious swimmer, he poked his toe in first, then gradually eased forward. The fact that he was living at home prevented him from making a swift plunge. The fact that he was only fifteen proved another obstacle. He enjoyed the company of the opposite sex, and his flowing conversation, handsome features and stout but sturdy build attracted their attention in return. Yet he felt more comfortable dating high school girls. Slowly he became increasingly involved with the four hundred other young men of Morehouse, and joined the football team, glee club and oratorical contests.

But it was not in individual activities that M. L. found his greatest zest. It was in the entire Morehouse spirit. It was a powerfully meshed feeling of hope, pride and determination. It did not matter what you selected as a future vocation. What really mattered was that you succeeded with the vocation. If you chose to be a store clerk, Morehouse demanded you be the best store clerk in the world. If you chose to be governor, the same standard applied. If you decided to become a garbage collector, second best was not good enough. You had to be the best garbage collector.

It was an atmosphere within which M. L. thrived. Instructors discussed any topic openly and freely. Always before M. L. had discussed the problems of being black only with his father and family at dinner. At Morehouse, instructors challenged students to share their inner feelings about being called "nigger" and "colored." Discussions were heated and heavy. Yet new ground was broken, fresh insights gained. Pent-up hostilities filled the air, after which teachers ordered students to suggest solutions for every human problem imaginable.

This time it was Daddy King who was doing most of the listening. Although they did not always agree on problems and solutions, both of them recognized the outstanding leadership qualities of the president of Morehouse.

Benjamin Mays had taken over the leadership of Morehouse College in 1940. His influence in the school and in Atlanta was soon felt. Tall and charismatic, Mays was a scholarly heavyweight and an orator of the first degree. Daddy King knew him from contributions made while serving on citywide committees. M. L. was immediately drawn to Mays by the force and depth of his Tuesday morning chapel presentations. To both the senior and junior Kings, Mays' message was virtually the same: "Whatever is done must be done well, that no man living and no man unborn could do it better." A powerful command, yet anyone listening was made to feel that such attainment was possible, and must be sought.

M. L. had already been introduced to such social reformers as Frederick Douglas and Mahatma Gandhi. Unwilling to commit himself totally to law as an intended profession, M. L. decided to pick sociology as a major. The selection quickly led him to still another champion of human rights—Henry David Thoreau. The ideas of Thoreau, as expressed in "Civil Disobedience," sent shivers of excitement through M. L. To Daddy King, the boy exclaimed, "a creative minority, even if it be just one honest man, could start an entire moral revolution." Daddy King was dubious. Had he not been battling for years, to try and better the living conditions for blacks in Atlanta? In so many arenas, so little had been accomplished. No, change demanded many people, the multitudes. Even Jesus Christ could not bring the multitudes to the better life he proposed. M. L. would learn, in time.

"Henry David Thoreau never lived in Atlanta," Daddy King quipped.

Still another voice at Morehouse College began to have an important effect on M. L. The director of the school's religion department, Professor George D. Kelsey, shared doubts about Protestant fundamentalist teachings so prevalent among Baptists in the South. "It is not a crime nor is it sinful to question the myths and legends of the Bible. It can strengthen one's faith, for beneath these very myths and legends lie the basic truths that can give direction and purpose to our lives." With this attitude and fresh interest, M. L. turned to the Bible with new perspective, finding Kelsey's ideas sound and helpful. The instructor also expressed feelings that today's clergymen must be armed with a knowledge of philosophy and sociology, ready to tackle social problems beyond strictly spiritual concerns. To simply enter a pulpit with only a background of scripture, attempting to reach the people with wild voice and gestures, was like attacking a killer bear with a slingshot . . . more, much more was needed.

Other instructors deposited new thoughts into the ever growing mind of Martin Luther King Jr. Sociology teacher Walter Chivers drew clear and frightening pictures of the capitalistic dangers encountered when a society is too caught up with monetary goals. "Money is not only the root of evil," noted Chivers; "it is the root of this particular evil—racism." But blame, the instructor insisted, had to be shared by both whites and blacks. "Whites have done the manipulating, and blacks have allowed themselves to be manipulated." From his English professor, Gladstone Lewis Chandle, M. L. developed even a greater respect for the effective use of language. "To know many words, " the teacher observed, "is to have a rather useless collection of nothingness. It is in the use of these words, in proper context and with appropriate emphasis, that vocabulary becomes the most useful tool of one's life."

M. L. sensed the dedication and devotion of his instructors at Morehouse College. Always meticulous about his own personal appearance, M. L. took even greater pains to dress in a manner appreciative and respectful of his teachers. His frequent wearing of handsome tweed jackets and coats earned him the nickname "Tweeds" among the other young men at the school.

Beyond the knowledge and understanding he learned within the Morehouse classrooms, M. L. was acquiring an empathy for his father. Daddy King had come from such a different background, each day of his youth struggling to exist in the crowded confines of a poor sharecropper's hut. The shadows of poverty had always hung over the family, and with it the fear of what more drinking might do to the confused mind of the head of the household. Surely such beginnings would have drowned the spirit of a lesser man, but not Daddy King. With vigor and determination, he became a preacher, a student, even a college graduate. For his wife, he selected one whom many might have placed "far above his station." Daddy King knew no stations. He wooed and won the lady he loved. He had provided a home for her and their children, while sharing his ministry to thousands of others. And always, yet always, he had placed God as his beacon, his light guiding each day. So what if he occasionally used the wrong grammar, mispronounced a few words, or hadn't read the latest theological literature? Was it wrong that he sometimes, even often, roared and ranted from the church pulpit? That was his way. It was what he knew. All points considered, Daddy King had made the very most of every opportunity. Yes, M. L. decided, this father of mine is quite a man. Quite a man indeed.

Despite M. L.'s growing appreciation of his father, the King house still harbored its share of heated disputes between the two men. Like any patriarch, Daddy King wanted what was best for his children. If his work among committees in behalf of bettering the black cause in Atlanta had paid any dividends, it was the contacts he had made among prominent black leaders, many of whom owned their own businesses. During summer breaks from Morehouse, M. L. decided to stay in Atlanta and work.

"No problem at all," Daddy King declared. "I've got plenty of friends who will give you a job."

M. L. shook his head. Making money to pay his college expenses was only one of the reasons he wanted to work. More importantly, he wanted to put his education to the test. Was the black worker really exploited when employed by whites? How was he treated? Were there solutions?

Daddy could not understand his son. He could recall when he was M. L.'s age, with no choice to shovel coal with blistered hands into the scorching heat of a train boiler. Here, M. L. could enjoy the comforts of a clean office job in employment that could challenge his mind and rest his body. Instead, he wanted none of that.

M. L. took a summer job working at the Atlanta Railway Express Company, unloading trains and trucks. It was heavy, grueling work in the blazing hot sun. Daddy King could only shake his head in wonder. But when the white foreman called M. L. "a nigger," he would have no part of such a degradation and quit the job. He headed to a spring and mattress company, hiring on again as a loading employee. There was no name-calling at the new job, but when the first paychecks came out, he saw that he and the other blacks were paid less than their white counterparts doing the same work. It had not been that way working the tobacco farm in Connecticut. Everyone had been paid the same. For the first time, reality hit M. L. in the gut. It was one thing to hear about the unfair practices in a classroom; it was another to hold a check in your hands and feel you had just been cheated.

"Why don't they open their eyes?" M. L. complained to his father. "Every day we're on that loading platform, sweating and aching just like the whites. We put in the same hours, take the same time for lunch, work just as hard. Can't they open their eyes and see we should get paid the same?"

"They see white and they see black," Daddy King answered, his voice tired and faltering. "Only the Lord and God sees us the same."

"True enough," M. L. conceded.

When M. L. returned to Morehouse, he became even more impressed with the work President Mays was trying to do. Education was a tool through which blacks could be intellectually free. No matter how physically oppressed, he was truly liberated, honestly free. Over and over President Mays shared that idea in his preaching during chapel. Calmly, rationally, intellectually—there were no loud rants and raves about the devil grabbing souls and the Lord's judgment. Yet there was prayer, a spiritual message, the love of God and the Savior.

At seventeen, while a junior at Morehouse College, Martin Luther King, Jr. made a major decision. He abandoned thoughts about other professions and began preparation to become a Baptist minister. He told his mother first, who then encouraged the young man to talk to his father about it. With no little trepidation, he shared the decision with Daddy King.

Daddy was overjoyed. His prayers had been answered. He could not imagine how many times he had hoped for this very moment.

But as Daddy looked into the innocent eyes of his seventeen-year-old son, his unlined face, his youthful features, the older man felt a nagging resistance. Did the boy truly understand the commitment of the ministry? Perhaps he had simply been influenced by a sermon or two from a minister at the college. Certainly, Benjamin Mays could offer a moving speech. Intellectual too. Or was M. L. merely trying to be an obedient son, sensing his duty?

Daddy King rubbed his chin. "It's all well and good to say you want to be a preacher. But I'll need some reassurance. Saying what you want to be and being it are two different things. A sermon in church might prove a good test for you. Yes, that's what we'll do. We'll give you a trial sermon."

The arrangements were made. One of the smaller auditorium units at Ebenezer Baptist was reserved. Anyone in the congregation who wished to attend could. It was not the audience that concerned M. L. It was Daddy King. Perhaps, M. L. thought, it might be a good idea to sprinkle in a few blustery phrases, a little fire and brimstone. That might please his father and some of the congregational leaders, and yet most of the sermon could be in M. L.'s own style, reaching for mind as well as spirit.

The day for the trial sermon finally arrived. As M. L. took his place in the pulpit, he glanced over at his father. Daddy King sat quietly, his face washed of any feeling or attitude. The few spectators in the pews turned their attention to the seventeen-year-old boy before them.

M. L. began slowly, hesitantly reaching for just the right words he wanted. From the moment he started, the thoughts of preaching to please his father slipped totally from his mind. This had to be his way, his own presentation. In a sense, a sermon was a conversation with God, with the people in the congregation listening in for their own value. As the boy spoke, he gained confidence. At first he had grasped the pulpit out of fear. Now his hands reached out in strength and purpose. His voice rose with fervor, asking God's direction for humankind. "What would you have us do with the lives you have given us?" M. L. asked.

As he spoke, more and more people filtered into the auditorium while no one left. Daddy King gazed out from where he sat, wondering if the people were simply attracted by the sight of such a youth in the pulpit. His son. Was it merely a novelty that held their attention?

As he turned back and listened, Daddy King knew it was something much more than novelty that captured the attention of the people in the auditorium. They were watching and listening closely. It was a different style than his own, no reaching for the "amens" and searching for just the right pause. But the sermon was clear and convincing, unified and meaningful.

"Reverend King? Reverend King?"

Daddy's thoughts were suddenly interrupted by the sound of a voice nearby. He turned to see that it was one of the church ushers.

"Yes?"

"Uh, the auditorium here is all filled up and there are more people wanting to get in to hear young M. L. Could we move to the main auditorium? Or maybe you want to stop the sermon. . . ."

Daddy King glanced out at the filled pews. Heads were nodding in agreement to M. L.'s words. Eyes staring intently forward, the congregation was caught up in every move and every word.

"No, we'll not stop him. We'll move to the main auditorium."

There was no doubt in anyone's mind that Martin Luther King, Jr's first sermon at Ebenezer Baptist Church was a resounding success. Men and women, old and young, swarmed around the boy when he had finished preaching. He smiled proudly, happy he had managed to share the Lord's words in his own style.

That night, M. L. lay awake a long time. Within himself he sensed a power to do something good for God and do something good for his people at the same time. It was a feeling that made the boy shiver and sink deeper beneath the covers on his bed. "Give me direction, Lord," the boy prayed. "Thank you for being beside me today, and please be with me every day in the future."

And in another room of the house, another voice whispered his own prayers of thanksgiving to God. On his knees beside his bed, Daddy King murmured his thanks for having a son named Martin Luther King, Jr.

10

As Americans struggled to rebuild their lives following World War II, Daddy King sensed that it was a perfect time to rededicate his efforts for change in Atlanta. Several of the local segregated black units of soldiers had distinguished themselves during military action overseas, and the entire country radiated a warm feeling of patriotism. It was not the sensationalistic propaganda that had stirred Americans into willing service and sacrifice during the years of combat, but a proud and strong awareness of the goodness of living within the boundaries of a secure nation. Yes, the time was right.

Furthermore, Daddy King had become more and more impressed with William B. Hartsfield. Most white candidates for political office sought little attention from the black community. Why should they? The white primary system prevented blacks from active participation in city and state elections. The whites controlled the political structure and gave little indication of wanting matters changed.

But William Hartsfield was different. He expressed the idea that Atlanta, and the rest of the South, could only grow and better itself by whites and blacks working together—on an equal footing. An old custom existed that whites spoke to blacks as if the latter were children: "Listen to me, boy," or "I'm talking to you, girl." Hartsfield broke the custom, respectfully addressing blacks as Mr., Mrs., or Miss. Daddy King encouraged Hartsfield's involvement with the black and white committees that met, and the Atlanta attorney happily accepted.

In 1946, with Daddy King's whole-hearted endorsement, William Hartsfield ran for mayor of Atlanta. His open association with the black community was criticized by many white leaders. But Hartsfield willingly visited Negro groups, agreeing to being photographed shaking hands with black leaders. Many believed that such action was political suicide. Not William Hartsfield. On the horizon he saw a new day dawning, a day when accomplishments would be achieved not through white or black power but through human power.

That same year, 1946, a Supreme Court ruling provided a catalyst for William Hartsfield, Daddy King, and the entire black community across the south. The white primary was ruled unconstitutional. Citizens who fulfilled proper age and residence requirements could no longer be prevented from voting because of their race. William Hartsfield was elected mayor of Atlanta.

Caught up in the flurry of political activity, Daddy had paid less time than usual to his family. But when he learned that M. L. was part of a newly formed Intercollegiate Council made up of black and white college students in Atlanta, Daddy had serious reservations. As intelligent as M. L. was, his father was certain whites would take advantage of any possible situation. Wisdom came from age, with experience. These black college students had simply not lived long enough or had enough encounters to know how easily they could be doublecrossed or hoodwinked.

"I don't like it, M. L.," Daddy King warned. "You don't need to risk any betrayals from them, and that's mainly what you'll get . . ."

M. L. listened, but he did not agree. "The easiest thing in the world would be to resent every white person. I know I don't have all the answers, but I think we can accomplish more by working together than staying apart."

"You don't know, M. L., how many times some fast talking white minister or businessman has made promises to pull his people closer to us. Then he runs into trouble, and before we know it, we're farther apart than before."

"So you give up?" M. L. parried.

"No, but you're sure a lot more cautious the next time," Daddy King fired back. "And sometimes caution comes with age and experience—"

"And sometimes caution, too much of it, prevents anything from happening," M. L. countered. "I believe there is a core of decency in all men, white and black. God put it there. If we start with a feeling of moral good in every person, we can build from there. I think that's what you do, and I believe that's what we are doing."

Daddy King did not like to lose arguments, especially with his own children. Now he realized, however, that there was much truth in what M. L. was saying. Granted he was young, a bit arrogant at times, but the boy was clear-thinking and sensitive. And confound it, he was right too!

Though convinced he was following a proper path, M. L. weighed his father's words carefully. "Caution" was a useful word to keep in mind, even a better word to put into action. Immersed in the reason and intellectual thinking that encased Morehouse, M. L. pondered the ultimate goals of education. He reached the conclusion that "the most dangerous criminal may be the man gifted with reason, but with no morals."

One recent figure in Georgia history troubled M. L. greatly. As a college student, Eugene Talmadge had earned a Phi Beta Kappa key, symbolizing the fine grades he had earned. Talmadge went on to become governor of the state. Yet he constantly ridiculed Negroes as being inferior.

M. L. reached the conclusion from Talmadge's examples that intelligence, of and by itself, is not enough. "The complete education," he wrote during his senior year at

Morehouse, "gives one not only the power of concentration, but worthy objectives upon which to concentrate." Yes, a man was not truly educated unless he was willing to assume moral responsibility, at least for himself, if not for others around him as well.

That moral responsibility was tested with his brother A. D. Christine sailed smoothly along with her preparation to become a teacher. M. L. found few obstacles in his educational pursuits. A. D. was different. He felt the pressure of being the youngest child who was held up to comparison with an outstanding brother and sister.

"Stay in school," Daddy King admonished him. "Whether or not you become a minister is not important to me. But you have to have an education."

Where Daddy King insisted and cajoled, M. L. simply talked. He could not help feeling somewhat guilty about his own success, realizing this had created part of the problem. For hours M. L. listened to his brother pour out his own dreams for his future. Much as he wished to please Daddy, those dreams did not include a college education. They centered more on a secure job, a wife and family. Clearly, A. D. felt ready to settle down.

As best as he could, M. L. acted as a middleman, carrying messages back and forth between his father and his brother. He felt awkward at times, yet he was glad to suffer awkwardness in order to maintain family harmony.

A. D. dropped out of Morehouse, choosing instead to sell insurance. The move provided a double-pronged resentment within Daddy King. It was bad enough that A. D. left school, but Daddy was incensed that his son did not use Daddy's influence to help establish him in the Atlanta business community.

"You work your butt off to smooth the road for your kids," Daddy ranted at Bunch one evening. "Then what do they do? They don't even stay on the road at all. They go off into a ditch."

As usual, the flames of anger gradually cooled under

the King roof. With Bunch's calm, collected influence and
M. L.'s placating reasoning, Daddy King could never stay
angry for long.

A few hardfought victories in behalf of Atlanta blacks
also helped soothe Daddy's temperament as well. After
eleven long years of courtroom squabbling, a decision was
reached that provided that black teachers were to be paid
equally with whites in the city's public schools. Atlanta's
black teachers had begun the case in 1936, and Daddy
King had persuaded the congregation of Ebenezer Baptist
Church to provide necessary finances. Finally, in 1947, the
black educators won the battle. Less than a year later,
Mayor Hartsfield managed to lead the way toward integrating the Atlanta police force. For the first time, blacks
donned law enforcement uniforms to patrol the city
streets and to hold clerical positions. They received the
same pay as whites also, but there was one drawback—
black officers could only arrest other blacks. It would be
another three years before Negro policemen were given
the power to arrest whites.

Still, these were steps moving in the right direction.
Daddy King felt that some of his time and effort was finally justified.

As for M. L., he felt the need for graduate study
away from Atlanta. By the time he received his degree in
sociology from Morehouse College in the spring of 1948,
M. L. had already applied for admission to Crozer Seminary in Chester, Pennsylvania.

"You're only nineteen," Daddy King reminded M. L.
"That's mighty young to be goin' so far away."

There were other reasons for Daddy King's reluctance to see M. L. leave Atlanta. So many blacks headed
north with every intention of returning home, but they
never did. The joy and freedom found out of the South
proved to be too comfortable. With relatively little effort,
M. L. had been ordained. He had accepted the invitation
to serve as co-pastor at Ebenezer Baptist. Now, before he

really had any opportunity to test his talents for pastoral ministry, he was leaving.

Not only that, M. L. had been dating a young black girl from a fine family. "You could do a lot worse," Daddy King reminded his son good naturedly but with some conviction. While M. L. was finishing school, Daddy promised to look after a new daughter-in-law. Then, when M. L. had completed his education, he could take over the pulpit of Ebenezer Baptist.

No thank you, no thank you, no, thank you. M. L. wanted no bonds that might tie him to Atlanta. He wanted to maintain his independence, free to plant new seeds of thought and to wait for the harvest. Memories of working and living in Connecticut years before remained fresh and clear. He needed to get away—no, had to escape from everything that was so familiar.

From the moment that he arrived on the Crozer campus, M. L. felt on trial. Among the student population of under one hundred, there were only six blacks. M. L. was well aware of the stereotype image of the Negro. Lazy. Loud. Late. Unclean. M. L. privately pledged to destroy that picture. He vowed to be on time for classes and appointments, always to be properly dressed, never to be noisy and obnoxious. It would not be easy, but in M. L.'s mind, it was absolutely necessary.

With this same serious manner, M. L. plunged headlong into his studies. No one would accuse him of laziness. The lights burned late every night in M. L.'s private room in the dormitory. Church history, Bible criticism, Christian ethics, social philosophy, the philosophy of religion—every course in the three-year Crozer program was attacked with equal intensity by the avid young scholar from Atlanta. Any B grade on a test or written assignment sent him back to the books to work harder. By the time grades were issued, the A had been earned. Seeking to cram as much learning into his mind as possible, M. L. enrolled in philosophy courses at the University of Pennsylvania in Philadelphia. The ideas of such great thinkers as Hegel, Sartre, Plato, Rousseau, Bentham, Mill and Locke flowed through his mind, leaving a theory here and a new thought there. M. L. took special interest in the theologian Walter Rauschenbusch, who felt that when Jesus Christ had called for a kingdom of God on earth, his hearers had not understood. Thus the institutional church emerged, rather than an earthly society of moral perfection based on love and sharing. To return to the intended vision would require the elimination or drastic modification of modern capitalism. M. L. did not agree with all of Rauschenbusch's "social gospel" thinking, but the ideas stretched his mind and offered additional topics for debate.

If the tenets of personal capitalism contained loopholes, perhaps then the political philosophers Marx and Lenin had the right answers in Communism. Hardly so, M. L. realized, after carefully scrutinizing *Das Kapital*, *The Communist Manifesto* and other works. The true Marxist accepted God as some imaginary figure, and religion was no more than a product of human stupidity and superstition. Humanity was its own savior, able to mold its own future. That future was interlocked with the government, the state. All that humankind was to create revolved around an allegiance to this state, thus robbing them of the freedom to think, to act and react. No, M. L. soon realized that communism held few if any answers for a better world.

Two names kept appearing and reappearing in his study, their ideas offering sense and reason to areas of injustice. Gandhi. Thoreau. Gandhi. Thoreau. Certainly, Gandhi himself had learned many lessons from the writing and actions of Thoreau. But what truly amazed M. L. was how much the two men had accomplished—Thoreau in the United States in the nineteenth century, Gandhi in India in the twentieth, without ever lifting a sword or shooting a gun. Not that their efforts had gone without violence. As Gandhi said, "Rivers of blood may have to flow before we gain our freedom, but it must be our blood." What courage, what calm, rational reasoning.

Even as he immersed himself in the philosophy of nonviolence, M. L. was thrown into a situation where, for an instant, he was convinced that his own blood would flow. The event jarred him from his readings of the world as it could be into the real world.

"Room raids" were common within the seminary dormitory. Most were harmless enough, the hasty ransacking of a student's living quarters by other students. Desks were overturned, mattresses tossed aside, chairs and tables toppled, personal effects scattered. Usually the victim of the raid and the perpetrators shared a few laughs within minutes of the discovery of the raid.

Such was not the case with one particular white student from North Carolina. Finding his room in a post tornado-like condition, the student came pounding on M. L.'s dormitory door. Totally unaware of what had taken place, M. L. answered to face a raging classmate.

"You darkie!" the youth shouted. "You dirty nigger. You come in and clean up my room before I beat your black ass right into the ground."

"Cool down, friend," M. L. suggested, trying desperately to remain calm himself. "I haven't been doing any room raiding tonight, if that's what you're getting at. I've just been here studying and—"

"Liar!" the accuser spat. "You filthy black pig. You're going to clean my room now or—"

The noise of the encounter had attracted several students to the hallway. A few of the actual pranksters exchanged worried looks, not knowing how safe it was to admit their guilt. Suddenly the North Carolinian brandished a pistol and aimed it directly at M. L.

His heart was beating so loud, M. L. was sure everyone around could hear its pounding. What to do, what to do.

"I think you're too excited," M. L. offered.

His accuser sneered, "I think I'm going to kill you, nigger!"

The students standing nearby could no longer remain silent. "Hey, put that gun away!" someone shouted. "King didn't do that to you!" another voice bellowed out. "Put the gun down!"

Slowly the angry student lowered his hand and slipped the pistol back into his jacket. M. L. released his breath, conscious now of the cold sweat soaking his clothing. He turned and closed his door, leaning against it for a full minute.

Within twenty-four hours, the encounter was brought to the attention of the Crozer student government. Students across the campus were outraged at the altercation. M. L. refused, though, to press charges. Under faculty and student pressure, the North Carolinian publicly apologized for his behavior, offering a personal apology to M. L. The apology was accepted, and within weeks, the two of them were friends.

As satisfied as he was with Crozer Seminary, M. L. looked forward to returning to Atlanta each summer. No one at home looked forward to his return as much as Daddy King. From the minute M. L. walked through the front door, he was no longer a student. He was co-pastor of Ebenezer Baptist Church. Daddy King was determined to impress upon M. L. how much he was needed by the congregation. Not that Daddy was ready to turn the pulpit over to his oldest son. That time had not yet arrived, but Daddy was willing to slow down a bit, as long as he was convinced the people of his church were being placed in capable hands. With M. L., Daddy needed no extra convincing. As his son shared highlights of his studies at Crozer, Daddy sat fascinated by how much M. L. had learned. The names, the ideas, all a giant picture puzzle, each piece slipping neatly into place. At times, as he himself sat in the chair near the pulpit and listened to M. L.

preach, he felt like standing up and shouting, "He's my son. Yes, he is. He's my son!" Glancing at Bunch, who was the church organist, he noticed her loving look of pride too. And Daddy knew, that Bunch was not only proud of the young man sharing his thoughts from the pulpit. She was proud of him, and Christine, and of A. D. too. Yes, that was Bunch, all right. Proud of the whole lot of them. Ah, that choir sounds mighty fine this morning, mighty fine.

> When Moses and his soldiers
>   from Egypt's land did flee,
> His enemies were in behind him,
>   and in front of him the sea,
> God raised the waters like a wall,
>   and opened up the way,
> And the God that lived in Moses' time
>   is jus' the same today.
> When Daniel, faithful to his God,
>   would not bow down to man,
> And by God's enemy he was hurled
>   into the lion's den,
> God locked the lion's jaw, we read,
>   and robbed him of his prey,
> And the God that lived in Daniel's time,
>   is jus' the same today.

Yes, there was a certain contentment in Daddy King as he approached and passed his fiftieth birthday. Half a century. Sometimes that sounded like a very long time. At other times, it seemed as if he'd barely started doing the things that needed doing. But he was mellowing a bit, just a trifle. When A. D. announced plans to marry a young girl named Naomi Barber from Dothan, Alabama, Daddy King expressed his wish that they would wait awhile. A. D. was in too big a hurry. He wanted to get married now, and that was final. Having voiced his objections, Daddy shrugged his shoulders and backed off. The wedding was held June 17, 1950, and Daddy was among the first to kiss the new bride.

Just about the time everything seemed to be settling in more quietly in the King household, an eruption would occur. At times, it would be minor, but when it had anything to do with a member of the family suffering a hurt at anyone else's hands, Daddy King became Mount Vesuvius. It was especially true when the victim was Christine, Daddy's only girl, who never caused him a moment's concern or worry.

Deciding very early that teaching was to be her profession, Christine had coasted smoothly through school, graduating from Spelman College and heading to Columbia University Teachers College in New York City to continue her studies. Once she had completed the requirements for a master's degree, Christine applied for a teaching job in Atlanta. Her request was denied.

Undaunted, Christine simply set out to earn a second master's degree. Surely a school system would not turn down an applicant with *two* advanced degrees. Sadly enough, Christine found out differently.

Despite the possibility of losing her job, Miss Bazoline Usher visited the King house. As supervisor of the Negro teachers in the Atlanta school system, she was privileged to inside information. Christine could earn ten master's degrees and fifty doctorates, but she would never have her own classroom in Atlanta. Why? Instead of answering aloud, Miss Usher simply looked over at Daddy King. No, it was not possible. Could his involvement in the court battle to gain equal pay for black teachers in Atlanta prevent his daughter from a teaching position? How ridiculous! But ridiculous or not, it was true.

Daddy King was livid. As he gazed at Christine's downcast face, he felt the rage of all fathers whose daughters had in any way been violated. How dare they, these unknown powers, refuse to even consider Christine's credentials simply because her father happened to be a fighter.

"Well, we'll just see about this!" Daddy promised,

heading to the telephone. Within minutes he had Mayor Hartsfield on the line. The conversation went back and forth tactfully with Daddy leading the way. First the men talked about the difficulties of raising children, and then Daddy asked how the mayor felt about political enemies seeking revenge on his family. Once Mayor Hartsfield declared his complete disgust with such a practice, Daddy launched into a discourse on Christine's personal situation.

"I may be a royal pain in the rear to a lot of people," Daddy King declared, "but I don't want my daughter penalized for what her old man is."

"Let me get back to you," Mayor Hartsfield promised. "And have Christine on the line too."

Daddy King agreed, and hung up the receiver. Within half an hour, Mayor Hartsfield returned Daddy's call. The news was good. Christine had a job, beginning with the fall term. She was assigned to W. H. Crogman School in the Pittsburgh section of Atlanta.

Usually calm and subdued as her mother was, Christine could not control her delight. Her joyous squeal echoed throughout the house. Daddy welcomed the grateful girl into his arms, patting her back gently.

But when she ran off to spread the news, a troubled Daddy King sat wondering why things had to happen this way. For years he had met with leaders of politics, business and religion. How many hours, how many countless meetings had been spent discussing the injustices incurred by blacks from whites? "Well, I think we've made some progress today." So often those words closed a session.

Yet how much progress had really been made? Or was the white leadership simply willing to do a few token favors for a small number of the black elite? Certainly, Daddy King was happy with the result he had achieved by calling the mayor. He would do anything for the good of his children, any of the members of his family. There was no question about that, but such a phone call should never have to be made. How could a school system not give consideration to a person with two master's degrees? It was one thing if the budget put the applicant out of reach in terms of salary, but this situation had nothing to do with money. It had to do with color, race, black versus white. When was Atlanta going to realize that it was never going to get anywhere as long as it was two cities instead of one? Every day there was news of a new medical advancement—a better way of treating cancer or an improved method for battling heart disease. There was talk that a box called a television would soon be entering people's homes, able to bring pictures and voices live from thousands of miles away into anyone's living room. There were rumors that America was planning a spaceship trip to the moon, with people aboard, Much was happening. There was movement forward. And Daddy King had the urge to go out and tear off every sign that read "Colored Only" and "White Only." He wanted to go into a white neighborhood, march up to a door, ring the bell, and announce to whoever answered. "I just bought the house next door." He wanted to plop down in the front seat of any bus, or restaurant, or public spot and say, "Yes, I do want to sit here. Why can't I? Ain't I one of God's children just like you?

In his head, Daddy heard a melody. It pounded, rolled and thundered. It was a memory from his childhood, and he had heard M. L. singing it too.

> You may talk about the man of Gideon
> You may talk about the man of Saul,
> Dere's none like good ole Joshua
> An' de battle of Jericho.
> > Joshua fit de battle of Jericho, Jericho,
> > Jericho; Joshua fit de battle of Jericho,
> > > an' de walls come tumblin' down.
> Up to the walls of Jericho
> He marched with spear in han ;

"Go blow dem ram horns," Joshua cried,
"For de battle am in my hand."
Den de lam' ram sheep horns 'gin to blow,
Trumpets begin to sound,
Joshua commanded de children to shout,
An' de walls come tumblin' down.
  Joshua fit de battle of Jericho, Jericho,
Jericho, Joshua fit de battle of Jericho,
  An' de walls come tumblin' down.

Yes, the walls were still there, waiting to be knocked down. Daddy King felt some embarrassment when M. L. and Bunch reminded him they had spoken about Christine's problem on several occasions. Apparently their conversation had been lost on Daddy's ears. He had been too busy fighting the war outside his own house to notice the battle that was being waged within.

Willing to accept personal responsibility for his oversight, Daddy turned the entire situation into a useful sermon which he delivered often in the years to come. "We may be too caught up swatting flies with a swatter," he shouted from the Ebenezer Baptist Church pulpit, "that we do not deal with the fly on our nose." It was a matter of "misplaced emphasis," as Daddy called it. "Or you may be so happy with a fine house, a new car and some snazzy, sporty outfit you're wearing, that you start to think all these fancy luxuries are what is important, really important in life. Beware. Yes, beware my children, 'cause that's the devil's blindness. The devil is hopin' to catch you up on all the fine things of his world."

M. L. listened to every word. He watched how his Daddy King fired up the people, shoveling coal in the furnace of their spirit. That old time religion that cast the devil out and brought the Lord in. All of us are God's children, and entitled to be treated as such. He can hold us in his hand, he can squash us with a slap. God's children, yes, all God's children.

When M. L. took his turn in the pulpit, the tone

changed. With softer voice, but with no less sincerity—
with cadenced flow, but without shouts—M. L. led the
way with soft words along a smooth even road of rea-
soned thought. "With hands and hearts joined together,"
he told the congregation, "we form a mighty chain to do
God's work. We are a mighty force. Standing alone, each
by himself, we have little strength. We must mold our
minds, offer worthy solutions to mend the problems of
our present lives. there is more to be won by displaying
the God's love that resides within us than to be ruled by
the devil's hate that is there too."

Daddy King nodded. Each time he listened to M. L.,
his dream of having his son take over the leadership at
Ebenezer Baptist grew stronger. Yet the work that M. L.
accomplished at Crozer Seminary drew him away from
Atlanta once more. When he graduated in June 1951, he
had been elected president of the senior class and had
won the Plaker Award as the most outstanding student.
His academic record consisted of all A's. Finally, he received the J. Lewis Crozer fellowship of $1200 for graduate
study at the university of his choice. He would not be
returning to Ebenezer Baptist for awhile.

11

Once more M. L. headed north, free from the shackled prejudice of the South, to pursue more education. Seated comfortably behind the steering wheel of a green Chevrolet, a gift from his parents upon his graduation from Crozer, the twenty-two-year-old junior minister headed toward Boston. Selecting philosophy as a major, M. L. began his studies at Boston University with the same vigor with which he always approached learning.

"My mind is like an empty glass," he wrote in one of his earliest papers. "I say to the instructor, 'Fill me up' with all you can, and I shall add what I can on my own."

Daddy King treasured each letter he received from Boston. His feelings for his son's mind had grown from admiration to amazement. Clearly the older man realized that M. L.'s ministry was more modern, sophisticated, learned. Yet the bond between the two men was that of respect. In spite of the fact that M. L. was obviously exploring levels of theology and philosophy that his father had never dreamed, the mutual goal of each was the same—to share a love of God with others.

Thankfully, M. L. was still able to preach while in Boston. A friend of his father was pastor of a church in the Roxbury section and invited M. L. to take over the pulpit now and then. It was an invitation he cheerfully accepted. Although Daddy was somewhat apprehensive when he first learned that M. L. was preaching in Boston, he soon relaxed.

"I guess what worried me was that I was thinkin' what I'd feel like if it were me," Daddy told Bunch. "But good old M. L. will fit in there just like he fits here."

M. L. kept in frequent contact with home with telephone calls too, and like most college students, he reversed the charges. Daddy seldom seemed to mind, even when the calls continued for hours at a time.

"The boy misses home," the proud father would tell his friends. "He'll be coming back here someday, you just mark my words. He'll have so much knowledge in that head of his we'll all have to help carry him around. But won't it be a pleasure, yessir, won't it be a pleasure?"

As a registered graduate student in philosophy, M. L. shared a small suite of rooms on Massachusetts Avenue with an old friend from Morehouse, Philip Lenud. Lenud was a divinity student at Tufts College, and the two young men spent hours merging book ideas with personal philosophy. Gradually, the Massachusetts Avenue living quarters became the "in" place for intellectual conversation among other black graduate students. A pot of coffee was always brewing.

"What is God's place in the world of today?"

"Is today's church meeting the needs of today's people?"

"What is the social responsibility of today's minister?"

One question alone might keep a discussion flowing all night long. As word traveled, more and more students made their way to the King-Lenud apartment. New visitors brought different backgrounds, different religious creeds, different standards of morality. The varying beliefs simply added fresh seasoning to the melting pot. At times, calm discussions turned into angry outbursts. It was usually M. L. who brought matters under control.

"Tantrums are for children," he would say quietly. "Yes, it is important that we feel deeply about our convictions. If our ideas mean nothing to us, then we are merely spouting words. But we must talk with logic and reason. One does not win an argument with the loudness of his voice or with a fist raised in anger. We must fight with our minds, lifting one thought upon another."

Gradually those persons who gathered in the apartment developed in to a club. Labeled the Philosophical Club, the group met at least once a week to read papers and reports, and then critique the manuscripts. The reputation of the club even attracted a number of area college and university professors. These educators who presented their own lectures, were eager to receive the comments of the group.

M. L. made new friends easily. Although at 5'7", he did not tower over many of his friends, his frame was strong and sturdy. More than one of the girls he had dated, and there had been many at Morehouse and Crozer, complimented him on the thin mustache he kept neatly trimmed. His eyes reflected curiosity and intellect, while a warm smile came readily to his lips. Keenly aware that his younger brother, A. D., appeared remarkably pleased with married life, M. L. began to entertain some serious thoughts of meeting a prospective mate himself. Through a friend he was given the name of a girl whom he might find congenial.

"But I'm not sure Coretta Scott is really the girl for you," Mary Powell declared. "She's pretty, intelligent, and has a wonderful voice. She's really not that into religion though."

"All I'm wanting is a name and telephone number," M. L. laughed. "I'm looking for a date, not a bride."

In February of 1952 M. L. and Coretta Scott had their first meeting. By the time it was over, M. L.'s position had changed considerably. The quiet, long-haired farmgirl from Marion, Alabama, completely won the young man's heart. While driving Coretta home, M. L. openly shared his feelings.

"I'd like to find four things in a wife," he admitted.

"They are character, intelligence, personality, and beauty. You have them all."

Surprised, Coretta Scott shook her head. "How can you say that? You don't even know me."

M. L. smiled. "I am a good judge of people. I know you, all right. And I want to see you again—soon."

Coretta did not want to appear overeager. "I'm very busy," she offered. "Call me later."

In the weeks and months that followed, M. L. found out a great deal about Coretta Scott. Although her parents were not wealthy, they had worked hard running a farm and a store so that their children could have good educations. Like M. L., she was the second of three children, and Coretta had decided early that music would be her vocation. As a child, she was a scrapper, ready to take on any kid, girl or boy, who challenged her toughness. She worked the Alabama soil, slinging a hoe and picking cotton. In school, she took to books quickly, recognizing that education offered the chance to be received as an equal to whites and to do something worthwhile for humanity. She earned the top grades in her class, and after graduation from Lincoln High School in Marion in 1945, she was awarded a scholarship to attend Antioch College in Yellow Springs, Ohio. Although she had some resentment of being a "token" black student in the midst of a giant majority of whites, Coretta enjoyed the work-study program at Antioch. Students attended classes half the year, the other half they worked full time on campus or in distant cities. Working gave Coretta a chance to earn money for school while testing her interest in a variety of areas. She worked as a librarian, a waitress, and a counselor. She majored in elementary education, while also nurturing a strong desire to be a professional singer someday.

Coretta experienced the usual hurts that came to a young black girl throughout her growing-up years. It was not until she was almost ready to graduate, though, that Coretta experienced a full dose of racial segregation.

When it came time for her to do her student teaching, she would have been assigned ordinarily to the public schools of Yellow Springs. But since no black had ever been assigned there, she was told she would student teach in the Antioch Demonstration School.

"Why?" Coretta demanded. "Just because I'm black?"

The answers she received did not satisfy the disappointed girl. She carried her objections and questions to higher authorities. Each time she was told that she had to accept the decision. It forced Coretta to face the fact that she was a black, and that fact would be a major obstacle. It was a disillusioning realization.

Yet it was this realization that aroused M. L.'s empathy for the young lady from Alabama. He knew exactly how she felt, and his anger at the white society which inflicted such hurts increased even more.

M. L. became more and more impressed with Coretta Scott. He sat in on a few of her rehearsals at the New England Conservatory of Music, and he invited her to attend church with him at the Twelfth Street Baptist Church when he preached there.

It was those Sunday dates that sent word south to Daddy King that M. L. was not spending every available moment studying and going to class. "She is a very attractive girl," Reverend William Hester volunteered when he spoke to Daddy King on the telephone. "I might be distracted if I were doing the preaching, but the young lady's presence does not bother your son a bit."

His friend's remarks made Daddy King curious. When M. L.'s phone calls suddenly dropped off, his curiosity grew even stronger. He was grateful that the Morehouse Board of Trustees was holding its next meeting in New York City. It provided a good excuse to go to Boston and see for himself what was happening.

Daddy and Bunch attended the New York meeting, then headed to Boston. They visited the Hesters and enjoyed sightseeing, but there was one sight Daddy came to see more than any other, Coretta Scott. He wanted to talk to her alone, to see just what the future might hold, and he finally managed to get her alone. The two of them met in the Boston apartment.

Coretta volunteered that her strong interest was in pursuing a career as a concert singer. Daddy King could not hide his disappointment. If M. L. was truly serious about this girl, and he certainly seemed to be from outward appearances, the idea of a minister with a concert singer did not mesh at all well.

"Perhaps you'll soon be growing tired of my son," Daddy offered, an artificial smile tracing his lips. "His interests are certainly not in your area, although I'm sure you'll find someone who does share your interests."

Coretta did not respond; she simply sipped the coffee from her cup. Daddy continued his attack.

"Oh, I think it's fine that you and M. L. are enjoying a little infatuation. He sometimes gets so intense with his studies. He needs some socializing."

Again Daddy waited for some response. Still there was no answer. Finally, he broached the matter head on.

"Miss Scott, do you take my son seriously?"

This time it was the artificial smile that traced Coretta's lips. "Why no," she replied, "not really."

Daddy King should have been delighted at the answer. Of course, there was no possibility that anything serious could ever come with the relationship between a dedicated student of theology and philosophy and a budding concert singer. Yet, the thought that someone, anyone, would dare not to take his son seriously angered him. As he noticed Bunch and M. L. coming in the door, Daddy expressed his approval that Coretta did not have any serious intentions about M. L.

"You might be interested in knowing that M. L. has gone out with some truly outstanding young ladies," Daddy boasted, lifting himself to his feet. "He has even proposed marriage to a few, and you can be sure every one of them was willing."

M. L. could not believe what his father was saying. Bunch stood shocked, then moved a few steps further into the room as if to caution Daddy about continuing. But the old country mule was loose in the man now, and he was not going to stop. "Yes, M. L. has enjoyed keeping company with the daughters of Atlanta's finest families, respected people, people who have much to share and much to offer."

This time it was Coretta who was on her feet. The smile was gone, replaced with blazing eyes. "*I* have something to offer, Reverend King. I know exactly what my relationship with your son is now and where it will go if I so decide."

Fire. Real fire. Daddy King was taken aback by the sudden outburst. He knew he had misjudged Coretta Scott. Whether or not anything serious would come of the relationship remained to be seen, but one thing was certain—this young girl had spirit and substance.

Pulling Daddy to a side room, M. L. managed to calm his father down. Once he was collected and cool, Daddy looked his son directly in the eye.

"How strongly do you feel about this girl, M. L.?"

"She's the most important person to come into my life, Dad. I love her more than anything." M. L.'s gaze dropped. "I know you may not approve, but I must marry Coretta. She's the one, Dad. The one."

Daddy King looked at M. L. for several moments. No words were spoken. Yet Daddy knew the tone of voice he was hearing. It was his own voice, of over twenty-five years ago. Yes, love had its own tone, strong and warm. If two people loved each other as much as M. L. was convinced he and Coretta could, and if it was God's wish, what else really mattered? Certainly not some grumpy Baptist preacher from Atlanta.

On June 18, 1953, Martin Luther King, Jr. married

Coretta Scott on the lawn of her parents' home in Marion,
Alabama. A. D. assisted his brother as best man, while
Martin Luther King, Sr. officiated.

12

M. L. was his own man. There was no doubt about it. Not only had he married Coretta Scott, he had taken a total independent step. Daddy had always assumed that M. L. would complete his studies and return to take over the pulpit at Ebenezer Baptist. He had also assumed that M. L. would likely settle down with one of the well-bred young quality girls of Atlanta.

But love sometimes takes its own direction. Whether or not that direction would ever lead M. L. back to Atlanta was completely uncertain. There was nothing wrong with hoping. Nobody knew that better than Daddy King.

The new bridegroom and bride found a four-room apartment not far from the conservatory in Boston. M. L. had completed most of the requirements for his Ph.D. Still, the dreaded thesis remained to be written. Coretta had no intention of giving up her studies either. Therefore, a schedule of shared household duties was set up.

"If you have classes, I cook," M. L. declared. "If I have to work at the library, you cook."

"We both do the washing, the ironing, and the cleaning," Coretta added.

"Fair enough!" came the reply.

The program worked smoothly. The beginning months of the marriage were not without minor spats and disagreements but most of the heated discussions were ended with loving words and a makeup kiss.

As 1954 opened, M. L. and Coretta began making

serious plans for their immediate future. In June, Coretta would complete her studies at the New England Conservatory of Music. M. L. knew the writing of his thesis would take some time longer. Having decided to investigate the philosophy of personalism as a topic by exploring the thinking of theologians Paul Tillich and Henry Nelson Wieman, M. L. saw the attainment of a doctorate as two or three years away. In the meantime, he was eager to find a church, his own church, from which he might share the results of twenty-one years of education. Eventually, he hoped to return to the classroom, not as a student, but as a teacher. Benjamin Mays, the preacher and president of Morehouse College, had left an indelible mark on M. L. Weighing the possibilities, he decided that he wanted a church pulpit more than he wanted a classroom podium.

The credentials M. L. had achieved brought in a number of job offers. Three teaching positions, a deanship, an administrator's role—all were available to him in the academic world. Two churches in the North sent him invitations, as did two churches in the South. And then there was always Ebenezer Baptist in Atlanta. Daddy King would welcome him home with open arms.

It was satisfying to have so many options. Yet it was difficult too. When one has fewer choices to make, decision-making is considerably less complicated. But one story, told about the departing pastor of Dexter Avenue Baptist Church of Montgomery, Alabama, intrigued M. L. greatly. The church was one that had offered M. L. a position, and the congregation was made up mostly of teachers and professional people at Alabama State College, the state-supported school for blacks. It seemed that the young preacher at Dexter, Rev. Vernon Johns, was once ordered to vacate a seat on a Montgomery bus. His refusal brought the irate driver storming back. "Nigger!" the bus driver shouted, "didn't you hear me tell you to get the hell out of that seat!" Johns returned the driver's fiery gaze with equal but calmer conviction. "And didn't you hear me tell you that I'm going to sit right god-damned here?" Flustered and confused, the driver retreated. The following Sunday, Reverend Johns told his congregation the entire story, word for word. The preacher said he was convinced God was not offended by the unauthorized use of his name. In truth, Johns summarized, God probably thought, "I'd better keep an eye on that boy; he's going to do a lot for Christianity down South."

M. L. still carried vivid memories of a night twelve years before when he had encountered such abuse and ugliness on a bus. He admired the bravery of Vernon Johns, and when the courageous preacher invited M. L. to deliver a trial sermon at the Dexter Avenue Church, M. L. accepted.

M. L. entitled his presentation, "The Three Dimensions of a Complete Life." As he spoke of the love of God, the love of self, and the love of neighbors, the congregation listened attentively. By April, they had issued a call for his fulltime services. The yearly salary offered of $4200 was the highest of any Negro minister in Montgomery.

The moment of decision had come. Certainly there were many points in favor of the Montgomery offer. The warmth of the people, the neat seven-room parsonage that accompanied the offer, the sturdy red-brick church itself, nestled so comfortably amid the mighty and proud white statehouse buildings of Alabama's capital city—all were positives. But on the more dismal side of the ledger was the fact that of the 130,000 citizens living in Montgomery, 50,000 were blacks. Of course, these people read about the Negroes of Atlanta and other Southern cities winning a right here and a right there on the ladder toward desegregation, but the thought of such things happening in Montgomery made whites and blacks both shake their heads. If ever there was a city of white supremacy, it was Montgomery, Alabama. What black in his right mind would want to live willingly in such a place, much less raise a family there?

M. L. and Coretta talked the matter through carefully. Both of them knew full well that if they had children, those children would suffer the shackles of segregation and institutionalized racism. They would experience the snips and snipes of day-to-day living, the inferior education, the fewer opportunities for work and pleasure. Yet, as M. L. and Coretta knew well, the South was home. Their families were there; their roots were there. What life had the Lord taken—the easy road—or the road plagued with heartbreak and danger? M. L. accepted the Dexter offer.

Having made this decision, M. L. knew an equally difficult task lay before him—telling Daddy King. "He might just understand exactly how I feel," M. L. told Coretta as he prepared to fly to Atlanta with the news. "Sometimes Daddy can surprise you."

This, unfortunately for M. L., was not one of those times. If the son had ever seen his father rant and rave from the pulpit, he had never seen him more fired up about M. L.'s choice than he was upon arriving home.

"You've been an associate pastor here at Ebenezer Baptist," Daddy said, loosening the collar from around his thick neck. "Naturally everyone in the congregation assumed you'd be coming home to Atlanta once you got your schoolin' finished. I know I did. What is wrong with you, boy? Dexter's not got the size congregation we got here at Ebenezer Baptist. This is a family church. Your Grandpa Williams, me, then you. Why you got to be taking over some church in Montgomery?"

"Daddy, you've done so much here, both in the church and in Atlanta. You got a good long time to be pastor at Ebenezer Baptist. But the people at Dexter want me badly. They're going to furnish the parsonage for Coretta and me, and give me time and money to help me finish my thesis. They want me there because I'm Martin Luther King, Jr., my own person, and what I am as a preacher. As for the city of Montgomery, everything I've heard and read makes me think that city is just about the same as it was when the Civil War ended. You and all your friends have done so much for blacks here in Atlanta. I can take some of what I've seen you do and try to get it into Montgomery."

"You're just blowing steam, boy. That city is the way it is because that's the way it wants to be. It took us years to get anything done here in Atlanta. Years of begging and pleading and coaxin' and waitin'. You think you're goin' into that city and turn everything upside down—"

M. L. shook his head. "I never said we would change everything overnight. But there's so much to do there. Atlanta has Martin Luther King, Sr. and Montgomery will have Martin Luther King, Jr. Now with that combination, we'll keep Georgia and Alabama hopping all right."

Daddy looked down at his hands. Suddenly he felt very tired, as if the years had come crashing down on his shoulders. In one way, he felt proud of his son for what he was doing. Yet again, it was the last thing on earth he wanted.

"M. L., don't you know a father wants to be able to do things for his children? I had to break away from my father because he would have just kept me takin' care of someone else's crops, mindin' someone else's land. I wanted to be able to give you something, to hand you the key to Ebenezer Baptist and say, here, boy, now you take over."

"Daddy, you've given me so much more than a key. You've given me the love and the help for me to find myself. Every night and day, I thank God for giving you and Mother Dear to me. No one could have had better parents. But I am what you made me, what you've let me be."

"But I—"

"Don't interrupt, Daddy. Let me finish. I don't know what life in Montgomery will be like. I know Coretta

would probably like to stay in Boston or at least live up
North. It hasn't been easy knowing that she'd like to live
entirely away from the South; you'd like me to come here
to Atlanta . . . but Daddy, there's another voice speaking
to me, deep inside, and it's that voice that gives direction
to all of us. I don't think you'd have me turn a deaf ear to
that voice, Daddy. And it's the voice that is telling me to
head to Montgomery."

Daddy King looked up, his eyes somewhat blurred
from the realization that the twenty-five-year-old kneeling
before him was considerably more than his son now. He
was a man, an independent follower of God, taking his
orders from the Lord as he understood them. Daddy
closed his arms around M. L.'s shoulders.

"Ah, boy, how many dreams we both have had. How
many more lie before us . . ."

M. L. nodded, feeling closer to his father than he
had in a long time. "But we are not only dreamers,
Daddy. We are doers. In that, you have led the way."

By September of 1954, M. L. and Coretta had moved
into the white frame house which was the residence for
the pastor of the Dexter Avenue Baptist Church. M. L.
was struck by the irony which his home and place of work
represented. His home was as white as white could be,
surrounded by dark, towering oaks. Yet his church was a
deep red brick, bordered across the street by the austere
white government structures of Alabama's capital.

The couple soon felt quite at home in their new sur-
roundings. Coretta was especially pleased by the baby
grand piano the congregation had cheerfully provided,
and she added a variety of the African and West Indian
art pieces that both she and M. L. enjoyed.

From the very beginning M. L. felt at home in the
pulpit at Dexter Avenue Baptist Church. His first sermons
reflected the scholarly climate from which he had just
come. He was sober, reflective, intellectual. But soon he
sensed the need for members of his congregation to re-

lease some of their emotions and frustrations. He found himself responding positively to the agreement in the "Amens" and "You tell us, Reverend." Why couldn't a worship service appeal to both mind and emotional spirit?

He adopted a similar tone when he counseled privately with members of the congregation. Whether it was a married couple trying to work out domestic problems or a factory worker unhappy with his foreman, M. L. asked for rational thinking and positive action.

"Violence is the devil's tool," he said often. "When you are hurt, your first reaction is to strike back—physically. This is seldom the best recourse. Better you take time to think, then take action. You will be less likely to make a mistake you'll regret."

Although some members of the congregation had trouble adjusting to M. L. because of his youthful appearance, his wise counseling soon won him a following, even among the church elders. "He looks young enough to be my grandson," noted one curt matron, "but he talks more like my grandfather."

Not merely content assisting the spiritual side of his congregation, M. L.'s efforts quickly spread into educational and social arenas. Student aid programs were established to help young people seeking more education find scholarships. Representatives of the National Council for the Advancement of Colored People made visits to the church organizations to inform people of activities. A committee network reached out effectively to the needy and sick.

As active as the inner workings of Dexter Baptist were, M. L. felt dissatisfied. Nothing was happening within the white and black framework of the city itself. The racial caste system flourished. "Our niggers are happy," observed city leaders, without feeling any shame at what they were saying. Worse yet was the apathetic attitudes of the blacks who saw themselves inferior because this was how they had been treated for so long.

If any favorable spotlight was shed on blacks in Montgomery, it was on January 1st. This was Emancipation Day, when blacks assembled to hear leaders praise Abraham Lincoln as their political "Father Abraham" and give eloquent testimony about the need for Negro rights.

"You wouldn't believe how strong and forceful they sound," M. L. told Daddy King on a long distance call home the next day. "But it is talk and nothing more. They give speeches for hours about what we should do and how much we should have, and then they go right back to the same way of life."

Daddy listened attentively, but he was eager to share the news that had traveled to Atlanta about M. L.'s success in the pulpit of Dexter Baptist. "Everyone tells me you preach circles around your old man. I'm not surprised. The acorn does not fall far from the oak."

Naturally, such compliments pleased M. L. So did Coretta's news that she was expecting a baby. But it was not enough. Even the completion of his thesis and his doctorate earned left M. L. with an empty feeling. The final draft of his thesis ran 343 pages. Yet he could not honestly say he had helped Montgomery take one step forward in knocking down the wall of segregation.

"If I've got brains enough to earn a doctorate," he confided to Daddy, "why can't I find the way to help our people make a little progress for themselves?"

Daddy understood M. L.'s impatience. He had traveled the same roads himself. "Time," Daddy offered. "Think of how long it took Montgomery to reach the point it has. You expect to undo in a year or two what it has taken generations to construct. The wall between whites and blacks is of solid structure. It is not loose sand. You must chip and pound away at it."

M. L. would never have dreamed that major help would come to his plan in the form of a fiesty department store seamstress named Rosa Parks. M. L. was caught up in the excitement of his firstborn, a girl Coretta and he decided to name Yolanda Denise, when Mrs. Rosa Parks made a move that would shake the South.

Of the many major obstacles in the path of blacks attaining personal rights and justice in Montgomery, the city bus service was but one. Northern-owned, the Montgomery City Lines crisscrossed the city, blacks making up almost seventy per cent of the system's passengers. Blacks boarding the buses automatically took their places at the rear and worked forward, while whites sat in the front and worked backward. Drivers enjoyed audibly labeling black riders as "black apes" and "black cows." An amusing prank among some drivers was to have blacks board the bus through the front door, pay their money and then order them out in order to board the bus by way of the rear door. While the blacks walked outside to the rear, drivers would drive away laughing, leaving the paid passengers stranded. Blacks who objected or protested were threatened, beaten, and sometimes put in jail.

On the afternoon of Thursday, December 1, 1955, a weary Rosa Parks boarded a Montgomery City Lines bus. The first four seats were always reserved for white passengers, so Mrs. Parks dutifully selected a seat in the middle of the bus. It had been a long day, and she was tired. As more and more whites boarded, the driver ordered the blacks to stand up and vacate their seats. This time Rosa Parks refused. The Montgomery police were summoned, and the determined seamstress was arrested.

"I was tired," the woman announced. "I was just tired."

For M. L., Rosa Parks' words sounded like a battle cry. If ever the time was right for movement forward, it was now. The Supreme Court had only recently ordered school systems across the country to end all segregation under the myth of the two systems being "separate but equal." In August, a fourteen-year-old black Chicago boy, Emmett Till, had been kidnapped and lynched while vacationing in Mississippi. Black sentiment was turning hostile. Rosa Parks, whether she knew it or not, was adding fuel to the fire.

"We are all tired!" M. L. told reporters. "Mrs. Rosa Parks speaks for us all."

It was a time for grassroots action. Montgomery's black leadership, men and women alike, gathered at the Dexter Avenue Baptist Church. A one-day boycott of the city line buses was set for Monday, December 5th. Leaflets were prepared to spread through the city. Black ministers would spread the word from their pulpits on Sunday. "Don't ride the city buses Monday" was the message.

Word traveled back to Atlanta. Concerned, Daddy King called M. L. to find out if everything was all right.

"I hope there won't be any violence," Daddy offered. "Uh, your mother was kind of concerned about that."

"*She* was, was she?" M. L. answered. "No, there is certainly no violence planned on this end. We've just asked our people not to ride the buses. It's as simple as that. We figure the best way of showing our feelings is to hurt the Montgomery bus lines right where it counts—in the pocketbook. We're all going to get together Monday night to evaluate the situation."

"Uh, huh. Well, you just take care, boy. We'll be a-prayin' for you."

"I know you will, Daddy. If there's anything I can be sure of, it's that."

M. L. and Coretta were up early the next morning. They were anxious to see the first bus that rolled by their front door at six in the morning. Inwardly, M. L. was hoping for sixty percent cooperation among the blacks. After all, they were used to riding the bus to work, to school and to shop in downtown Montgomery. To ask them to change their whole way of life, even just for a day, was asking for sacrifice.

"Martin!" Coretta shouted, seeing the early morning bus. "Look!"

His eyes widening in disbelief, M. L. yelled a joyful

"Hallelujah!" The only passenger on the bus was the driver himself! The bus was usually filled.

Was it just a fluke? Jumping in to his car, M. L. drove around the city. Everywhere he went, he saw small groups of blacks walking along the sidewalks. Every bus he saw was empty. "Hallelujah!" he whooped again. "It's a miracle! God be praised!"

That morning Rosa Parks was convicted of violating the city segregation code. She was fined ten dollars and court costs.

Black leaders and ministers met at the Mount Zion AME Church before a scheduled meeting on Monday night to evaluate the results of the bus boycott. A new organization was formed, its name suggested by another Baptist minister whom M. L. admired, Dr. Ralph Abernathy. The group called itself the Montgomery Improvement Association. M. L. was unanimously elected president. The leaders voted to extend the bus boycott.

The Monday night meeting was set for seven p.m. at Holt Street Baptist Church. M. L. was nervous. All afternoon when he thought about the gathering sweat soaked his clothes. How desperately he wanted to find the right words to share with the people. After all, this was not a small incident. This was open rebellion, out and out revolution. Blacks were standing up and being counted. It was important to give a speech that would keep them aroused and willing to maintain positive action without losing control and destroying their goals.

M. L. had only a half of an hour between the Mount Zion and Holt Street meetings. "Give me the words, Lord," he prayed. "Stand beside me and offer direction."

By the time M. L. arrived at Holt Street Baptist Church, the building was filled and thousands more stood outside under the loudspeakers. It took little time for the crowd to decide to continue the bus boycott. Immediately, the people began shouting and singing:

148

> Onward, Christian soldiers, marching as
>   to war
> With the cross of Jesus, going on before,
> Christ, our loyal Master, leads against the
>   fray
> Onward into battle, hear our voices
>   pray . . .
> Onward, Christian soldiers, marching as
>   to war
> With the cross of Jesus, going on
>   before . . .

The voices of the people swelled with pride and determination. Once introduced, M. L. matched that feeling with his words. He recited a litany of abuses placed upon blacks by the city bus line, then expanded the list of grievances suffered by blacks throughout American history. He knew the people were listening. He saw it in their faces, and heard their voices in agreement. "Our method will be that of persuasion, not coercion," he insisted, sensing his audience's need for direction. "We will only say to the people, 'let your conscience be your guide.' " M. L. had never before felt the desperate need to capture just the right tone, sharing guidance and understanding, offering comfort and hope. "Love must be our regulating ideal. Once again we must hear the words of Jesus echoing across the centuries: 'Love your enemies, bless those that curse you, and pray for them that despitefully use you.' If we fail to do this, our protest will end up as a meaningless drama on the stage of history, and its memory will be shrouded with the ugly garments of shame. In spite of the mistreatment that we have confronted we must not become bitter and end up hating our white brothers." M. L. swallowed deeply, wiping his damp forehead with his handkerchief. "As Booker T. Washington said, 'Let no man pull you down so low as to make you hate him.'" Applause shook the church rafters. M. L. paused, praying that God indeed would carry him to the end. "If you will protest courageously, and yet with dignity and Christian love, when the history books are written in future generations, the historians will have to pause and say, 'There lived a great people—a black people—who injected new meaning and dignity into the veins of civilization.' This is our challenge, and our overwhelming responsibility."

M. L. turned, but the thunderous applause held him captive. Everywhere people rose in their seats, showing their support and approval. Happily, joyously, M. L. raised his hands and smiled. Truly, he thought, truly God was standing beside him.

Later that night, as M. L. spoke with Daddy King on the phone, the son tried to recapture the feeling of the moment. "It was magnificent, Daddy, we were all standing together for one cause, peacefully."

"But breaking laws—isn't there a better way? Maybe if you sat down with the right people, negotiated—"

"No," M. L. answered. "Alabama is different from Georgia. You have people there who are listening and changing things. The only way we have to change the law here is to break it. Rosa Parks took the first step. If we boycott the bus line, we can break it. Daddy, sometimes you can change things a political way, sometimes an economic way. We will do it however we can."

"It can be dangerous, son."

"I know, but there is no violence in our plan. None at all."

"I'll tell your mother you are fine. Take care, son. God bless . . ."

"You too, Daddy."

As Daddy King turned away from the phone, he felt Bunch's gentle hand on his shoulder. Her questions were in her face. She did not need to say a word.

"He's fine," Daddy offered. "Everything is all right."

Bunch slipped into Daddy's arms. "Oh, I'm so glad it's over."

Daddy held his wife close, sensing her tenseness dissolve. But somehow he knew that the struggle was not over. In fact, it was just beginning.

13

One day became two, two became three, and the Montgomery bus boycott was a week old. Across the city, car pools had sprung up. Empty city buses rolled along the streets passing clusters of blacks filling the sidewalks on their way to work.

"It won't last," white civic leaders said. "It can't. Those black lazy no-goods will be riding the buses soon enough."

It did last. The Christmas season came and went with no sign of the end of the boycott.

M. L.'s intense study of India's Gandhi proved highly useful. Once he had overcome the initial fear that comes from taking a first dramatic step, M. L. realized that the next steps came more easily. It was like riding a bicycle, learning to swim, or giving a speech. The first attempt was scary, then much of the fear disappeared. He taught his supporters to overcome their fears too.

"We know we are in the right," he told his congregation at Dexter Avenue Baptist. "Jesus has shown us the way. Hate can never drive out hate. But love can drive out hate. We must love those who make us suffer. It is not people we are trying to change as much as it is a system. We must resist the ways of the past. There is no need for violence. We simply stop doing what we have been doing. Changes will come."

If M. L. thought all the changes would come without any problems, he was sadly mistaken. By January of 1956,

Montgomery police started issuing tickets to any black driver for the slightest violation. "Ride the bus!" policemen ordered. M. L. was arrested for driving five miles over the speed limit. Shoved into a patrol car, he was driven to the city jail where he was tossed into a cell with murderers, drunks, and thieves.

The experience was unforgettable. M. L. gazed around at men sprawled on the floor near open, filthy toilets. The ugliness, the depression, the emptiness pulled him down. Human beings should not be treated this way, no matter what they had done. M. L. was taken to a small room, fingerprinted, and told to report for trial the next week. Concerned about the angry crowd outside, officials released him on his own recognizance. A loud, joyful cry greeted M. L. when he emerged from jail.

To counter all the cries of support, there were the missiles of hate. Obscene threats arrived in the mail daily at the King house. *GET OUT OF MONTGOMERY, NIGGER* was typical. *YOU WANT YOUR FAMILY BLOWN TO HELL?* Others were longer, filthy, and more graphic. The message of hate was the same: *IF YOU THINK YOU ARE AS GOOD AS A WHITE MAN, YOU ARE SO DAMN WRONG YOU NEED A NEW HEAD. MAYBE WHEN WE GET DONE POUNDING IN YOUR SKULL, YOU WILL KNOW YOU AIN'T EVER GOING TO GET ANYTHING YOU WANT!*

Phone calls were equally revolting. No matter how many times M. L. listened to someone curse at him, threaten him or degrade him on the telephone, he could not imagine the kind of person who would do such a thing. Callers accused him of lusting after white women, wanting personal power, seeking attention and the spotlight of fame . . . "You don't give a damn about black people," one caller declared. "You just want to be looked at yourself. Well, maybe people will be looking at you in your casket pretty damn soon."

The anonymous letters and calls troubled M. L. tremendously. Often he came home from meetings to find Coretta trembling and upset. Both of them feared for little Yolanda's safety.

On the anniversary of Gandhi's birth, M. L. was giving a speech to a group of followers. "From this noble, kindly man of another country, we can learn much," M. L. emphasized. "Though he be small in stature, he was seen around the world."

Moments after M. L. had finished speaking, a friend brought him fearful news. "Your house has been bombed," came the whisper. In a dazed stupor, M. L. hurried home. When he arrived, he found a wild crowd of shouting blacks surrounding the white frame house, whom policemen were having little success in calming. Many held guns, knives, and sticks.

Thankfully, Coretta and Yolanda were safe. The baby had been sleeping in a back bedroom. Coretta had been sitting in the living room with a visitor when what sounded like a brick hit the front porch. Coretta wisely suggested moving to the rear of the house, and just as they did, the bomb exploded. A porch support was split and all of the front windows broken, but no one was hurt. The crowd of blacks outside the house swelled quickly to a thousand. "Let's rip this city apart!" someone shouted. "You got your .38 and I got mine," one black told a white policeman, "so let's battle it out." Mayor W. A. Gayle arrived at the scene and joined the Kings inside, as did other Montgomery officials. The appearance of these white civic leaders brought a deafening roar of boos from the crowd.

Like dry leaves and dead wood in a forest the angry crowd was ready to ignite into a giant flame of hatred and bloodshed with the slightest spark. M. L. felt the tension. It was choking, stifling. He asked Mayor Gayle and the others to follow him out on to the porch.

The people quieted as M. L. raised his hands to speak. He gazed from one side to the other at the desperate crowd. "Don't get panicky!" he shouted. "We need no weapons here. He who lives by the sword shall die by the sword." People exchanged puzzled looks. Wasn't this the man whose wife, child, and home had just been violated by a vicious act? Surely he would want revenge on his attackers. "We are not advocating violence," M. L. continued. "We must be good to our enemies. I did not start this boycott, and I want it known the length and breadth of this land that even if I am stopped, the movement will not stop. What we are doing is right. What we are doing is just, and God is with us."

"Amen!" a man shouted. "God bless you, son!" another yelled. Slowly the people began to move away from the house. If M. L. could speak for love and justice after what had happened, who were they to feel differently? It was one thing to speak of loving one's enemies, but M. L. had demonstrated that love visibly. There was no question that Martin Luther King, Jr. was a symbol of Christian forgiveness. And as newspapers, television, and radio carried the news of what had happened in Montgomery that night, he also became known as the leader of a whole movement—a movement of blacks seeking their civil rights—history was being made.

In Atlanta, Daddy King accepted the news of the violence with mixed feelings. He had been involved in the battle for civil rights long enough to realize the bombing would bring a mighty outburst of support for the campaign for equality. Few human beings could accept such an attack on the wife and infant of a man fighting for what he believes. Yes, people would be willing to make financial contributions, sign petitions, lend their voices in meetings. All that was good. Still, M. L. was now the acknowledged leader of a movement that divided friends and neighbors, quickly turned discussion to argument, brought feelings from indifference to rage. M. L. was now clearly an open target, and there would always be assassins with words or weapons waiting to score a bullseye.

"It will not be as easy to sleep at night," Daddy told Bunch. Bunch nodded. "But he is doing what he must do," she murmured.

As the bus boycott swept into its second month, the atmosphere in Montgomery became even worse. White drivers roamed the streets, yelling obscenities at every black they passed. Rallies were held, with white city officials openly attacking the NAACP and all efforts to promote equal rights. Handbills spilled from printing presses, carrying slander and hate against every Negro leader, especially Martin Luther King, Jr. One handbill read: "When in the course of human events it becomes necessary to abolish the Negro race, proper methods should be used. Among these are guns, bows and arrows, sling shots and knives. We hold these truths to be self evident: that all whites are created equal with certain rights, among these are life, liberty and the pursuit of dead niggers. In every stage of the bus boycott we have been oppressed and degraded because of black, slimy, juicy, unbearably stinking niggers. Their conduct should not be dwelt upon because behind them they have an ancestral background of Pygmies, head hunters, snot suckers . . . If we don't stop helping these African flesh eaters, we will soon wake up and find Reverend King in the White House."

Never had M. L. read such gutter talk, such horrendous, vicious trash. But it was typical of the mood growing in Montgomery. For the time being, M. L. took Coretta and Yolanda to Atlanta to stay with Daddy King and Bunch.

The city officials and bus company leaders sought to find any way possible to end the boycott. Actually, all that M. L. and the other black leaders wanted was equal treatment and respect given anyone riding the buses. It was asking too much. One white lawyer found an antique law in the books that forbade boycotts. M. L. was out of town when the grand jury handed down indictments against the black ministers of the city and all of the drivers in the car pools. Returning to Montgomery to be arrested, M. L. stopped in Atlanta to make sure Coretta and Yolanda were all right. Daddy King was waiting for him.

"You can't go on like this, son. Your momma is sick with worry. You've got a wife and child to care for. There's ways of doin' things like we are here in Atlanta. But your ways are dangerous. They could arrest you and take you out someplace and kill you."

M. L. shook his head. "There's others, Daddy. I'm not the only one."

"You're the main one they're after. You know that. Why can't you take things slow and easy? Things change. I know. I had to learn patience."

"You and I are different that way, Daddy. We both want the same things, but our ways are different. I can't do your way just as you can't do mine."

Daddy would not give in. In desperation, he immediately called together the black leaders of Atlanta to talk with M. L. Even Dr. Mays was there, a man whom M. L. had always idolized. All of them spoke of the dangers of returning to Montgomery.

How badly M. L. wanted to agree. These were the people he had grown up with in Atlanta. He respected them and everything they had done. Educators, businessmen, ministers—and they had reached their goals by hard work and sacrifice. And Daddy, good, loving Daddy. What a tower of strength and determination he was, had always been. Now this loving man sat, his eyes filled with tears of worry and concern, begging to be understood.

Finally, M. L. spoke.

"I have to go back to Montgomery," he insisted. "To stay away when my friends and associates are being arrested would be total cowardice." Turning to face Daddy, M. L. continued. "I might have to go to jail, but I would rather be there with my people than desert them now. I have begun the struggle and I can't turn back now. I've passed the point of no return." Daddy King was devastated. He had been convinced that M. L. would alter his plans when he realized what everyone in this distinguished group thought. A terrible premonition shook Daddy's body—the fear that next time an unknown bomber would destroy M. L. and his wonderful little family. This thought caused Daddy to sob out loud. M. L. wanted desperately to console his father, and to tell him everything would be fine. He turned to Dr. Mays.

Tall, gray-haired and scholarly, Benjamin Mays had listened to every word spoken. Somehow, a story kept coming back to him of a young boy speaking to his elders and teachers in a temple. It was not his intention to concern his parents, but he did anyway. There was no other choice. He had to do what he had to do. And now, like a young Jesus of so long ago, Martin Luther King, Jr. stood before those who loved him and declared his need to be about his Father's business. Strangely enough, this did not seem so different. "Martin must do what he feels is right," Dr. Mays offered. "No leader runs away from battle."

How grateful M. L. was for May's words. Others in the room nodded in agreement. Finally, Daddy looked up. "If it is what you must do, I will not try and stop you. But you must grant me one favor."

"Anything," M. L. agreed.

"Let me return to Montgomery with you. Your momma will feel better about it," Daddy lowered his eyes. "And I will too."

"Request granted," M. L. answered.

Cheerful news awaited M. L. on his return to Montgomery. To show their unity and fearlessness, many of the black ministers and car pool drivers had already turned themselves in. M. L. went immediately to the jail. While thousands of his followers stood near, M. L. was fingerprinted and had his trial date set. There was no doubt now that the movement for civil rights was rolling.

The trial began on March 19. For three days black witnesses testified to the numerous abuses that they had suffered at the hands of white bus drivers and city officials. Their grammar was sometimes incorrect, their language tangled and confused, but black after black shared accounts of harrassment when riding the buses. Prosecution witnesses simply reported facts about the boycott, that blacks had stopped riding the buses and that Martin Luther King, Jr. was behind the action.

The verdict came as no surprise. M. L. was found guilty, fined $500 and court costs—the equivalent of 386 days at hard labor. M. L. felt anything but a convicted criminal. The legal decision was the first step in taking the entire matter to a higher court, even the United States Supreme Court. Not only that, blacks had maintained a unified force, a towering wall of resistance and power. A minor battle may have been lost, but the real war lay ahead.

14

SUPREME COURT DECLARES ALABAMA BUS
LAWS UNCONSTITUTIONAL

Newspaper headlines of November 13, 1956 brought
cheers of joy from the blacks of Montgomery. For months,
they had been waiting, praying, hoping for just such a
decision. Finally, it came. With the news, ten thousand
blacks gathered in simultaneous meetings held in two city
churches and voted to end the boycott.

"We have fought the battle as Christians, with the
firm belief that God looks at all men as equal," M. L. told
the people of Dexter Avenue Baptist. "We have fought
with no bitterness, no hate, but with a conviction that
what we were doing was right and just. Now, we may go
back to the buses with humility and meekness. We have
won no victory over whites, and if you return to the buses
with such an attitude, all we have accomplished will be
lost. What we have done is to make a change in a system,
made a correction where a correction needed to be made.
We are weary from the journey, yet we rejoice with the
outcome."

There is little doubt that at twenty-seven years of age,
Martin Luther King, Jr. had assumed the role of champion
for civil rights for blacks. National magazines ran cover
stories about him; television and radio reporters tripped
over themselves trying to get feature information on the
air; political figures sought close identification with the
new black leader.

"You are no longer a person," Daddy King told his son. "You are a symbol, a product. This carries power with it, but it carries a dark side too. Many folks will be your friend, and you'll be able to spot them. But not all your enemies will be wearing a Ku Klux Klan outfit."

M. L. knew there was truth in Daddy's words. A church minister not wanting to stir up his congregation—a city mayor wanting re-election more than innovating just policies—a businessman desiring customers over fairness—yes, these were major obstacles in the pathway to justice.

But for the moment, there was a special joy in watching Coretta turn a wall of their home into a "Wall of Fame" for the certificates of honor and awards that flowed in. There was pride in returning to Morehouse College and receiving an honorary degree from President Mays. There was delight in seeing the twinkle in Daddy's eyes as he observed each accomplishment that his son achieved.

Because of all the attention, M. L. faced serious questions about his future. Offers of new jobs and lecture tours flooded the mailbox. Not only did black business leaders and church congregations seek his leadership, but opportunities came from the white sector as well. Could he be more useful as a college dean, a pastor, a professional speaker, a writer—which direction was best? Finally, M. L. resolved that first of all, he was a pastor, a preacher, a shepherd gathering the Lord's sheep. Secondly, he was a black leader, seeking fairness and justice for the oppressed.

Accepting that realization, M. L. willingly took on the presidency of the Southern Christian Leadership Conference early in 1957. He forcefully called upon blacks to claim their right to human dignity by avoiding any further cooperation with the evil of racism. M. L. encouraged those writing the cornerstone documents of the SCLC to acknowledge Jesus as an example for all that can be accomplished by nonviolence. "Nonviolent resistance," asserted M. L., "transforms weakness into strength and breeds courage in the face of danger."

In May, 35,000 blacks surrounded the Lincoln Monument in Washington, D.C. for a Prayer Pilgrimage. One after another, black leaders were introduced in order to share their feelings. The loudest applause came for M. L., wearing a long, black robe, who sensed the importance of the moment and felt the eyes of millions of Americans upon him by way of their television sets. With cool and calculated eloquence, like a drum rallying forces before a mighty battle, M. L. pounded out a forceful indictment. Government leaders he called "silent," "apathetic," and "hypocritical." He pleaded for the powers that could "Give us the ballot . . . so that blacks could choose better officials, make better laws, transform misdeeds into good deeds. Again, M. L. warned against hate, emphasizing that it would be a step backward. "We must meet hate with love," M. L. insisted, "physical force with soul force."

In October of 1957, M. L. and Coretta welcomed a new addition to their family. Martin III, immediately called "Marty" joined sister Yolanda, who had acquired the nickname "Yoki." Having a son brought M. L. a special joy, but he worried that he was not spending enough time with his family. It was no small task, leading a movement, and the thought that he was with strangers more than he was with his family troubled him.

Equally troublesome were the grumbles and complaints of some black leaders who resented the meteoric rise of M. L. to the forefront of the civil rights movement. Within the membership and leadership positions of the NAACP, the National Urban League and other organizations aimed at prompting Negro rights were countless men and women who had spent years laboring for the cause. But many lacked the instant charisma, the magnetic hold that M. L. possessed each time he spoke. A. Philip Randolph, Roy Wilkins, Martin Luther King, Sr.—

yes, even Daddy King was numbered among the giants of the freedom movement—could never captivate an audience immediately as M. L. could. It was a powerful tool, a rare gift, but even as it won friends and supporters for the civil rights movements, it created inner friction as well.

As sensitive as M. L. was to the feelings of those with whom he worked, he knew that he could not spend time trying to be certain he did not offend others. There were bigger things to be done. Through a "Crusade for Citizenship Campaign," he announced a drive that would get five million new black voters in the South. He met with President Dwight Eisenhower and Vice President Richard Nixon, attempting to increase their interest on behalf of blacks throughout the country. He flew to wherever an audience could be assembled to carry the word for a better understanding of black needs. On one flight, he and Coretta went as official representatives of the United States government. Ghana became the first African colony to win its independence, and President Eisenhower felt no other American citizen would serve as a better ambassador of good will for the occasion than Martin Luther King, Jr. He accompanied Vice President Nixon on the trip.

Always conscious of the power of words, spoken or written, M. L. recorded the events that had occurred in Montgomery. In 1958, his first book *Stride Toward Freedom* was published. Encouraged to promote the book, M. L. visited cities across the country. Crowds in Detroit and Chicago were enthusiastic and large. When he visited a department store in Harlem, however, the welcome was not as cordial. Black nationalists, unimpressed with M. L.'s strategy of "love thy neighbor," shouted insults. Other blacks yelled insults because M. L. was going into a store owned by whites.

Once inside, M. L. seated himself at a desk and began autographing copies of his book. Customers were pleasant and cheerful. One woman made her way forward, eager to meet the visiting author. Izola Curry was a heavy-set woman wearing a bright-patterned dress and gold earrings. "Is this Martin Luther King?" she asked a nearby clerk. "Yes, it is," the store employee answered. Pushing her way forward, Mrs. Curry stood directly in front of M. L. "Are you Mr. King?" she asked. Receiving an affirmative nod, the woman suddenly reached inside her dress and pulled out a letter opener of Japanese design. "I have been after you for five years!" she exclaimed, thrusting the steel letter opener down into the upper left side of M. L.'s chest. Screams and frantic cries filled the air while Mrs. Curry pounded her victim with her fists. Finally, onlookers managed to pull the frenzied woman away and hold her for the police.

M. L. was rushed to Harlem Hospital, the letter opener still in his chest. Surgery was needed at once. When notified in Montgomery, Coretta gave permission, then boarded a plane immediately, unsure whether when she arrived that her husband would be alive or not.

While the doctors operated, New York police learned that Izola Curry was from a broken home, had failed in her own marriage, and could not hold a job. She saw the highly publicized Dr. King as a total success, the opposite of her own existence. That was the reason she tried to kill him.

After three hours of surgery, M. L. was taken from the operating room into an intensive care unit where he was placed on the critical list. "He's lucky to be alive at all," doctors admitted. "The tip of the weapon had penetrated to the aorta. Just one sneeze or cough and he'd have been a goner."

Thousands of telegrams, letters and cards flooded the hospital. Governor Averell Harriman of New York visited M. L., as did black leader A. Philip Randolph. President Dwight Eisenhower sent get well wishes.

M. L. waged a valiant recovery campaign and soon he left the hospital to convalesce at the home of a friend in

Brooklyn. Doctors warned about an immediate return to the South fearing that M. L. would be swamped with well-wishers. He bore no feelings of revenge toward his attacker. "Don't hurt her," he pleaded. "Get her help and treatment."

Daddy King, at home in Atlanta, was not surprised by M. L.'s remarks. "No, my son ain't the 'get even' kind. He knows the Lord's mercy."

But there was little doubt that Daddy and Mother Dear shared some feelings about M. L. He was in too much of a hurry, too anxious to bring the black community "into the full sunlight." If only M. L. would be willing to slow his step a bit, allow people to think about what he was saying. He was in such a hurry, running into the shadows of danger.

Regaining his health, M. L. took the counsel of Daddy and others. A trip to India had been planned for a long time. There were always speeches to give, or the church needed special tending or a meeting was scheduled. But this time the doctors ordered M. L. to slow his pace. With that in mind, he and Coretta set off for India, homeland of his hero—Gandhi.

The trip was invigorating. Under Prime Minister Nehru, the government of India was working hard to tear down much of the long established caste system. The untouchables were protected by the Indian Constitution, and the laws were backed by money to help the lowest caste peasants. "We will never make up for all the injustices the untouchables have suffered," Nehru noted, "but we will do everything we can." Not only were the people of India, from rich and powerful leaders to the most humble servants, directing their material means and efforts to change, their hearts and spirit were behind the movement too. In many ways, the untouchables of India were much like the blacks of America. M. L. returned to America more committed than ever to a program of nonviolence in the civil rights movement. This commitment would demand drastic changes in his life.

"Is the job still open as co-pastor of Ebenezer Baptist?" M. L. asked Daddy King.

"You betcha!" came a joyful answer.

M. L.'s decision to return to Atlanta was not merely a personal move to appease Daddy King. The Southern Christian Leadership Conference, with its headquarters in Atlanta, was floundering. Leadership and financial support were badly needed. In Montgomery, M. L. felt he was trying to do at Dexter Avenue Church what five or six staff members should be doing. There were too many demands as president of the Montgomery Improvement Association. He felt more could be accomplished in Atlanta.

Announcing his resignation as pastor of the Dexter Avenue Church was not easy—for M. L. or his loyal congregation. Some members voted "no," in order to show their reluctance at losing a beloved leader. As the final pages closed on the 1950s, and a new decade began, M. L. offered these final thoughts to his friends in Montgomery.

"You have come far," he declared. "Yet we have only begun our journey. Freedom has never been free. It is won with sacrifice and suffering. But let there be no mistake. We shall win. No matter how long it takes, we shall win."

A new decade. A new home. And with the new broom sweeping clean came a fresh burst of enthusiasm for energized action. M. L. sensed something in the air, a willingness to break away the harness of the past and gallop freely into the future. Few could have predicted that such galloping would be accomplished with inactive movement—the taking of a seat in a white public facility and refusing to move when ordered. Mrs. Rosa Parks' sit-in lit a spark. She had selected a vehicle intended for use by blacks and white alike, and she was alone in her decision to ignore commands. What might happen if an organized group of blacks planted themselves at a totally white restaurant counter, department store, or in a public library?

Such an event occurred in February of 1960. Four college students in Greensboro, North Carolina, positioned themselves in a dining area reserved for whites' use only. When service was refused, the men simply opened books and quietly began to read.

The next day, more black students returned to join the sit-in, and this idea spread quickly across the South. At university and college campuses, young men and women organized themselves to stage similar protests at those public facilities which excluded blacks. White students came from the North to aid in demonstrations.

M. L. welcomed the efforts of the young to the fight for desegregation. But he worried that the new army of rebels would get so caught up in the physical tactics of their sit-in demonstrations that they would forget the whole purpose of their actions.

"Mere resistance and nonviolence are not good in themselves," M. L. told gatherings of student leaders. "It is the reconciliation that follows, the willingness to live together in love and understanding that we are working for."

Student leaders listened to M. L. Under the guidance of Ella Baker they formed their own organization, the Student Nonviolent Coordinating Committee (SNCC). Pockets of segregation were carefully targeted so that demonstrations and sit-ins could achieve maximum attention and effect. But always, as M. L. emphasized to the young men and women, "resist in a firm but nonviolent manner. Give them no reason, no justification for physical violence."

Areas of dissension popped up here and there. Some student leaders felt M. L.'s code was too soft, too conciliatory. "To behave in a manner that Martin Luther King, Jr. advocates is to behave like a coward," one fiery leader protested. "To gain action, we must fight for change, physically, if necessary. King is too weak. We must be strong."

M. L. would not alter his stance. To such charges, he merely noted, "There is power and strength in turning the other cheek. We must show that the Negro American has been mistreated. You do not fight violence with violence. Understanding and love are the keys. We are not merely wishing to change the minds of people; we are seeking to change their hearts and spirits as well."

With M. L.'s move to Atlanta, Daddy King became swept up in the flurry of activity surrounding his son. It was not easy to reconcile himself to the more frantic pace. In truth, the older man could not grasp the need for moving quickly in so many areas. Discussion became arguments. M. L. scolded his father for taking too long to achieve too little result. Daddy fired back, admonishing M. L. to pay closer attention to the wisdom of his elders and less to the youthful voices of college rebels.

But when sheriff's deputies arrested M. L. in connection with perjury charges dealing with income tax returns, Daddy King was furious. "Some people will trump up anything to get a person out of circulation or discredit his reputation," the older man protested. And he insisted on accompanying M. L. to court. The two men stood side by side before the judge, each one declaring M. L.'s innocence.

M. L. was revolted by the whole situation. He was prepared to be arrested, fined, jailed or whatever was necessary in behalf of the civil rights movement. But the charges he faced now dealt with stealing and lying. He was accused of giving false information on his Alabama state income tax returns in 1956 and 1958.

"The charges are lies," M. L. told his father. "All lies. But what difference will that make? Everyone I talk to will be wondering—'Did he' or 'Didn't he?' Who will believe me? Who will trust me?"

Daddy King shook his head. "Just don't get so caught up in what you're doing here that you forget who the final Judge is. He knows, and he will always know. I believe you, and anyone who knows you at all believes you. They will trust you. But just remember—even if they don't, they are merely witnesses using the evidence they can see. God is the judge, and he knows all."

As Daddy spoke, M. L. felt like a small boy again, listening to his father share the joys and beauty of another time. It was easy to get caught up in the ways of this world, forgetting how little it truly matters. Yes, M. L. had forgotten. How fortunate he was to have someone to remind him. Perhaps a jury might believe him too.

That is exactly what happened. To add even greater joy to the triumph was the fact that all twelve men on the jury were white. But the acquittal, handed down in May of 1960, left its mark on M. L. His honesty, his personal character had been attacked. No words from Daddy or anyone else could completely wipe away the hurt that he had suffered.

Across the South and beyond it, people were sitting-in, marching, and speaking out in behalf of civil rights. The funnel cloud was mushrooming, and M. L. was in the eye of the funnel.

Conscious of M. L.'s efforts on behalf of blacks and concerned with his personal tribulations and trials, Democratic presidential candidate John Kennedy contacted him. "I'll help you all I can," the youthful Kennedy declared. "So will my brother Bobby. I hope you can help us too."

M. L. carefully researched the background of Kennedy, who was presently serving as a senator from Massachusetts. Impressed with what he found, M. L. sought further contact. Kennedy had important plans for the future of blacks in his programs, if he were elected. But

M. L. hesitated at coming out publicly for Kennedy. As Daddy King said, "You are a product as well as a person. What you say and do will be imitated by our people across the country. You must watch every word you express."

M. L. and Senator Kennedy had breakfast together. They talked about the need for a strong push for civil rights from the executive office. Clearly, Eisenhower had not provided enough energy. Senator Kennedy pledged to do more. But M. L. did not want to endorse any political candidate. He worried that his support might offend Republicans. What would happen then if Nixon were elected?

On the other hand, Daddy King was leaning toward Nixon. Not satisfied with what the Republican administration had done for blacks, Daddy at least felt he knew what to expect from Vice President Nixon. Kennedy was an unknown commodity, and Catholic. Daddy had serious doubts whether a Catholic President could govern freely.

Although politics occupied much attention from both Daddy and M. L. during the summer of 1960, family matters were even more in the spotlight. Both men welcomed A. D. into the movement for civil rights. Unhappy with life as a businessman, A. D. decided that he, too, wanted to become a preacher. Not only that, he also wanted to be a part of the planned sit-in and marching demonstrations.

"I was always a little bit slower to get my direction," he told his friends. "But now I feel at home. Daddy smiles a lot more too, now that I'm a preacher."

Life for Christine was changing directions also. She had been dating a young journalist from Missouri named Isaac Newton Ferris. Now a teacher at Spelman College, Christine informed the family that she and Isaac planned to get married. The ceremony took place August 19, 1960, with M. L. and A. D. officiating, while a proud Daddy King and Mother Dear beamed their approval.

As record heat submerged much of the country, the

presidential campaign got hotter too. Even astute political analysts hesitated to make predictions. There were too many unknown factors. But no one could have guessed that events in Atlanta's Rich's Department Store would have a decisive effect.

On October 19, M. L. joined a large group of other blacks in staging a sit-in. The demonstrators were immediately arrested. A sympathetic Mayor Hartsfield saw that all but one of the demonstrators were released, everyone except M. L. Judge Oscar Mitchell ruled that M. L.'s actions clearly violated a probationary sentence he had received for driving with an expired Georgia driver's license. He had forgotten to renew his Georgia license after moving back from Montgomery. The judge ordered M. L. to serve his four-month sentence doing hard labor at the Reidsville Work Camp.

When Daddy King heard of the sentence, he could not believe it. Reidsville was a penitentiary located three hundred miles from Atlanta. The institution was filled with convicted murderers and hard-core lawbreakers.

Daddy King was shocked. He contacted Judge Oliver immediately, demanding a real hearing on the case. "I don't have time," the judge answered. "I'm going fishing."

M. L. was taken to Reidsville in the middle of the night. He was chained and handcuffed. Daddy received word that a plan was being set up that would have M. L. killed in a fight with another inmate. Everything would be covered up. Daddy tried desperately to comfort Coretta, who now was carrying a third child. In struggling to find some help, Daddy contacted a well-known lawyer in Atlanta named Morris Abram.

Attorney Abram did not waste a moment. Although the White House had been apprised of the situation, no help seemed to be forthcoming. Republican candidate Nixon shrugged a terse "No comment!" when reporters asked him about M. L.'s arrest. But Abram found the Kennedy organization much more sympathetic—and willing to help. John Kennedy personally called Coretta, offering his interest and expressing a desire to be useful. Meanwhile, Bobby Kennedy called Judge Oliver and asked why bail hadn't been granted on such a trivial matter.

The wheels of justice suddenly spun forward. Within hours, papers were signed that brought about M. L.'s release. Wherever they were, blacks shouted cheers of joy upon learning the news.

At Ebenezer Baptist Church, a special prayer service was held. People filled the pews and lined the aisles to give thanks for the safe return of their co-pastor. Happy voices rang out.

> O Peter, go ring them bells,
> Peter, go ring them bells,
> I heard from heaven today.
> I thank God, and I thank you, too,
> I heard from heaven today.

Thunderous applause greeted M. L. as he took his place at the pulpit. Smiling faces were a welcome sight after what he had been through. Choosing his words carefully, M. L. expressed his gratitude to Senator Kennedy as "a great force in making my release possible."

M. L. refrained from making any official endorsement of Senator Kennedy. But Daddy King did not hold back. Gone were all the reservations he had expressed about the possible problems of a Catholic serving as President of the United States. "John Kennedy had the moral courage to take a stand on what was right," Daddy declared, waving his hands forcefully from the pulpit. "If I had a suitcase full of votes, I'd hand them over to John Kennedy, hoping he could use them in the forthcoming election."

The words spoken that night in Ebenezer Baptist Church reached far beyond the 800 members of the congregation who were present. News media carried the story across the South, across the country. In the November election, John Kennedy squeaked out a narrow victory, 34,226,925 to 34,108,662, for Nixon. To most people, that represented a loss of 112,881 votes for the Vice President. "Yes, Richard Nixon lost by that number of votes," observed a politically astute President Eisenhower, "but it might be more accurate to say that John Kennedy won by two telephone calls."

After the election, there were many claims that the Kennedy brothers had used Martin Luther King, Jr. and Sr. to help their campaign. Statistics revealed John Kennedy had won three-fourths of the black vote. When interviewed about their personal feelings concerning the outcome, Daddy King was exuberant. "You're damn right I'm happy Kennedy won!" he said. Standing next to his father, M. L. just smiled.

15

"Let the word go forth from this time and place, to friend and foe alike, that the torch has been passed to a new generation of Americans—born in this century, tempered by war, disciplined by a hard and bitter peace, proud of our ancient heritage . . ."

The strong, vibrant words rolled easily from the newly inaugurated John Fitzgerald Kennedy, at forty-four, the youngest man ever to assume the office of the Presidency. Washington, D.C. shivered in twenty degree temperatures as the inaugural platform provided a picture of contrast. The older spectators—outgoing President Eisenhower, Richard Cardinal Cushing, Chief Justice Earl Warren, poet Robert Frost—passing the torch to a powerful, eager Kennedy and his band of youthful knights. Or was the torch being torn away, not passed?

"So let us begin anew—Let us never negotiate out of fear. But let us never fear to negotiate . . ."

"Amen," M. L. murmured, his head nodding as he listened to the new leader. "Never fear to negotiate." It was a code M. L. fervently believed, lived his life by, and guided a movement with. Now the same feeling was being expressed by the leader of the nation. One hundred years before, in this same city in 1861, another new president accepted the standard of authority. Perhaps Kennedy could attack the web of prejudice just as Abraham Lincoln had done a century ago.

"All this will not be finished in the first one hundred days. Nor will it be finished in the first one thousand days, nor in the life of this Administration, nor even perhaps in our lifetime on this planet. But let us begin."

This thought caused Daddy King to nod in agreement as he sat in a large, overstuffed chair at his home in Atlanta. "At least he isn't in such a big hurry," the older man offered, still aware that he was in that assemblage born in the previous century, and in a sense therefore, passing the torch rather than receiving it. Bunch smiled, resting a hand on her husband's, providing that loving tenderness and comfort she sensed he needed at moments like this. "And so, my fellow Americans: ask not what your country can do for you—ask what you can do for your country."

As thunderous applause greeted President Kennedy's closing remarks, M. L. felt his own pulse quicken. This was not merely oratory he had heard; it was the challenge of a fighter, a summons to action, a call to re-energize. It was a new time, a fresh beginning.

And while the sound of Kennedy's words still echoed in his mind, M. L. welcomed another member of his own family into the world. It did not evade his thoughts that someday he, Martin Luther King, Jr., would pass the torch to the next generation. Dexter Scott King was born on January 30, 1961.

Caught up with the fervor of a new Presidential administration, M. L. rededicated his efforts on behalf of blacks. Whenever meetings were held, whenever sit-ins took place, an anthem of unity for the entire civil rights movement was sung. "We shall overcome," the people promised, their voices raised in strength and determination. "We shall overcome . . . someday."

But within M. L.'s mind, the beat of yet another old song echoed in the background. "Joshua fit de battle of Jericho . . ." and the words and melody crescendoed, "and de walls come tumblin' down . . ."

With the swearing in of the Kennedy administration, the workers for the National Association for the Advancement of Colored People, the staff of the Southern Christian Leadership Conference, the team at the Congress of Racial Equality, the young leaders of the Student Nonviolent Coordinating Committee were fired with new zest and spirit. "Now we are going to move!" one civil rights chief declared. "We been inchin' along for too long. We got some mighty big catchin' up to do."

M. L. eagerly welcomed a circle of new lieutenants to work closely with him. His longtime colleague, Ralph Abernathy, moved to Atlanta in order to be closer to the center of the action. From SNCC and the SCLC came Bernard Lee and James Bevel; from the National Council of Churches in New York came Andrew Young.

"Make sure you let some of your helpers do their share," Daddy King admonished M. L. "You got to make people feel they're useful. With all these workers, you got more time to spend with your family at home. You *do* remember you got a family at home, don't you, M. L.?"

The son looked at his father, knowing that Daddy King was teasing. Yet in the teasing, there was an element of honest truth in the way Daddy felt. M. L. was always writing a speech, talking to somebody, flying here and flying there. It was a tremendous pace, exhausting. Yet there seemed to be no way of slowing him down. The constant hurry-scurry troubled Daddy, more than he could bring himself to say. And Daddy King was seldom without words.

It troubled M. L. too. He knew, though, that no one else could give a talk and pull in thousands of dollars for any one of the civil rights organizations. Other black leaders could write magazine articles, but that Martin Luther King, Jr. byline caught immediate attention among readers, both black and white. In an essay written for the *Nation* magazine, which appeared in February, 1961, M. L. forcefully encouraged President Kennedy to fight for a

176

strong civil rights bill and to help knock down the walls of segregation. Joshua was not the only one who could fight battles. Eloquent statements of reason and logic could win over countless minds and attitudes. Not only were the black forces strengthened, but white civil rights workers streamed down from northern states. The volunteers gave rise to a new device for putting the inequality of human rights into the spotlight. "Freedom rides" they were called, with blacks and whites boarding buses, sitting and eating together in highway restaurants. They ignored the signs aimed at keeping whites and blacks apart. When they were arrested, the freedom riders went peacefully, filling the jails with their songs of peace and love.

> You are my brother and my sister too.
> I don't mind goin' to jail for you,
> 'Cause someday the Lord will smile and
>   say,
> Love, my children, is the only way . . .

M. L. found himself being arrested frequently too. Often he knew that the attention his arrest would draw across the country might produce rich dividends. Another family might read the newspaper and become aware of the unfair voting laws of the South. A minister, priest, or rabbi might feel compelled to speak out publicly against segregation and injustice. Students might hold an open discussion about the current plight of Negroes in America. The message had to be taken to the people. M. L. calculated each step carefully.

But even careful calculation can be misunderstood—especially by young children. It was confusing to learn their father was in jail for Yoki and Marty, attending nursery school in Atlanta. Wasn't jail for bad people?

"Your daddy is brave and kind," Coretta explained to her children. "Some people need his help so they can have food to eat and homes to live in. The only way he can help these people is by going to jail."

Daddy King nodded. "He's helping you too. What he is doing now will help you later on. He's already helped lots of folks. And he's going to help more and more."

The children tried to understand, but it was not easy. Just as it was not easy understanding why they could not go to Funtown, the giant amusement park in Atlanta. Television commercials blared constantly about the wonderful rides at Funtown, and encouraged children to bring their parents for a full day of delight. Yet when Yoki suggested they all go, M. L. had to sit down and explain that Funtown was not open to everyone.

"Can't we ever go?" the five-year-old girl asked, her eyes clouding.

M. L. smiled, glancing over at Daddy King. "Someday we will *all* go, Yoki. And we'll laugh louder than anyone else there!"

But days of laughter did not come often. Compared to the sit-ins, the freedom rides posed constant potential dangers. The fact that segregated transportation was outlawed by the Supreme Court did not prevent troublemakers from taking their own stand. It was one thing to stage a sit-in within the confines of a public restaurant, but it was yet another to ride a bus, especially at night, through the hills and valleys of the South. Just as the organizations supporting civil rights enjoyed fresh growth and new life, so too did groups like the black-hating Ku Klux Klan. Hiding under the double cover of white robes and dark night, Klan members and others set out to terrorize any freedom rider traveling after dark. Black and white riders alike were pulled off buses and beaten. Others were thrown into jail. In Anniston, Alabama, a Greyhound bus was attacked by an inflamed mob. Using iron bars to smash the windows, the crowd shouted, "Kill those damn niggers—and their white son of a bitch friends! Burn 'em up!" With that, an incendiary bomb was tossed inside and exploded. Frantically, the passengers scrambled for their lives.

"We are not asking for special privileges," M. L. told the reporters. "We simply want those rights guaranteed us under the Constitution. We want to vote, to enjoy public accommodations, to raise our children in the free and blessed country that is America."

And from the pulpit of Ebenezer Baptist Church, Daddy King called for prayers on behalf of his son and the troubled times in which they were passing. "No, I do not always understand why my son Martin does all that he does," Daddy King said. "I know he is on the side of the Lord and the side of what is right and just. I only wish that side did not hold so many dangers."

Dangers, indeed. Not only did M. L. face attack in the open, but from sources within his own being and unknown enemies as well. Everywhere he went, there were those who would surround him offering to take his direction and answer to his needs. The separations from Coretta were long and frequent. There were eager helpers in each city and town he visited for a meeting or speech. Some were women, drawn to the immediate charisma and strength of M. L. as a man as well as the leader of a cause. Desperately M. L. fought to cast aside lustful desires. He did not always win those battles.

Within the organized framework of the United States government, there were dangers too. J. Edgar Hoover, longtime chief of the Federal Bureau of Investigation, was convinced M. L. had Communist connections. At the mere mention of M. L.'s name, Hoover's blood would turn to venom, and he unleashed every tool at his command to topple the black leader. "King's more Red than he is black," the FBI head declared. "He can't fool me." With gleeful delight, Hoover shared his suspicions with top government officials as well as the media.

Hoover's personal feelings about M. L. circulated freely among FBI agents across the country. There were not many who were interested in defying the crusty lawman who ran the bureau with an iron hand. Countless complaints from blacks, charging civil rights violations, flooded the national FBI office. Few, if any, received any official attention.

"One of the greatest problems we face with the FBI in the South," M. L. told reporters, "is that the agents are white southerners who have been influenced by the mores of their community. To maintain their status, they have to be friendly with the local police and people who are promoting segregation."

"Humbug and poppycock!" Hoover huffed publicly. But in private, his anger was far more vehement. Any criticism of the FBI was taken as a personal insult. Hoover raved and ranted to every legislator and public official who would listen.

"King is a threat to every American," the FBI chief declared. "He's a puppet for the Communists. Wherever he goes, there's trouble. That's what he is supposed to do—cause trouble."

Anti-King reports made their way regularly from Hoover's desk to the desk of Attorney General Robert Kennedy at the Justice Department. At a mass rally, M. L. would only have to nod at someone who was suspected of having socialistic sympathies, and off would go an FBI memo that a private meeting had taken place. If M. L. spoke to any young woman, suggestions of a sexual tryst would appear in an official report. Hoover knew the power he enjoyed, and he directed it in a full assault at destroying Martin Luther King, Jr. The black leader's name was added to the list of known dangerous individuals who were to be taken into custody immediately in the event of any national emergency.

Associates frequently reminded M. L. of the actions of the FBI chief and his agency. Yet M. L. seemed unable to comprehend fully the depth of Hoover's personal vendetta. The civil rights movement was too big with too much to do. Constant concern about one man, despite his power, seemed a waste of time and energy to M. L. Surely a man who had dedicated his life to law and victim protection would someday recognize the needs of the black man in America, M. L. thought.

"Sometimes a spider can get caught up in his own web," Hoover told one associate. "He might even strangle himself. Now wouldn't that be too bad if such a thing happened to Mr. Martin Luther King, Jr.? Wouldn't that be too bad?"

Within this dangerous web, M. L. continued to wage the fight for black equal rights. In Montgomery, freedom riders departed on a bus, only to be jeered and insulted by a crowd of three hundred. The first rider off, a white university student named James Zwerg, was knocked to the ground and beaten unconscious. Zwerg had known the risks involved. He had signed the pledge of nonviolence, the pledge M. L. insisted was essential to forward the cause. Zwerg did not fight back. It was an hour before an ambulance arrived to take him to a hospital. Throughout the encounter, Montgomery policemen did nothing to stop the attacks.

M. L. arrived the next day and in the evening as twelve hundred white and blacks gathered for a rally in the First Baptist Church of the city, thousands of yelling men and women surrounded the building. Rocks crashed through the stained glass windows, showering the people within with jagged pieces of glass. Knowing the fear among those people in the church, King went to the pulpit.

"We must fight hate with love!" he said. "Remember him who said, 'Forgive them, for they know not what they do.' Let us never forget the strength of our Lord. It is ours to copy, to imitate. He is always our example for living."

With full voice and spirit, M. L. led the people in prayer and song. Hearing the joyful songs coming from within incensed the crowd outside even more. Throughout the night, missiles of stone and rock bombarded the sanctuary. "Burn the church down!" someone shouted. "Roast that big nigger King!" another joined in. Still, the songs continued. "We shall overcome . . . someday."

M. L. knew that some marshals were trying to keep order outside the church. But as the mob's shouts grew louder and more threatening, he decided to take action to defend the people assembled. Quickly he put in a call to Attorney General Robert Kennedy. "Can you call in more marshals here?" M. L. queried. Kennedy acted immediately. The additional marshals began dispersing the crowd soon after they arrived on the scene. By daybreak, everyone had left the church safely.

Freedom rides continued throughout the South. Among the most energetic participants were college students, often joined by white church people of various denominations. "Our cause is not Catholic, Protestant or Jewish," M. L. told an audience one night in Albany, Georgia. "It is a human cause. But rest assured, the Lord stands with us. He is in our hearts and souls. If we be arrested, so be it. We shall carry the Lord wherever we must. Let us not forget his suffering. He faced his enemies with love and kindness. He laid the pattern for nonviolence. What better way is there to live than the Lord's?"

With each speech he gave, with every article he wrote, M. L. managed to win more supporters to the movement. "I do believe that the good Lord climbs right inside my boy's skin each time he gets behind a podium or desk," Daddy King observed wryly. But when others made similar comparisons of M. L. to Jesus Christ, and there were many who did, Daddy recoiled. "He's a good man doing the Lord's work, but let us not carry it any further than that. After all, if Martin Luther King, Jr. is Jesus Christ, just think what that makes me! That should end that discussion!"

More and more followers began to climb aboard the

civil rights train. Some accepted leadership duties with SCLC, while others dedicated themselves to service with SNCC. Many of them were young, impatient, wanting change tomorrow rather than next week. Hosea Williams, Bernard Lee, Lonnie King, Julian Bond, Jesse Jackson— the list of volunteers was endless and forever growing. "They've all got the energy from bein' young," noted Daddy King, "but they can't see around the corner. If they could just realize, some things take time."

The conflict between the old and the young, the patient and the impatient, reached a head in March of 1961. Daddy King and the old guard of Atlanta black leadership had worked out a plan with the all-white Atlanta Chamber of Commerce. Under the guidelines of the supreme Court decision, Atlanta schools would integrate at the opening of the fall term. Within thirty days of that happening, downtown Atlanta stores and businesses would open their lunch counters and services to blacks also. Daddy King was proud of the agreement. But youthful demonstrators wanted action immediately. M. L. attended a meeting in an Atlanta church. Tension was high. Even when Daddy King rose to speak, the angry shouts did not stop.

"Now I've been workin' in this town for thirty years," he said, pausing for emphasis, but before he could continue, a youthful shout rang out. "That's what's wrong!" Applause followed this outburst and then more angry shouts. Slowly, sadly, helplessly, Daddy looked around. His eyes filled with tears. Where had the years gone, he wondered. Have I really grown so old, so far away? What are these voices, who are they? Confused, he sat down and stayed silent.

Everyone turned to M. L. What would he say? How did he feel about all this? When he rose and stood behind the pulpit, he looked into the audience for a full minute without uttering a word. It was an uneasy silence, with both old and young fidgeting and squirming.

"Is this why we have come here?" M. L. finally asked. "Are we here to fight among ourselves? If we make enemies of each other, how do we ever hope to fight the battle outside these walls?"

With careful precision, M. L. recited the contributions that his father and others had made for the cause of the civil rights movement. "Before many of you were born," M. L. declared, "this man and his peers were struggling. We have all waited for one hundred years for justice. Could we not wait for four or five more months?"

When he had finished, M. L. quietly left the church. The mood of unrest and discontent was gone, vanished into the air. Replacing it was unity, peace, understanding. Old and young shook hands, hugged, and promised to try harder.

It was not the first time M. L. had brought tears of love and pride to his father's eyes, nor would it be the last.

If M. L. recognized the need for patience, he also felt a need for immediate action. As optimistic as he had been when President Kennedy took office, M. L. felt that not enough was being done by the administration in behalf of the black people. His initial assessment that Kennedy was a leader "unafraid of change" was retracted. M. L. called on the American leader to issue a presidential order banning all racial segregation in public facilities. In addition, M. L. recommended a Secretary of Integration be appointed to the presidential cabinet. "The president proposes a ten-year plan to put a man on the moon. We do not have a plan to put a Negro in the state legislature of Alabama," M. L. noted.

Although President Kennedy failed to act on M. L.'s requests, he did invite the black leader to Washington for a meeting. The President again restated his commitment to civil rights, but M. L. left the meeting with a feeling of emptiness.

"He just doesn't understand the depth and evil of

segregation," M. L. told Daddy King upon his return to Atlanta.

Daddy shook his head. "Then you'll just have to keep after him until he does."

If M. L. seriously had hoped that President Kennedy would step up his civil rights involvement, the black leader was in for great disappointment. International events, from the Bay of Pigs invasion to the traumatic deceptions of the Soviet Union, occupied much of the President's time and attention. As sincere as Kennedy was about pushing for strong civil rights legislation, he felt the timing had to be just right. On a personal note, Kennedy was also concerned about the FBI notes that highlighted M. L.'s associations with possible Communists. "I've learned how closely you are under inspection," the President noted. "Being a leader opens you to microscopic observation from every angle. Believe me, I know."

M. L. did not question President Kennedy's sincerity. But the need for action within the civil rights movement was vital. To dramatize the evil of segregation that still thrived in the South, it was decided to target a city which represented the greatest level of inequality to blacks. Existing in its own world of darkness, ignoring the efforts of other major Southern cities to integrate, Birmingham, Alabama seemed proud of its image. It ever there was a Jericho whose walls needed tumbling down, it was Birmingham, Alabama.

Attempts to change had been made. A young Baptist minister, Fred Shuttlesworth, had been fighting for years against the strangling tentacles of segregation. The fight had almost cost him his life in a bombing, but Shuttlesworth would not give in. Again and again he pleaded for the support of the SCLC. "We are coming," M. L. declared, and Shuttlesworth cried out in joy.

With the methodical skills of gifted surgeons, M. L., Shuttlesworth and another aide, Wyatt Tee Walker, plotted a plan of action. Workshops were set up for volunteers to study nonviolent techniques. Everyone taking part signed a pledge, promising to refrain from violence of "fist, tongue or heart." The overall plan, with every activity cautiously and carefully drawn, was labelled "Project C." The "C" stood for confrontation, for it reflected M. L.'s fresh vision of encounter. Blacks would take totally nonaggressive, nonviolent action. If any violence occurred, it would not be their doing. "If Birmingham loses its cool, our entire movement will take a giant step forward. As Birmingham goes, so goes the South."

Many long months went into the planning. By the early spring of 1963, everything was ready. "Your timing is fine," observed Daddy King. "One hundred years after the Emancipation Proclamation. Yes, indeed. That's good timing." To give the entire plan of action more meaning, events were set to start at the beginning of the Easter season.

On March 28, 1963, shortly before "Project C" rolled into motion, M. L. and Coretta welcomed their fourth child, Bernice Albertine, nicknamed Bunny.

"Project C" did not get off to a flying start. Even the blacks of Birmingham, so long used to living as second class citizens, were confused about this new plan aimed at turning their lives around. White city leaders spoke of "outsiders" who were causing the concern presented by scheduled marches to City Hall and demands for voting rights. "Outsiders?" countered M. L. "A person would have to be outside the human race not to be concerned with the suffering of Birmingham's black people." Commissioner of Public Safety Eugene "Bull" O'Connor announced defiantly, "I'll keep the Negroes in their place."

On April 6, 1963, the first Birmingham march began. Dressed in their finest clothes, the marchers headed downtown toward City Hall. Three blocks away from their destination, police blocked their way. "Halt!" a police captain ordered. Ignoring the command, the marchers proceeded. Quickly they were herded into police vans. "We shall overcome," they began singing, "We shall overcome . . ."

Only forty-two were arrested that first day, charged with unlawful assembly. But the word spread. Momentum grew. The next day there were more marchers. Fifty became a hundred—a hundred became a thousand. In a week of marches, 3,300 blacks were arrested. M. L. was thrown into jail on Good Friday. When his brother A. D. arrived, wearing ministerial robes with Bible in hand to pray for him on Easter Sunday, he was also arrested.

"Project C" fell into place perfectly. Not only were many of the marchers arrested, they were attacked by snapping dogs held by police. Fire hoses were turned on the marchers, tossing men and women to the ground while powerful streams of water pounded their bodies. It was painful punishment, and the newspaper and television coverage horrified people around the world. Donations rolled in, and black singer-actor Harry Belafonte supervised bail payments for the marchers.

M. L. put his jail time to the best of use. Borrowing paper from a jail guard, he addressed a letter to his fellow ministers. "I am in Birmingham because injustice is here. There are two types of laws: There are just laws and there are unjust laws." Knowing there might be some who would criticize his actions as illegal, M. L. reminded people that everything Hitler did in Germany was "legal" and everything the Hungarian freedom fighters did in Hungary was "illegal." M. L. continued, "My friends, I must say to you that we have not made a single gain in civil rights without determined legal and nonviolent pressure. . . . We know through painful experience that freedom is never voluntarily given by the oppressor; it must be demanded by the oppressed." To those who would simply label him an extremist, M. L. countered, citing the extremist of love, Jesus; the extremist for justice, Amos; an extremist for Christ's gospel, Paul; Abraham Lincoln and Thomas Jefferson, both extremists. In the 9,000 words labeled "Letter from a Birmingham Jail," M. L. provided a moving plea for equality and freedom. Some called it "The Living Bible of the Freedom Movement."

But the struggle was not over when M. L. was released on bail. Bull Connor continued to misplay his hand. When a group of one thousand children marched toward the Sixteenth Street Church to pray, Connor ordered the fire hoses opened and the dogs turned loose once again. Boys and girls sprawled onto the ground, as the force of the jet sprays of water ripped their clothes. Dogs bit at their faces, arms and legs. Wild screams filled the air. An angry nation watched with disgust. President Kennedy was pressured to take action.

The governmental and business leaders of Birmingham gave in. Segregation at all public places was outlawed; there was to be no discrimination in the hiring of blacks; the jailed marchers were to be released, and a committee composed of whites and blacks was to be set up to discuss all of the problem areas. Bull Connor was removed from office, and soundly defeated when he ran for mayor.

The victory was not without tragedy. White extremists bombed the home of A. D. and his wife. Medgar Evers, an NAACP official, was murdered by white men in Mississippi. Another freedom marcher, William Moore, was shot and killed.

But the message of Birmingham had been carried across the country. "The events in Birmingham and elsewhere have so increased the cries for equal rights that no city or state can fail to hear them," declared President Kennedy. With that, he sent a sweeping civil rights bill to Congress, urging its passage. "Justice requires us to assure the blessings of liberty for all Americans—not merely for reasons of economic efficiency, world diplomacy and domestic tranquillity—but above all, because it is right."

In cities and towns everywhere across the South, local and community laws underwent drastic changes even before any federal civil rights legislation was passed. Public accommodations were thrown open to blacks and whites alike, unfair voting restrictions were cast aside, attitudes and ideas were examined and altered. "Can you hear that sound out in America?" Daddy King shouted from the Ebenezer Baptist pulpit. "The walls of Jericho are tumblin' down, yessir, tumblin' down. And what a joyful sound it is, good people, what a joyful sound it is."

The time seemed perfect for a giant victory rally, a huge peaceful demonstration to celebrate what had been accomplished and to put pressure on Congress to pass President Kennedy's Civil Rights Bill. A leadership meeting was held, pulling together many of those who had worked long and hard in the movement for civil rights. A. Philip Randolph and Roy Wilkins of the NAACP were there; John Lewis of SNCC, James Farmer of CORE, Whitney Young of the Urban League, Dorothy Height of the National Council of Negro Women. Following Randolph's suggestion, plans were put in motion for a march on Washington, D.C. in August.

It was hoped the Washington rally would attract one hundred thousand people. But when August 28 arrived, two hundred and fifty thousand Americans flooded the city to attend the event. They came from all parts of the country, by car, plane, bus and on foot. Over one quarter of the marchers were white. Gathering first on the slope of the Washington Monument, the massive crowd then marched to the Lincoln Memorial. It was an appropriate location, this being the 100th anniversary of the Emancipation Proclamation.

There were policemen and soldiers on duty everywhere. Some feared violence would break out with such a huge crowd. But there was no need for fear. The people had come to celebrate the achievement of nonviolent action. They had come to hear speakers and singers share the phrases and melodies of peace, freedom and love.

God bless America, land that I love
Stand beside her and guide her
Through the night with a light from
    above . . .

From warm patriotic tunes to deeply moving spirituals, well known performers led the audience in song. Lilting rhetoric swept the people into frenzies of happiness and pride. The best was saved for last. Everyone strained to hear and see M. L. who had taken his place at the speaker's stand. With the mighty statue of Abraham Lincoln in the background, it appeared as if the Great Emancipator himself was listening too.

"Five score years ago," M. L. began, his notes cradled in his hands," a great American, in whose symbolic shadow we stand, signed the Emancipation Proclamation. This momentous decree came as a great beacon light of hope to millions of Negro slaves who had been seared in the flames of withering injustice." Carefully timing each phrase, his eyes searching the multitudes before him, M. L. traced the history of blacks in America. No longer speaking from the notes he had prepared, the voice of his heart and spirit took over. "I have a dream today," he offered. "I have a dream that my four little children will one day live in a nation where they will not be judged by the color of their skin but by the content of their character. I have a dream," he repeated, his voice gaining in force, "that one day every valley shall be raised, every hill and mountain shall be made low, the rough places will be made plain, and the crooked places will be made straight, and the glory of the Lord shall be revealed, and all flesh shall see it together . . ." Despite the size of the crowd, there was little sound except for the cadenced, full voice of the man in the black robe standing before the microphone. The sun bathed the gathering with heat, yet few people fanned themselves in order to hear every word being spoken. ". . . When we let freedom ring, when we let it ring from every village and every town, from every state and every city, we will be able to speed up that day when all of God's children, black men and white men, Jews and Gentiles, Protestants and Catholics, will be able to join hands and sing in the words of that old Negro song, 'Free at last! Free at last! Thank God Almighty, we are free at last!' "

Cheers rolled across the Potomac as M. L. stepped away from the speaker's stand. Tears dampened the cheeks of many in the crowd. "The Holy Spirit had hold of you in that speech!" Ralph Abernathy said, embracing his longtime friend and co-worker. Coretta slipped an arm inside her husband's, smiling an 'I love you,' message.

"The Lord truly blessed us when he sent that boy to us," Daddy King murmured to Bunch, holding her close. "Truly he did!"

16

July 2, 1964.

With silent satisfaction, M. L. watched the man sign the document lying before him. Then, turning in his chair, President Lyndon Baines Johnson extended the pen he had used to sign the civil rights bill into law. "I believe you have earned this," the President said.

Nodding gratefully, M. L. took the pen. He could not hide the feeling of sadness that swept through him. Only a sniper's bullet had prevented the signing from happening the previous November. With Kennedy's assassination the torch had once more been passed. The new president had immediately indicated his own support of the civil rights law when he addressed Congress. "No speech could better honor President Kennedy's memory than the earliest possible passage of the civil rights bill for which he fought so long," President Johnson declared.

"How do you feel?" a reporter asked M. L. "Now that you've got what you've worked for all this time?"

M. L. thought a moment. "I think I can sum it up by quoting an old Negro slave preacher. 'We ain't what we ought to be, and we ain't what we want to be, and we ain't what we're going to be. But thank God, we ain't what we was.' "

Daddy King chuckled as he read M. L.'s words in the *Atlanta Constitution*. "The boy sure does know how to answer those questions, don't he, Bunch? Maybe we just might be seein' and hearin' him around here more often."

Bunch lowered her coffee cup to the breakfast table. "That would please you a lot, wouldn't it, Daddy?"

No answer was needed. At sixty-five, it was no secret that Daddy King was thinking more about the time when he might turn the chores at Ebenezer Baptist over to M. L., not get out of harness completely, of course, but ease up a bit. Enjoy life. Spend time with the twelve grandchildren he now had. But returning to Ebenezer Baptist was not in M. L.'s immediate plans. Although the new civil rights bill cleared the way for blacks of the nation to enjoy the rights they had been denied, there was still much work to be done. A major goal lay in getting blacks registered to vote. Many blacks especially in the southern states, had never voted in their lives. M. L. helped map out a campaign to sign them up for the November elections. He spoke at both the Democratic and Republican conventions that summer, urging both parties to put civil rights planks in their platforms.

In September, a special memorial service was held in West Germany in honor of54resident Kennedy. The mayor of West Berlin invited M. L. to attend. Following the visit to Germany, M. L. went on to have a private meeting with Pope Paul VI in Rome. The Pope shared his concern about the black struggle in America, commending M. L. for his "efforts to solve problems through peace and love."

The following month brought news that M. L. had been awarded the Nobel Peace Prize. At 35, he was the youngest person ever to be selected for the prestigious award, and only the third Negro. Established in 1895 by Alfred Nobel, the Swedish inventor of dynamite, the prize carried a cash award of $56,400. Immediately M. L. declared that all the money would go toward continuing the work of the civil rights movement.

M. L. set another record when he was named a Nobel Prize recipient. He also brought the biggest entourage. There was little doubt about who was the proudest among the twenty-six people in the King party flying to

Oslo, Norway, where the presentations were scheduled. Daddy King seemed to be one giant smile. When the assemblage arrived in Oslo, parties and receptions were held. At one such event, Daddy shared his personal feelings before the entire group. ("I always wanted to make a contribution, and all you got to do if you want to contribute, you got to ask the Lord, and let him know, and the Lord heard me and in some special kind of way I don't even know, he came through Georgia and he laid his hand on me and my wife and he gave us Martin Luther King and our prayers were answered, and when my head is cold and my bones are bleached the King family will go down not only in American history but in world history as well because Martin King is a Nobel prize winner."

It was a stirring tribute, one that left M. L. not knowing what to say. His past mistakes troubled him greatly. He had sinned, and sins of the flesh especially haunted him. Why had he not been able to fight off the temptations of the flesh, thrown before him in the form of willing women? He knew God's commandments. What had happened to the moral and spiritual strength he needed to refuse that which was sinful? The questions haunted M. L. What was done was done; the past was over. With all his spirit and mind, M. L. pledged to himself to fight off any temptations in the future. The Nobel Peace Prize, more than ever, put him in the position of a moral leader. M. L. promised God that for the sake of all people who looked to him for an example in living, that he, Martin Luther King, Jr. would try to provide just that.

In accepting the award in Oslo, M. L. recounted the long, often treacherous road the blacks had followed to the present point in history. In his thoughts were workers for freedom who became martyrs, four innocent little girls who died in a bombing while Sunday School was being held in a Birmingham church, the beatings, the bombings, the threats, the jeers. "I believe that wounded justice, lying prostrate on the blood-flowing streets of our nations can be lifted from this dust of shame to reign supreme among the children of men." M. L. paused, surveying the richness and splendor of the people listening and watching. "I have the audacity to believe that peoples everywhere can have three meals a day for their bodies, education and culture for their minds, and dignity, equality and freedom for their spirits. I believe that what self-centered men have torn down other-centered men can build up. I still believe that one day mankind will bow before the altars of God and be crowned triumphant over war and bloodshed, and nonviolent redemptive good will proclaimed the rule of the land. 'And the lion and the lamb shall lie down together and every man shall sit under his own vine and fig tree and none shall be afraid.' I still believe that we shall overcome!" With a humble smile, M. L. finished his remarks. ". . . I accept this award . . . in trust for its true owners—all those to whom beauty is truth and truth beauty—and in whose eyes the beauty of genuine brotherhood and peace is more precious than diamonds or silver or gold."

After the ceremonies in Oslo, M. L. enjoyed a brief vacation in Europe. He was surprised at the hero's reception he received wherever he went. But he knew there was more work waiting at home in America. Again, the crowds turned out to cheer and welcome him. In Atlanta, 1500 attended a special hotel banquet in his honor. Through tears, he thanked his family and friends. "I confess that I have enjoyed being on this mountain top. I am tempted to stay here and retreat to a more quiet and serene life." M. L. glanced over at Daddy King, knowing how eagerly his father would welcome such a decision. Shaking his head, M. L. looked at the crowd. "But something within me reminds me that the valley calls me."

The call of the "valley" was a crusade to get blacks registered to vote. Although the Civil Rights Bill of 1964 was in full force, millions of blacks in the South still did not have their names on voting registers. It had to change.

M. L. went to Selma, Alabama, a city where only two percent of its black population had even been allowed to register to vote.

"We don't need no Martin 'Looser' King runnin' around our town," one Selma official declared. "We got enough blackbirds flyin' around the farm fields."

M. L. had heard all such tripe before. It did not faze him. Even death threats, by mail and telephone, did not slow him down.

"Having the right to vote is having power in your hand," he told a meeting of supporters. "If public officials deny you the right to proper housing, jobs and education because you are black, you can vote those people out. But you must be registered first. You must go to the county court house and register."

"Lead the way, Brother King!" one man shouted. "Show us how!" yelled another. M. L. smiled. "Just follow me!" he hollered back, his eyes flashing the excitement.

Thus, M. L. led another march, this time on the Selma County Court House. Once again, he was thrown in jail. Suffering the same consequences were five hundred school children and two hundred and sixty-three adults. Once more, M. L. took pen in hand and composed a "Letter from a Selma, Alabama Jail." He knew that some people might be confused as to why a man who had received the Nobel Peace Prize in December would be sitting in a jail cell only sixty days later. The answer was simple. "This is Selma, Alabama," M. L. wrote. "There are more Negroes in jail with me than here on the voting rolls." A march was organized from Selma to Montgomery. The purpose? It would further dramatize the need for blacks to vote. Danger hung in the air. A civil rights march in nearby Marion had caused one black, Jimmie Lee Jackson, to be shot and killed. An angry Alabama Governor George Wallace said further marches would not be allowed.

But M. L. would not turn back. "The march will go on," he declared.

Alabama state police were ready. Ordering the marchers to break up, and not getting a satisfactory response, the state police attacked. Some rode horses. The officers swung bull whips and clubs. They shot tear gas pellets. Seventeen marchers were taken to the hospital.

But once again the American people, witnessing the encounter through their televisions and newspapers, became aroused and angry. With new plans announced for marching, supporters from every state headed to Alabama. Several hundred of the nonviolent freedom marchers were white ministers.

"Ministers or not, they better stay out of Alabama!" one racist leader warned. "A nigger got killed here last time. We can kill white nigger lovers too."

Warning became prophecy when one of the white ministers, Reverend James Reeb of Boston, was beaten and died from his injuries. The death of Jamie Lee Jackson had caused a ripple of public attention and outcry, but the death of Reverend Reeb caused a thunderous roar across the nation. On the day that M. L. conducted memorial services for Reverend Reeb in Selma, President Johnson went before Congress in Washington, D. C. "I speak tonight for the dignity of man," said the president. "At times history and fate meet at a single time in a single place to shape a turning point in man's search for freedom. So it was at Lexington and Concord. So it was a century ago at Appomattox. So it was the last week at Selma, Alabama." Again and again the Congress interrupted the president's speech with applause in approval. He explained why it was important that the voting rights bill he was presenting be passed, sharing even a bit of his own personal touches with racism when he was growing up in Texas. He had been poor and understood their suffering. "Their cause must be our cause too. Because it's not just Negroes, but it's really all of us who must overcome the crippling legacy of bigotry and injustice." Taking a deep breath, President Johnson concluded, "And we shall overcome."

On March 21, a triumphant victory march began in Selma and proceeded to the capitol city of Montgomery. This time, there were no state police to interfere. President Johnson had sent 4,000 U. S. Army soldiers to make sure there was no violence. The 54-mile trip took four days, but when the hundreds of marchers reached Montgomery, they were joined by thousands of others. Happily, yet in an orderly manner, the giant crowd entered Montgomery. Governor Wallace refused to talk personally with the gathering, but few persons seemed to care. They would rather hear M. L.

"We are on the move now," he shouted to everyone standing in the city square. "Let us continue our triumph. Let us march on segregated schools. Let us march on poverty. Let us march on the ballot boxes . . . Our aim must never be to defeat . . . the white man but to win his friendship and understanding. We must come to see that the end we seek is a society at peace with itself, a society that can live with its conscience. That will not be a day of the white man, not of the black man. That will be the day of man as man."

On August 6, 1965, President Johnson officially signed the Voting Rights Act after if had been passed by Congress. Coupled with the Civil Rights Act of 1964, American blacks had truly begun to experience a new way of life. The walls of Jericho were falling.

"You have earned a rest," Daddy King told M. L. "Come home to us. Watch your children grow up. Why, just last week Marty was asking me when that man was coming home again to stay for a few days."

M. L. knew his father was joking. Daddy had been singing the same song for years. There was never enough time for M. L. to be with the children and Coretta. What a joy it would be to gather around the piano for a happy songfest or to listen to Mama play the church organ and Daddy shiver the spines of the congregation with an old fire and brimstone sermon. If only there were time to jump into a swimming pool and challenge those muscles so long neglected. What stimulation there would be to explore the thoughts of great theologians and philosophers by reading their books.

And yet there was a thought that nagged in M. L.'s mind, a persistent re-occurring and frightening idea that time was running out. The thought had come fleetingly at first, the day when the news came over television that John F. Kennedy had been shot in Dallas. M. L. called Coretta to his side, and they listened together to each minute-by-minute report. Finally, the announcement came that President Kennedy was dead. In a somber tone, M. L. said, "This is what is going to happen to me also. I keep telling you, this is a sick society." As much as she wanted to, Coretta could not bring herself to say anything. All she could do was move closer and grip her husband's hand in hers.

For months M. L. struggled with the decision of what direction to take with his life. "You are not merely a person," Daddy reminded M. L. "You are a beacon. Whatever you do, people will follow."

It was true. As M. L. heard his father's words, he knew there was nothing he could do solely as an individual. When he spoke, he spoke as the movement. Whether he was shaking a stranger's hand or walking across the street, he was the movement.

And yet, despite the power M. L. commanded, there were those within the civil rights movement who constantly challenged his authority, who threatened to undo much of what had been accomplished. "Black Power!" became much more than a chant shouted here and there at meetings and rallies. It represented an idea for immediate change and action. It meant violence.

"It is not the black man who supports Martin Luther

King Jr.," declared Malcolm X, a fiery advocate of Black Nationalism. "It is the white man. The white man pays King to keep the black man defenseless. Oh, you may call it nonviolence because that sounds noble. But it still means defenseless."

Another supporter of black Nationalism was Stokeley Carmichael. "I'm not going to beg any white man for rights I have coming to me," he insisted. "I'm going to take them."

M. L. understood their anger and impatience. But he would not bend to his critics. "If we must have slogans, can we not use 'Black Equality' or 'Black Consciousness'? With 'Black Power,' it sounds as if we seek domination. We're not seeking a nation of black supremacy. We want a nation where all people share the same rights, the same responsibilities, the same freedom to dream."

M. L. believed every word that he said. Somehow, a drum within him seemed to pound out the logical and sensible tempo of progress, of taking one step at a time in an orderly progression. "Black Power!" was a jarring staccato note, a beat out of rhythm. If only everyone could hear the music, march to the same drum beat.

But there was still another noise drowning out the melody of the movement. The sounds of guns and exploding bombs in Southeast Asia grew louder and louder. An American military presence began there quietly enough in the mid 1950s, and now as the conflict continued to escalate a decade later, President Johnson seemed committed to a military solution.

The Vietnam conflict troubled M. L. more deeply with each passing day. Who was always made to suffer the most in times of war? It was the poor, the homeless, those who possessed no way or means to flee or find security. Was there anyone listening to the cries of the helpless? He knew he would have to speak out.

"We read facts and statistics of what is happening in Vietnam," M. L. told his friends. "Yet too many of us are merely reading numbers. These people are mothers and fathers, children, grandmothers. They are tossed around like toys in a game. They are confused, poor, frustrated. We have them in our own cities, here in America. The only difference is that of geography."

And while the bombs fell from the sky in Vietnam, bombs exploded too in America. Race riots broke out in Harlem, July 1964, and in Watts, a ghetto area of Los Angeles, August, 1965. Thirty-four were killed, 900 injured in Watts. As he surveyed the torn buildings and littered streets, M. L.'s eyes filled with tears. He labeled rioting "the language of the unheard."

He did not intend to go unheard. Despite the advice of many of his close supporters, M. L. knew he had to make his feelings public. "Violence answers nothing," M. L. told reporters. "It is a useless, destructive force. Oppression of any people, whether it be through active warfare as it is in Vietnam or racial prejudice, as it is in America, is wrong, wrong, wrong. Let us stop the bombing in Vietnam. Let us face the needs of the poor and hungry in our own country. I offer to do anything and everything I can do in either case."

Daddy King was among the first to react to his son's criticism of the war in Southeast Asia. "You're trying to do too much. You can't be all things to all people, son. No one can. You're doin' so good, movin' this civil rights along. You got the President working with you. Why do you want to go shootin' off your mouth about this Vietnam thing?"

M. L. shook his head. "Daddy, it's all part of the same thing. It's all tied together."

"I don't see it, son."

"Here, let's look at just one thing. What young man in this country is most likely to be sent off to Vietnam, possibly to get shot down thousands of miles away from home? It's the poor, black boy, that's who. While white boys go to college and are deferred from service, the black boys go to war. And that's just a part of the injustice, Daddy. We're spending all this money for weapons, for guns, bullets and bombs. That money should be going toward constructive projects, not for destroying people and places we don't even know."

M. L. was attacked by many other black notables. Civil rights leaders Roy Wilkins and Whitney Young, baseball star Jackie Robinson, Senator Edward Brooke—each denounced the "broadside slap" M. L. had taken at the United States military involvement in Vietnam. With renewed zest, J. Edgar Hoover circulated the FBI files hinting at M. L.'s association with known Communists, his questionable moral behavior and his financial resources. President Johnson, who had displayed much support for the Civil Rights Movement, made little attempt to hide his disgust at M. L.'s Vietnam attacks.

But M. L. stood firm. With Daddy sitting nearby, M. L. took the pulpit at Ebenezer Baptist and tried to explain his thinking. "As a minister of God," he said, "and as a winner of the Nobel Peace Prize, I feel guided by a voice within. Oh, I hear the voices around me. I feel the sting of words hurled in anger and criticism. But I must listen to the voice within, because I know who is speaking."

The momentum of civil rights movement continued. With renewed energy, M. L. sought to find a plan early in 1966 that would highlight the pulpit of the poor living in big city ghettos. Sometimes at night M. L. was haunted by the hopeless, tired faces of those he had seen living, no not living, but existing in rundown tenements and scarred, shabby apartments. Chicago, that would be a place to focus upon. Too often people thought only of blacks struggling in the South. It was past time to show the ugliness of life in the Northern urban centers.

And so the movement headed north to a major American city. M. L. approved plans to lead marches and institute boycotts to protest segregated housing, discrimination, and unfair hiring practices in Chicago. The city's mayor, Richard Daley, openly feared violence. "It will not come from my people," M. L. promised.

Violence came anyway. As M. L. spoke in Chicago's streets and parks, he saw hate on the faces of blacks and whites alike. Blacks hurled obscentities at Jews, whites screamed threats at blacks. Puerto Ricans condemned Poles, Swedes ridiculed Germans. The tension spread far beyond race, into nationality differences, politics, and religion. Anger and frustration boiled over in Chicago's West Side ghetto neighborhoods in hot July and August days. This brought Mayor Daley and other city leaders to a meeting with M. L. and agreements promising change were signed. The Chicago campaign ended; M. L. left the city weary and disappointed. He was not sure whites really wanted integration—and he had many doubts about blacks as well. Meanwhile, the war continued to intensify. "Just quit talking about Vietnam," one top government leader told M. L. "It's none of your business."

"Human life *is* my business," M. L. snapped back. "I shall speak out whenever I feel I must."

In the spring of 1967, a national religious peace organization, Clergy and Laity Concerned About Vietnam, asked M. L. to accept the co-chairmanship. A call went out for 10,000 volunteers willing to promote peace in 500 communities across the nation.

Criticism of King, Jr. increased. More and more people demanded further explanations from him regarding his criticism of American foreign affairs. He decided to answer all of his critics, once and for all, at New York's Riverside Church in April of 1967.

Three thousand people jammed the church to hear the major address. After giving him a standing ovation, the audience seated themselves. M. L. looked at the crowd, realizing how badly he wanted to make them all understand his thinking.

With care and precision, King presented the rationale that had forced him to speak out about the Vietnam conflict. Calling himself "a preacher by trade," he reminded those listening of a few years before, when "it seemed as if there was a real promise of hope for the poor—both black and white—through the Poverty Program. There were experiments, hopes, new beginnings. Then came the build-up in Vietnam and I watched the program broken and eviscerated as if it were some political plaything of a society gone mad on war, and I knew America would never invest the necessary funds or energies in rehabilitation of its poor as long as adventures like Vietnam continued to draw men and skills and money like some demoniacal destructive suction tube."

M. L. paused, allowing the audience to consider his words. A few heads were nodding in agreement. Next, he went on to note the high percentages of black men who were being sent to Vietnam compared to the white population. In America, these same soldiers could not even attend the same schools, and yet they were dying side by side on the battlefield.

The more M. L. spoke, the more it became clear why he felt obligated to speak out. Was it so surprising that a Christian minister should be speaking out against war? Was it surprising that a winner of the Nobel Peace Prize should be speaking out against war? Didn't the Vietnamese people, who had lived with war for almost three decades, deserve someone to speak for them?

With sensitive accuracy, M. L. catalogued the history of warfare in Vietnam. He accused America of turning a civil war into a major struggle over Communism. "We must stop now. I speak as a child of God and brother to the suffering poor of Vietnam. . . . I speak as an American to the leaders of my own nation."

And in speaking to America's leaders, M. L. called for a halt to the bombing, a unilateral ceasefire, and a date to be set for the removal of American troops. "If we do not act," he declared, "we shall surely be dragged down the long dark and shameful corridors of time reserved for those who possess power without compassion, might without morality, and strength without sight."

The audience in the Riverside Church was clearly moved. The applause at the end of M. L.'s speech thundered through the rafters.

But the thunder had barely quieted when fresh explosions shook the ghetto areas of Newark and Detroit in early summer, the worst outbreak of violence in the century. Federal troops were called in and M. L. defended President Johnson's actions in doing so. "But we have created the conditions from which these riots spring," M. L. declared. "We should have been developing government programs to get rid of slums, provide more jobs . . . Instead, our time and money is directed to a country on the other side of the world." "When will we take positive action?" M. L. demanded. "We breed these nests of frustration and rage, then we must deal with the results. If only we might seek to cure instead of applying order and force after the disease strikes . . ."

What to do? Perhaps it was time for another march on Washington. The last time such a march was held, it had helped to oil the tracks for smooth passage of the Civil Rights Act. This time the march could focus on the poor, revealing to the country the evils of poverty—a "Poor People's March." It might push legislation forward to help the poor. Why not build a giant shantytown, right in front of everyone? The government would have to do something to answer the demands of the people.

As plans for the "Poor People's March" were being made, a call for help came in March, 1968 from the Memphis garbage workers, 90 percent of whom were black. They were striking for better pay and improved working conditions. Young Black Nationalists were stirring up trouble. "We must maintain nonviolence," M. L. urged again. But when he attempted to lead a peaceful march, problems broke out. One man was killed, many injured and over two hundred people were arrested. Buildings were vandalized and tempers flared. Returning to Atlanta, M. L. gathered his top SCLC aides. "We belong where we are needed," he told his friends. "At first I didn't think we should be there, but now I'm convinced it's where we belong."

The trip to Memphis got off to a shaky start when the airplane flight from Atlanta was delayed at takeoff. There had been a bomb threat, and every article of luggage was searched. Accustomed to such supposed dangers M. L. laughed the threat off. Meetings began as soon as the party checked into the Lorraine Motel in Memphis. A march was scheduled for Friday, and M. L. wanted to make sure every detail was checked out. This time there would be no violence, and he wanted that to be a fact!

A rally was set for the night of April 3, but M. L. begged off attending. Sheets of rain plummeted the city with sharp cracks of thunder rolling across the sky. The crowd at Mason Temple would likely be a small one, and M. L. felt tired. Ralph Abernathy agreed to fill in for him.

But within a short time, M. L. was summoned by phone to the Temple. A crowd of two thousand had braved the bad weather, and media coverage was heavy. "They want you!" Abernathy insisted. M. L. gave in, dressed, and drove to the Temple.

Rain pelted the roof of the auditorium when M. L. mounted to the speaker's platform. The lights were bright, causing him to squint. He spoke without script, referring to the troubles and confusion which filled the nation. It was just such trouble and confusion, the poverty, hurt and neglect experienced by those present, which had brought M. L. to Memphis . . . and he was happy that God had allowed him to come. Slowly M. L. mentioned in brief many major events of his life—the stabbing in New York City ten years before, student sit-ins,

Freedom rides, the Birmingham and Selma marches, the civil rights gathering at the Lincoln Memorial. He touched on the bomb threat to his plane that morning and other threats he had received. "Well, he said, "I don't know what will happen now. We've got some difficult days ahead. But it really doesn't matter with me now. Because I've been to the mountaintop."

The cries and applause blended with the rolls of thunder. No longer did M. L. feel tired. People, yes, people, always made his juices come alive. He wanted to share, to touch the spirit and mind of everyone present. "Like anybody I would like to live a long life," he continued. "Longevity has its place. But I'm not concerned about that now. I just want to do God's will. And he's allowed me to go up to the mountain. And I've looked over. And I've seen the Promised Land. And I may not get there with you, but I want you to know tonight that we as a people *will* get to the Promised Land. So I'm happy tonight. I'm not worried about anything. I'm not fearing any man. Mine eyes have seen the glory of the coming of the Lord. I have a dream this afternoon that the brotherhood of man will become a reality. With this faith, I will go out and carve a tunnel of hope from a mountain of despair . . . With this faith, we will be able to achieve this new day, when all of God's children—black men and white men, Jews and Gentiles, Protestants and Catholics—will be able to join hands and sing with the Negroes in the spiritual of old, 'Free at last! Free at last! Thank God Almighty, we are free at last.' "

M. L.'s words, punctuated frequently by loud cries from his audience, thrilled those listening, although some of his staff members were surprised at its morbid undertones. Perhaps the bomb scare at the airport that morning had more of an effect on M. L. than anyone thought. Whatever the case, the response to the speech was positive.

April 4 was spent in meetings at the motel. After lunch, M. L. and A. D. called Atlanta and chatted with their mother. She was always pleased when the two boys were together. Later in the afternoon, the meetings broke up, and M. L. cleaned up. The Reverend Samuel Kyles was host for supper at his home. He arrived to pick up M. L. and whoever else wished to go. The early evening air was chilly. Leaving his balcony room, M. L. turned and asked Ralph Abernathy to bring his topcoat. Glancing down at the group of staff members waiting in the parking lot below, M. L. smiled at Jesse Jackson. "I want you to go to dinner with us this evening. And be sure to dress up a little tonight okay, Jesse? No blue jeans, all right?"

M. L. stood beside the iron railing. A light breeze danced through the trees. Across the street sat a row of dilapidated buildings along Mulberry Street. M. L. started to turn when suddenly—crack!—the sound of a rifle shot broke the quiet of dusk. A bullet ripped into his face, forcing his husky body backward. Reaching desperately for his throat, M. L. collapsed to the balcony floor. It was over.

While Martin Luther King, Jr. took his final breaths on a motel balcony in Memphis, Martin Luther King, Sr. was hurrying Bunch into the family car in Atlanta. As one of the church organists at Ebenezer Baptist, Bunch practiced often, sometimes with a soloist, other times with a group. On this particular evening, the senior Kings were running slightly behind schedule. Daddy had a counseling appointment and he did not like to be late. The conversation in the car was cheerful and light. Bunch was especially pleased about the telephone call she had received that afternoon. No matter how old the boys grew, they would always remain her little boys. She was also greatly to blame for the hefty waistlines on both M. L. and A. D. It was a blame she carried with pride.

Arriving at the church parking lot, Daddy's attention

was drawn to a woman who seemed to be wildly yelling and gesturing from her car. Since her window was rolled up, Daddy could not hear what she was saying. The sight of several other cars backed up along Auburn Avenue made his pulse quicken. Something was wrong. He could sense it strongly. After parking the car, he and Bunch hurried into the building. They did not speak but rushed upstairs to Daddy's study. Without a moment's thought, Daddy switched on the radio. An announcer was saying that Martin Luther King had suffered a serious wound by gunfire in Memphis. Daddy looked at Bunch as she sat stoic and unmoving, except for the tears that slid down her face. ". . . King was shot in the shoulder," a local announcer stated, "but he is said to still be alive." Daddy King shook his head, his hands trembling. "Lord, let him live, let him be alive." It was not to be. In moments, the announcer, his own voice cracking with emotion, carried the somber bulletin that Martin Luther King, Jr. was dead. Daddy turned to Bunch. They had thought often of the possibility of this very moment. Yet, there was always something that told them it could never happen, it was too ugly to happen. In a few seconds of radio time, it was all over. The child, the scholar, the preacher, the boy singing and smiling—all of it was gone.

In the minutes and hours that followed, a daze clouded Daddy King's mind. Faces, voices, soft words, comforting hands—all were there, and yet there was an emptiness, a void, that no one could touch. Like a mindless statue, he functioned, consoling, and being consoled. As always, Bunch remained strong, or at least appeared strong to the unknowing observer. But Daddy understood what she was going through. Someone had come along and snatched the hearts out of their bodies.

M. L. came home to Atlanta a final time. Never had the city witnessed such an outpouring of grief. Rich and poor, the powerful and the unknown—they came to say farewell to one who had fought the good fight with weapons of love and kindness.

Seeing his son's body in the casket, Daddy King was once more a father trying to wake his son from a nap. "Answer me, M. L.! Answer me!" Knowing there would be no answer, Daddy King collapsed sobbing. "He never hated anybody," the old man softly cried. "He never hated anybody."

17

Another April, another spring.

Daddy King stood before the marble crypt. A smile came to his lips as he read the words hewn into the precious rock: Free at last, free at last, thank God almighty, I'm free at last.

Silently Bunch slipped to his side. "You're smiling, Daddy. Why?"

Daddy King put his arm out and pulled Bunch closer. "I was just thinking about M. L. a long time ago when your mother died. He asked me if she was wearing a robe in heaven. 'Of course,' I answered. Now I was just thinking what a fine robe he must be wearing."

Bunch smiled. "Free at last, free at last, thank God Almighty, I'm free at last." How true those words were. Free from the marches, the pain, the angry words, the hurts. Yes, surely M. L. was free at last!

Daddy nodded, sensing Bunch's thoughts as he so often did. "M. L. is so much better off than we are. He's at peace with the Lord. Let's go see if any of our grandchildren would like to go to Funtown today."

It was a different world for Daddy King. No one could fill the void that M. L.'s death had caused. But when A. D. accepted the position of co-pastor at Ebenezer Baptist, that certainly helped. Having all of his grandchildren living in Atlanta helped Daddy too. He loved being with the rapidly growing youngsters and delighted in spoiling every one of them. In her own quiet manner,

Bunch was a dedicated accomplice in that regard. The family helped to ease the pain, for each one felt the emptiness, the loneliness and despair of what they had lost. Only through the support of one another could the pain be eased, that, and the abiding faith in an ever loving, everlasting Savior.

And then, without any warning at all, death struck again. In the early morning hours of July 21, 1969, Daddy awoke to a ringing phone. It was seventeen-year-old Al, the oldest son of A. D. "There's trouble here at the house!" Al shouted hysterically. "Trouble! Trouble!"

Daddy dressed quickly. Bunch did not go with him to A. D.'s home. She had had enough of trouble. She could not force herself to go along. So Daddy King drove by himself.

When Daddy arrived at A. D.'s home, a fire department unit was also pulling up. Rushing inside, Daddy was greeted with hugs and kisses. But they carried with them a feeling of loss and suffering. The news came quickly. A. D. had drowned. Al had found him that morning in the family swimming pool. Holding his grandchildren close, Daddy closed his eyes. For a moment he was lost in a world of the past. He could hear the laughter of two young boys at play, "Now quit teasing your sister!" Daddy heard himself saying. "You boys know better than that!" Gone. Over. "I don't care if you boys become preachers," his voice echoed from years past, "but it sure would please me and your momma if you do some thinkin' about it." Finished. Through. And as Daddy King opened his eyes, he knew the most difficult task still lay before him, telling Bunch. "Help me, Lord," he murmured to himself, "I need just a little help, my Lord."

Daddy King and Bunch remained strong with shared strength and understanding. They accepted their pain as a duty. For those who might ask "Why?" and many did, Daddy was ready with an answer. "God did not bring us tragedy, he has brought us opportunity," Daddy explained. "We can make ourselves stronger and better. Our faith is with us. Yes, I have lost much, but I have a great deal left." Once more, Daddy pulled the family closer, knowing a feeling of emptiness would always remain, actually should always remain, but that the future was in God's hands—hands that would provide comfort to ease the pain.

At seventy, Daddy King found his second wind. Although he was content to spend all of his free time with Bunch and the family when he was not ministering at Ebenezer Baptist, he was often invited to give lectures and guest sermons. Few individuals had been so long and so closely connected with the civil rights movement. Daddy liked the image of "an elder statesman" and enjoyed visiting college campuses and civic groups. "They don't even mind that I ruin the English language," he told Bunch. "When you're an old man, people make allowances for a lot of things."

When Daddy spoke, he emphasized values, ethics and rights. In discussions and conversations with young people, he sensed a need for instilling moral concepts. He tried to avoid preaching to his listeners, but there was no question that his remarks were more spiritual than political. "I can't do much about that," he told one observer. "God controls my tongue, and I do believe he cares more about souls and sinning than about Democrats and Republicans."

Staying busy helps soothe the loneliness, comforts the spirit. Daddy was grateful for his good health. Other than a little prostrate trouble, his body functioned pretty well. But so often when everything seems to be going so smoothly, another test appears. For Daddy King, this one came June 30, 1974, the last Sunday of the month.

Bunch was sleeping when Daddy King awoke that morning. After the morning services at Ebenezer, he was scheduled to board a plane for New Jersey and deliver a talk there that afternoon. He dressed quietly, feeling a special pleasure that he could slip away without waking her. Suitcase in hand, he headed out the door and drove to church. Old friends gathered in the parking lot, sharing stories of bygone times and how the world was "going to the dogs." Daddy mingled as long as he could, then headed upstairs to the study. Skimming through some letters, Daddy felt a restlessness come over him. He closed his eyes, organizing his thoughts for the day and thanking God for providing strength for all that needed doing.

Leaving his study, Daddy went down to the basement. He enjoyed visiting Sunday School classes, but most were over now, and boys and girls spilled into the hallways. As he turned to go upstairs, he sensed someone watching him. Glancing around, he saw nothing but a sea of faces, none who really returned his stare.

When Daddy returned to his study, the church organ could be heard. Daddy recognized Bunch's style, her agile fingers pressing the keys for the glory of the Lord. It was a good sound. Rich. Full. Daddy hummed the hymn tune as he walked toward the main sanctuary. A guest speaker would fill the pulpit, Reverend Calvin Morris. Daddy was glad he could save his voice for the afternoon presentation.

Christine sat in the left front pew, the pulpit directly in view. Daddy moved toward her. Suddenly, he stopped. He gazed over at Bunch, while in the background the reciting of the Lord's Prayer continued in the service. Over the sound of the music, a shrieking voice was heard: "I'm taking over here this morning!" The shout was followed by a popping sound, then a scream. Daddy did not know who screamed first, but the second voice he recognized at once. It was Bunch. Her hand flew to cover her face, and as Daddy watched, blood flowed through her fingers. A strange man stood near her, his hand wildly waving a pistol. Rushing to help Bunch, Daddy felt a bullet whistle by his head. Bunch fell forward, then Daddy could see nothing but bodies scrambling in every direction. Arms reached out and pulled him backward. "I can't leave here without Bunch!" Daddy insisted.

Minutes later, Daddy sat in a police car rushing behind an ambulance on its way to Grady Memorial Hospital. People were talking, but he did not hear the words. "God, help her!" he prayed. "Please help her." His head dropped forward, painfully recalling the blood pouring from her face. This couldn't be happening. It was all a nightmare. It was time to wake up. Time to wake up.

As the police car halted, Daddy King bounded out. He ran to the ambulance as Bunch was being carried off. She tried to speak, but the words would not come.

Daddy King sat alone in a small office. Seconds became minutes. They seemed like hours, days, months. Finally, a young doctor entered the room. "I'm sorry, Reverend King, we just couldn't save her."

She was gone. Forty-seven years of sharing, loving, discovering, burying, ended.

Once more Daddy King endured the ordeal of saying goodbye to one whom he had loved dearly. Once more he called upon God to lend the strength needed, and just as before, strength was provided.

"I shall never understand how any person can get through life without spiritual faith," Daddy told a friend later. "I recall a well-meaning caller who said, "It must be terrible being alone like you are. A man never needs to be alone. The Lord accepts any and all invitations to be a companion."

In spite of the spiritual strength provided by the Lord, Daddy King grieved deeply. Thankfully, his family offered constant support. Daughter Christine and her husband Issac, Coretta, and Naomi, A. D.'s wife. The grandchildren. They all were so practiced at sharing and suffering. Too practiced.

With some regret, but with relief as well, Daddy King said farewell to his pastorate at Ebenezer Baptist Church. There would be no King to take over the pulpit, but it gave Daddy special comfort to witness Joseph Lawrence Roberts, Sr. deliver the installation sermon for his son, Joseph Lawrence Roberts, Jr.

There was still work to be done, years to be lived. What a thrill it was for Daddy to be the first black to address a joint session of the Alabama state legislature. On the same day, he spoke at M. L.'s old church, Dexter Avenue Baptist. From his son's former pulpit, Daddy King looked back. "Once," he said, "as a young preacher I worked hard at preaching to move people. Now I want to preach and have people think." Wistfully, he added, "You and I know these are bewildering times we live in. But don't you lose your way and don't you ever let it get too dark you cannot promote a song."

His steps were slowing, and he needed a cane to use for balance now. But Daddy King's spirit still sought usefulness and service. When former Georgia Governor Jimmy Carter sought his political help, he agreed. In Carter, Daddy saw a good, honest man, a symbol of how much the South had changed. Carter's Presidential victory pleased Daddy King. "M. L. was always hesitant to speak out for a candidate," Daddy King recalled. "But my mouth was always a tad bigger than M. L.'s."

Time was running out. In August of 1976, Daddy found himself in a coronary care unit. The following year he was treated for congestive heart failure. Despite the seriousness of his illnesses, Daddy King offered a light touch. "I've been using this body of mine for a long time now," he noted. "It was never the most handsome product around, but it always worked pretty good. I suppose it's about time it's starting to fall apart here and there. I'll be ready to go whenever the Maker calls me. Even if I weren't, I don't think it would make any difference."

On the morning of November 11, 1984, Daddy attended services at Salem Baptist Church in Atlanta. That afternoon, he suffered a heart attack and was rushed to Crawford W. Long Memorial Hospital. He died at 5:41 in the afternoon, with his daughter Christine and his grandson, Derek King, at his side.

"Dr. King lived a rich, full life dedicated to the noblest principles of our people," observed President Ronald Reagan. "His sense of family and community, his spirit and charity and neighborliness, and above all his dedication to the ideals of justice and equality, leave a shining legacy for others to follow. The achievements of Dr. King and his family will live in the hearts not only of the American people but of all those who hunger for freedom and equality everywhere in the world."

Blacks and whites stood side by side in Ebenezer Baptist Church on Thursday, November 16, 1984. One by one, leaders of the nation came to offer memories and tributes to the man who had occupied the pulpit in the southern church for forty-four years. Former President Carter spoke, as did Vice President Bush, Reverend Ralph David Abernathy, Jesse Jackson, and Atlanta Mayor Andrew Young, a close friend and colleague of M. L. They remembered Daddy King with warmth and sincerity.

Finally, Christine King Farris, Daddy's sole surviving child, spoke to her father. "I pledge to carry out your legacy of love and service," she murmured. "Dad, we will keep the faith and we will keep looking up."

"Looking up." It was the way Daddy King would have wanted it.

> I've got a robe, you've got a robe, all of
>   God's children got a robe
> When I get to Heaven, goin' to put on my
>   robe,
> Goin' to shout all over God's heav'n,
>   heav'n, heav'n—

When I get to heav'n, goin' to put on my
     robe,
Goin' to shout all over God's heav'n.

A Chronology of the Lives and Times of
Martin Luther King, Sr. and
Martin Luther King, Jr.

Timeline

1896

May 18. With *Plessy v. Ferguson*, the U.S. Supreme Court upholds the doctrine of "separate but equal" treatment for the races, providing the legal justification for segregation.

1898

April 25 to December 10. The Spanish-American War. Spain cedes the Philippines, Puerto Rico, and Guam to the United States and gives up all claims to Cuba.

May 12. Louisiana adopts a new constitution with a "grandfather clause" designed to eliminate black voters.

November 10. Eight blacks are killed in a race riot in Wilmington, North Carolina.

1899

June 2. Black Americans observe a day of fasting called by the National Afro-American Council to protest lynchings and racial massacres.

December 19. Martin Luther (Michael) King is born to James and Delia King, sharecroppers in Stockbridge, Georgia.

1900

July 23–25. The Pan-African Congress meets in London; among the leaders is W. E. B. DuBois.

August 23–24. The National Negro Business League is established, and Booker T. Washington elected president.

1901

November 11. Alabama adopts a new constitution with a "grandfather clause."

1903

With the publication of *The Souls of Black Folk*, W. E. B. DuBois gives voice to the opposition to the social and political subordination by blacks to whites espoused by Booker T. Washington.

1905

July 11–13. Black intellectuals and activists, led by W. E. B. DuBois, organize the Niagara Movement and demand the abolition of all distinctions based on race.

1906

September 22–24. A race riot in Atlanta, Georgia, leads to the deaths of ten blacks and two whites. The black community responds by forming the Atlanta Civic League, under the leadership of Rev. Adam Daniel Williams, who will become Michael King's father-in-law.

1908

The eight-year-old Michael King witnesses a lynching. Eighty-nine blacks are reported lynched during this year.

1909

February 12. W. E. B. DuBois, Ida Wells-Barnett, Mary Church Terrell, Jane Addams, John Dewey, Lincoln Steffens, Rabbi Steven Wise, and others found the National Association for the Advancement of Colored People (NAACP).

April 6. Commander Robert E. Peary reaches the North Pole; the only American with him is his black assistant, Matthew Henson.

May 17. White firemen on the Georgia Railroad strike to protest the employment of blacks.

1910

December 19. The Baltimore City Council passes the first city ordinance requiring white and black residential areas. Similar laws will be passed in Norfolk, Richmond, Roanoke, Greensboro, St. Louis, Oklahoma City, Dallas, and Louisville.

1911

October. The National Urban League is founded, and Eugene Kinckle Jones is named executive secretary.

1912

September 27. The first published blues composition, "Memphis Blues" by W.C. Handy, goes on sale in Memphis.

1913

April. President Woodrow Wilson's administration begins segregating blacks and whites in government departments.

1914

February. The Church Peace Union is founded, an interfaith organization of prominent religious peace seekers.

June 28. Firing the first shot in what is to become World War I, Gabriel Princips assassinates the Crown Prince of Austria.

Michael King leaves home to go to work in Atlanta's Southern Railroad Yards, until his mother comes to retrieve him.

Michael King delivers his first sermon in Floyd's Chapel in Stockbridge and gets his preacher's license.

1915

January 10. Jane Addams and Carrie Chapman Catt initiate the Women's Peace Party.

April. Jane Addams heads the U.S. delegation to the International Congress of Women at The Hague, meeting with leading European women whose countries are at war. They form a committee that will become the women's International League for Peace and Freedom (WILPF) in 1919.

June 21. The U.S. Supreme Court (*Guinn v. United States*) rules that the "grandfather clauses" in the Oklahoma and Maryland constitutions violate the Fifteenth Amendment.

November. Norman Thomas and 40 other Christian absolute pacifists found the U.S. section of the Fellowship of Reconciliation (FOR).

December. Henry Ford's "peace ship," *S.S. Oscar II*, sails to Europe with a delegation of citizen-mediators seeking an end to World War I.

The Great Migration begins. Some 2 million Southern blacks will move to Northern industrial centers in the following decades.

The NAACP leads demonstration against showings of the movie, *Birth of a Nation* because of its depiction of blacks.

1917

April 2. Saying "the world must be made safe for democracy," President Woodrow Wilson asks Congress to declare war on Germany.

April. The American Friends Service Committee (AFSC) is formed to give Quaker conscientious objectors options for alternative service.

May 18. In the first conscription since the Civil War, Congress passes the Selective Service Act.

July 1–3. A race riot in East St. Louis, Illinois, kills between forty and two hundred people.

July 28. Ten thousand blacks march down Fifth Avenue, New York City, to protest lynchings and racial indignities.

August 23. Thirteen are killed in a race riot between black and white soldiers in Houston; eighteen black soldiers will be hanged for alleged participation.

1918

January 8. President Wilson sets forth his "Fourteen Points" for peace in the world, including a "general association of nations."

224

June 1. A board of inquiry is constituted to examine all conscientious objectors and recommend them for alternative service; there are 4,000 COs during World War I.

Michael King moves to Atlanta, where he will work at a variety of jobs—in an auto tire shop, loading bales of cotton, and driving a truck. He also will become a preacher for a number of Stockbridge families who have moved to the East Point section of Atlanta.

November 11. The German government signs an armistice treaty. The war cost the United States $41.7 billion; 130,174 U.S. soldiers died.

1919

February 19-21. The Pan-African Congress, organized by W. E. B. DuBois meets in Paris with delegates from Africa and the U.S.

March. The Supreme Court holds that freedom of speech does not apply to draft resistance, and Socialist labor leader Eugene Debs is imprisoned under this ruling for opposing U.S. entry into World War I.

November. The U.S. Senate refuses to ratify the Versailles Treaty officially ending the war because it includes a provision to create the League of Nations.

1920

August 2. Marcus Garvey addresses 25,000 blacks in Madison Square Garden; his nationalist movement, the Universal Negro Improvement Association, reaches its height in 1920-21.

August 16. Women win the vote with the ratification of the Nineteenth Amendment.

Michael King enrolls in the fifth grade at the Bryant Elementary School, taking night classes.

November 6. James Weldon Johnson becomes the first black executive secretary of the NAACP.

November 15. The League of Nations meets for the first time in its new headquarters in Geneva, Switzerland.

1921

After a struggle of several months, Michael King obtains his voter registration card.

For the first time, black women are awarded Ph.D. degrees—Eva Dykes, English, Radcliffe; Sadie Mossell, Economics, University of Pennsylvania; and Georgiana Simpson, German, University of Chicago.

1922

January 26. The Dyer antilynching bill is passed in the House, 230-119, but killed in the Senate by a filibuster.

1923
March 29. The War Resisters League (WRL) is founded by Jessie Wallace Hughan, Tracy Mygatt, and Frances Witherspoon to work with nonreligious conscientious objectors.

June 21. Marcus Garvey is sentenced to five years in prison for using the mail to defraud; he says the charges are political.

September 15. The governor says Oklahoma is in a "state of virtual rebellion and insurrection" because of KKK activities, and he declares martial law.

October 24. According to the Department of Labor, some 500,000 blacks have left the South during the year.

1924
Spring. Michael King's mother dies.

Fall. Booker T. Washington High School opens, the first high school for blacks in Atlanta.

1925
August 25. A. Philip Randolph is elected president of the newly organized Brotherhood of Sleeping Car Porters.

1926
February. Carter G. Woodson organizes the first Negro History Week celebration, which will later be expanded into Black History Month.

Fall. Michael King is admitted to Morehouse College.

November 25. Michael King and Alberta Williams are married in the sanctuary of the Ebenezer Baptist Church, where her father is the minister.

1927
March 7. The Supreme Court, in *Nixon v. Herndon*, strikes down the Texas law that barred blacks from voting in the "white primary."

September. Willie Christine, the first child of Michael and Alberta King, is born.

1928
November 6. Oscar DePriest of Chicago becomes the first black member of Congress from the North, and the first black in Congress since 1901.

1929
January 15. Michael King, Jr., is born in Atlanta, Georgia. In 1933 he will officially be named Martin Luther King, Jr., (and his father, Martin Luther King, Sr.) at the wish of his dying grandfather, James King.

Fall. A Jobs-for-Negroes campaign begins in Chicago; it will become the "Spend Your Money Where You Can Work" campaign and spread to New York, Cleveland, and Los Angeles.

October 29. The Stock Market Crash signals the beginning of the Great Depression.

Harlem Renaissance: During the decade there has been a flowering of black genius in the arts with Langston Hughes, Countee Cullen, Josephine Baker, Florence Mills, Eubie Blake, Noble Sissel, Arna Bontemps, and Paul Robeson. Also a period of growing race pride and consciousness of the African past.

1930

June 30. Michael King receives his bachelor's degree in theology from Morehouse College.

July 30. Alfred Daniel (A. D.) King is born, the youngest child of Michael and Alberta King.

FOR organizes the American League for India's Freedom to provide financial support for Gandhi's March to the Sea.

1931

April 6. First of the Scottsoboro trials begins in Scottsboro, Alabama. Nine black youths are accused of raping two white women and are subsequently railroaded into jail.

Spring. Rev. Williams, Alberta King's father, dies.

Fall. Michael King takes over the pastorate of the Ebenezer Baptist Church.

December 7. Hundreds of "hunger marchers" are turned away from the White House when they try to present their petition seeking employment at a minimum wage.

The Nobel Peace Prize is awarded to Jane Addams and Nicholas Murray Butler.

1932

February 2. The World Disarmament Conference, sponsored by the League of Nations, opens in Geneva, Switzerland.

November 8. Franklin Roosevelt is elected president; through the New Deal, he will establish federal agencies to ease unemployment and revive the economy. The number of unemployed has reached 13 million, and wages are 60% less than in 1929. Among the members of Roosevelt's "Black Cabinet," an unofficial body of black advisors, are Robert Vann, editor of the *Pittsburgh Courier*, and William H. Hastie, dean of Howard Law School.

1933

January 30. Adolf Hitler is named chancellor of Germany. Later in the year he will begin to send political opponents, Jews, and other "undesirables" to concentration camps.

Peter Maurin and Dorothy Day found the Catholic Worker Movement, which becomes the leading Catholic voice for militant pacifism. Between 25% and 40% of blacks in most urban centers are on relief.

1934

April 12. The Senate establishes the Nye Committee to investigate the extent to which munitions manufacturers influenced and profited from WWI.

W. E. B. DuBois leaves the NAACP. Since he is no longer editing *Crisis*, the NAACP journal, nor providing ideological leadership, the organization's focus on Pan-Africanism and black history decreases.

1935

August 14. President Roosevelt signs the Social Security Act.

August 31. President Roosevelt signs the Neutrality Act, which forbids the shipment of arms and munitions to belligerents in the growing conflicts in Europe.

Martin Luther King, Jr., has one of his first encounters with racism when a shoe-store clerk refuses to serve him and his father in the front part of the store.

September. Martin Luther King, Jr., enters elementary school.

October 2. Italy invades Ethiopia; U.S. black groups will protest and raise funds for Ethiopia.

November 5. The Maryland Court of Appeals orders the University of Maryland to admit Donald Murray, a black student.

December 5. The National Council of Negro Women is founded in New York with Mary McLeod Bethune as president.

The Swing Age begins—the heyday of the big bands of Chick Webb, Andy Kirk, Cab Calloway, Count Basie, Jimmie Lunceford, and Duke Ellington.

While teaching at Atlanta University, W. E. B. DuBois publishes *Black Reconstruction*, a landmark in black history.

1936

August 9. Track star Jesse Owens wins four gold medals at the Olympic Games in Berlin. Embarrassed at the defeat of Germany's "master race" athletes by an Afro-American, Chancellor Adolf Hitler leaves the stadium and has someone else present Owens his medals.

December 8. In Atlanta the NAACP files the first suit in its campaign to eliminate wage differentials between black and white teachers. At the request of Michael King, Ebenezer Baptist Church provides essential financial assistance for the eleven-year legal battle, which will be won in 1947.

1937

February 12. Representatives of the Historic Peace Churches visit the

White House regarding a possible military draft.

September 26. The great blues singer Bessie Smith dies in Clarksdale, Mississippi. It is widely believed that her death was due to being turned away from white hospitals while there was still time for treatment.

Joe Louis wins the heavyweight boxing championship.

A. Philip Randolph's Brotherhood of Sleeping Car Porters wins full recognition as the bargaining agent for porters and maids employed by the Pullman Company.

1938

November 8. Crystal Bird Fauset, the first black woman legislator, is elected to the Pennsylvania House of Representatives.

1939

September 1. World War II begins with the German invasion of Poland. On September 5, the United States declares its neutrality in the war spreading across Europe.

Singer Marian Anderson is denied use of Constitution Hall in Washington, D.C.; First Lady Eleanor Roosevelt protests and resigns from the Daughters of the American Revolution, who own the hall.

December. The movie, *Gone With the Wind*, is released, putting Atlanta in the headlines and causing discontent in Atlanta's black community about the stereotyping of blacks in the movie.

1940

September 16. Congress enacts the first peacetime draft, requiring all men between 21 and 35 to register for military training.

October 1. Dr. Charles Drew, a black physician who pioneered the technique for producing blood plasma, is appointed director of the plasma project in Great Britain.

October. The Historic Peace Churches and other pacifist organizations form the National Service Board for Religious Objectors, which sets up Civilian Public Service (CPS) camps as an alternative service program for conscientious objectors.

Chicago City Council member and attorney Earl Dickerson wins a Supreme Court decision declaring restrictive housing covenants illegal in a Chicago neighborhood; in 1948, the Court will outlaw all such covenants in the United States.

Richard Wright publishes *Native Son*, a revelation of the spirit of black rebellion.

1941

A. J. Muste and Rev. Jay Holmes Smith establish the Harlem Ashram (which will continue until 1947) to apply Gandhi's teachings about nonviolent action to problems in U.S. society.

April 18. New York City bus companies agree to hire black drivers and mechanics, ending a four-week boycott. In Chicago, Earl Dickerson leads a successful fight for the employment of black conductors in streetcars.

April 28. The Supreme Court rules that separate facilities on trains must be substantially equal for blacks and whites.

May. Alberta King's mother dies.

The King family moves into their own home on Boulevard.

June 25. As the result of a planned march on Washington, led by A. Philip Randolph, the Fair Employment Practices Committee is established to prevent discrimination in defense-related work.

December 7, Japan attacks Pearl Harbor, and the United States declares war on Japan the next day; the sole dissenting vote in Congress is cast by Rep. Jeannette Rankin, who had been one of 50 House members to vote against entry into World War I. The United States declares war on Germany a few days later.

1942

February 20. Roosevelt authorizes a program to move Japanese-Americans from the West Coast to inland internment camps; 120,000 will be forcibly relocated.

June. A group of black and white believers in direct, nonviolent action—including FOR members Bayard Rustin, George Houser, and Bernice Fisher—organize the Congress of Racial Equality (CORE) in Chicago, and they stage the first sit-in in a segregated restaurant in Chicago.

Peace activists form the Provisional Committee Toward a Democratic Peace to promote civil rights and a more equitable distribution of the costs of the war among U.S. citizens.

Fall. Martin Luther King, Jr., enters Booker T. Washington High School as a sophomore, skipping his freshman year.

December 2. The first nuclear chain reaction is achieved at the University of Chicago and will lead to the Manhattan Project to develop the nuclear bomb.

1943

October 19. Paul Robeson opens in the title role of *Othello*; it will run for 296 performances, setting a record for Shakespearean drama on Broadway.

November. AFSC leader E. Raymond Wilson and other East Coast Quakers form the Friends Committee on National Legislation as a Washington lobby for civil liberties, racial justice, relief and reconciliation.

1944

Martin Luther King, Jr., wins a speech contest with "The Negro and the Constitution" but encounters racism on the bus on the way home from Valdosta, Georgia.

Martin Luther King, Jr., enters Morehouse College. He spends the summer working in tobacco fields in Connecticut, his first time out of the South.

August 1. Adam Clayton Powell is elected the first black member of Congress from the East.

Birth of the Bebop school of music in New York City, with Charlie Parker, Dizzy Gillespie, Miles Davis, Max Roach, and Thelonius Monk.

1945

May 7. Germany surrenders.

June 26. Fifty nations attend the San Francisco meeting to found the United Nations. W. E. B. DuBois represents the NAACP at this event.

August 6, 9. The U.S. drops an atom bomb on Hiroshima, a few days later on Nagasaki.

September 2. Japan formally surrenders.

1946

March 5. In a speech in Fulton, Missouri, Prime Minister Winston Churchill remarks that "an iron curtain descended across the continent allowing 'police governments' to rule Eastern Europe."

September. The International Tribunal in Nuremberg, Germany, convicts 22 German leaders for war crimes.

September 23. Paul Robeson, spokesman for the American Crusade Against Lynching, a coalition of some 50 groups, leads a delegation to the White House and asks President Truman to establish a "definite legislative and educational program to end the disgrace of mob violence."

Martin Luther King, Jr., decides to become a minister.

1947

March 12. Ushering in the Cold War era, President Truman introduces the Truman Doctrine with a $400-million aid package for Greece and Turkey to aid their recovery from the war and prevent the spread of communism. Later in the month he will institute a loyalty program for government employees.

April 9. CORE and Fellowship of Reconciliation send the first Freedom Riders to the South to test the 1946 Supreme Court decision banning segregation in interstate bus travel. Leaders of the "Journey of Reconciliation" include Bayard Rustin and FOR activists George Houser and James Farmer.

April 11. Jackie Robinson joins the Brooklyn Dodgers, the first black player in major league baseball.

August 15. India gains its independence from England. Mahatma Gandhi's nonviolent campaigns have been central to the struggle for self-determination.

December 19. The Nobel Peace Prize is shared by the British Friends Service Council and the American Friends Service Committee.

Martin Luther King, Jr., is licensed to preach; assists his father at Ebenezer Baptist.

Ralph Ellison publishes *The Invisible Man*, which wins the National Book Award for Fiction.

1948

January 30. Mahatma Gandhi is assassinated.

February. Martin Luther King, Jr., is ordained into the Baptist ministry and accepts the invitation to serve as co-pastor at the Ebenezer Baptist Church.

April. The Emergency Committee of Atomic Scientists, led by Albert Einstein, warns that a policy of "armed peace in a two-bloc world" would mean "tremendous and steadily accelerating armaments expenditures over an indefinite period."

June. Martin Luther King, Jr., receives his bachelor's degree in sociology from Morehouse College.

June 26. Black labor leader A. Philip Randolph forms the League for Non-Violent Civil Disobedience Against Military Segregation. Eight months earlier, Bayard Rustin and journalist William Worthy had formed the Committee Against Discrimination in Military Training.

July 26. An executive order bars segregation in the U.S. armed forces and calls for an end to racial discrimination in federal employment.

August. In response to the Selective Service Act requiring all men between 18 and 25 to register for the armed forces, the Central Committee for Conscientious Objectors (CCCO) is founded, and will provide draft counseling services around the country.

September. Martin Luther King, Jr., enters Crozer Theological Seminary in Chester, Pennsylvania. After hearing Dr. A. J. Muste and Dr. Mordecai Johnson preach on the life and teachings of Mahatma Gandhi, he begins to study Gandhi seriously.

The Atlanta police force is integrated, but black officers will not be allowed to arrest white citizens until 1951.

1949

April 20. Paul Robeson and W. E. B. DuBois are among the delegates from 60 countries to the World Congress of Partisans of Peace in Paris. Robeson delivers a speech in which he says, "It is unthinkable that American Negroes would go to war on behalf of those who have oppressed us for generations . . . against a country [the Soviet Union] which in one generation has raised our people to full human dignity."

July 18. In an appearance before HUAC, Jackie Robinson attacks Robeson's statement. Subsequently, criticisms come from A. Philip

Randolph, Roy Wilkins, and Lester Granger of the Urban League.

August 24. Nine Western European nations, the United States, and Canada establish the North Atlantic Treaty Organization (NATO). In 1955, Eastern European nations will form a counterpart military alliance, the Warsaw Treaty Organization.

August 27. Many in the audience are injured by rock-throwers who disrupt a concert at Peekskill, New York, featuring Paul Robeson.

1950

March. W. .E. B. DuBois and others found the Peace Information Center, which circulates the Stockholm Peace Appeal to abolish the atom bomb and collects some two million signatures. In February 1951, a grand jury will indict the Peace Information Center and DuBois for "failure to register as an agent of a foreign principal," but in November, a judge will decide there is no substance to the charge.

June 30. President Truman sends U.S. ground troops to South Korea. The Korean War will last until 1953.

June 27. The United States sends 35 military advisers to South Vietnam and agrees to provide military and economic aid to the anticommunist government.

July 28. The State Department demands that Paul Robeson turn in his passport because his "travel abroad at this time would be contrary to the best interests of the United States."

September 22. Ralph Bunche wins the Nobel Peace Prize for his attempt to bring Arabs and Jews together when he was U.N. mediator in Palestine.

1951

June. Martin Luther King, Jr., graduates first in his class from Crozer Theological Seminary with a B.D. degree.

July 12. Governor Adlai Stevenson calls out the National Guard to quell rioting in Cicero, Illinois, where a mob of 3,500 attempts to prevent a black family from moving into the all-white city.

September. Martin Luther King, Jr., begins graduate studies in philosophy at Boston University and occasionally preaches at a church in the Roxbury section.

December 17. Paul Robeson presents a petition to the United Nations secretary-general, charging the United States with genocide against black Americans.

The government revokes W. E. B. Dubois's passport.

1952

November 1. The first hydrogen bomb is exploded at Eniwetok Atoll in the Pacific.

December 30. The Tuskegee Institute reports that 1952 was the first year in 71 years of tabulation in which there were no lynchings.

1953

March 26. President Eisenhower makes a commitment to aid France in its war in Indochina. In 1954, it will be announced that the United States is paying more than three-fourths of the war's costs.

June 18. Martin Luther King, Jr., and Coretta Scott are married in Marion, Alabama, with Martin Luther King, Sr., officiating.

August 4. The movement of black families into the Trumbull Park housing project in Chicago precipitates three years of rioting and will require the assignment of over 1,000 policemen to keep order.

1954

April 7. President Eisenhower supports foreign aid for France in Indochina, saying that without it, Southeast Asia would succumb to communism like a "falling row of dominoes."

April 22–June 17. Senator Joseph McCarthy leads televised hearings into alleged communist influence in the Army.

May 17. In the *Brown v. Board of Education* decision, the Supreme Court declares that separate-but-equal facilities are inherently unequal, overturning *Plessy v. Ferguson* (1896).

July 11. The White Citizens Council is founded in Indianola, Mississippi.

July 21. The Geneva agreement is signed by the Big Four countries, ending France's war in Indochina.

September 8. The Southeast Asian Treaty Organization (SEATO), a collective defense pact for the Pacific, is formed.

October 31. Martin Luther King, Jr., is installed by his father as the pastor of the Dexter Avenue Church in Montgomery, Alabama.

December 2. The Senate censures Senator Joseph McCarthy.

1955

February 12. The United States agrees to help train the South Vietnamese army.

March 10. President Eisenhower indicates that in the event of war, the United States would use nuclear weapons.

May 31. The Supreme Court orders "all deliberate speed" in integrating public schools.

June 5. Martin Luther King, Jr., receives a Ph.D. degree in systematic theology from Boston University.

August 28. Emmett Till, a black 14-year-old, is kidnapped by two white men in LeFlore County, Mississippi. It had been rumored that he had "whistled at a white woman." Four days later, his body, tied in barbed wire, will be recovered from the Tallahatchie River. An all-white jury will acquit the two men accused of the crime.

November 17. The Kings' first child, Yolanda Denise, is born in Montgomery.

December 1. Rosa Parks refuses to yield her seat to a white man, sparking the Montgomery bus boycott.

December 5. The Montgomery Improvement Association is formed, and Martin Luther King, Jr., is chosen to be its head.

December 10. The Montgomery Bus Company suspends service in black neighborhoods.

1956

January 30. A bomb is thrown on the porch of the Kings' home in Montgomery; no one is injured.

February 3. Autherine Lucy is admitted to the University of Alabama; after a riot on February 7, she will be suspended and, on February 29, expelled.

February 21. Dr. King is indicted with several others in the Montgomery bus boycott on the charge of being party to a conspiracy to hinder and prevent the operation of business without "just or legal cause."

March 12. A call for massive resistance to Supreme Court desegregation rulings is issued by 101 Southern members of Congress.

August 10. Dr. King speaks before the platform committee of the Democratic Party in Chicago.

November 13. The Supreme Court rules that Alabama's state and local laws requiring segregation on buses is unconstitutional.

December 21. The Montgomery bus boycott ends—281 days after it began.

December 25. The home of Rev. Fred Shuttlesworth, Birmingham protest leader, is destroyed by a dynamite bomb.

December 26. Birmingham blacks begin mass defiance of Jim Crow bus laws; 21 are arrested.

1957

January 10–11. The Southern Christian Leadership Conference (SCLC) is formed at the Ebenezer Baptist Church in Atlanta, and Dr. King is elected president in February.

February 18. *Time* puts Dr. King on its cover.

March 5. Ghana becomes independent, the first of over two dozen African nations to do so between 1957 and 1962. Coretta and Dr. King represent the United States at the independence celebration.

May 17. SCLC sponsors the Prayer Pilgrimage for Freedom in Washington, D.C., to celebrate the third anniversary of the Supreme Court's desegregation decision. A crowd of some 30,000, the biggest civil rights demonstration staged to date, hears Dr. King's speech, "Give Us the Ballot."

June. FOR's A. J. Muste and AFSC's Lawrence Scott form the Committee for Non-Violent Action (CNVA), whose members will engage in civil disobedience to protest nuclear testing.

June 13. Dr. King has a conference with Vice President Nixon about civil rights.

September 4. National Guardsmen, called out by Arkansas Governor Orval Faubus, bar nine black students from the all-white Central High School in Little Rock. On September 24, President Eisenhower will send in Federal troops to insure the black students' rights to attend the school, the first time federal troops are used to protect the rights of black citizens.

October 23. A second child, Martin Luther King III, is born to Dr. and Mrs. King.

November. SANE (National Committee for a Sane Nuclear Policy) is founded to call for an end to nuclear testing.

1958

February 12. Dr. King kicks off SCLC's Crusade for Citizenship Campaign to register black voters in the South.

June 23. Dr. King, along with Roy Wilkins of the NAACP, A. Philip Randolph, and Lester Granger of the Urban League, meet with President Eisenhower.

September 3. Dr. King is arrested in Montgomery on a charge of loitering. The fine is paid, over Dr. King's objections, by the Montgomery police commissioner.

September 17. Dr. King's first book, *Stride Toward Freedom: The Montgomery Story,* is published.

September 20. While autographing his recently published book in a Harlem department store, Dr. King is stabbed in the chest by a woman who will later be diagnosed as mentally unstable.

W. E. B. DuBois's passport is returned by order of the Supreme Court.

1959

February 3. Dr. and Mrs. King and L. D. Reddick leave for a month in India. They will retrace Gandhi's campaigns on an itinerary arranged by the American Friends Service Committee and meet with followers of Gandhi, including Prime Minister Jawaharlal Nehru.

March 11. *Raisin in the Sun,* by Lorraine Hansberry, the first play written by a black woman to reach Broadway, opens with Sidney Poitier and Claudia McNeil.

April. The first major student peace organization of the 1960s, the Student Peace Union (SPU), is founded in Chicago to work for the dismantling of the arms race and international militarism.

April 25. Charles Mack Parker is dragged from jail and lynched by a mob in Poplarville, Mississippi. This prompts novelist William Faulkner to advise blacks to "go slow now" in an article in *Look.*

W. E. B. DuBois challenges him to debate the question on the courthouse steps in Sumpter, Mississippi.

September 15–27. Soviet Premier Nikita Khrushchev pays an unprecedented visit to the United States, making a transcontinental tour.

Fall. James Lawson, first Southern Field Secretary for the Fellowship of Reconciliation, holds a workshop on nonviolence at Nashville's Vanderbilt University. His students—including Diane Nash, Marion Barry, John Lewis, and James Bevel—will stage sit-ins in an unsuccessful attempt to prod Nashville businessmen to desegregate voluntarily.

Their rules of conduct for demonstrations becomes a model for other protests in the South: "Don't strike back if cursed and abused . . . Show yourself courteous and friendly at all times . . . Report all serious incidents to your leader in a polite manner. Remember love and nonviolence."

November 29. Dr. King submits his resignation, effective at the end of January, as pastor of the Dexter Avenue Baptist Church in Montgomery.

January 24. Dr. King becomes co-pastor with Rev. Martin Luther King, Sr., of the Ebenezer Baptist Church in Atlanta.

February 1. The sit-in movement begins when four students from North Carolina A. and T. College refuse to move from a Woolworth lunch counter after they are denied service. By February 10, the movement will spread to 15 cities in five Southern states. By September 1961, more than 70,000 students—black and white—will have participated in the sit-ins, and Northern supporters will picket and boycott Woolworth's stores as well.

April 15. At a conference at Shaw University in Raleigh, North Carolina, called by SCLC and its executive director Ella Baker, the Student Nonviolent Coordinating Committee (SNCC) is founded to coordinate student protests. Keynote speakers are Dr. King and Rev. James Lawson, the author of SNCC's original statement of purpose. In the early 1950s, Lawson had gone to prison rather than serve in the military during the Korean War. Later, he spent three years as a missionary in India and studied Gandhi's use of nonviolence to achieve political change.

May 6. President Eisenhower signs a Civil Rights Act authorizing federal referees where there are patterns of discrimination against black voters.

June 10. Dr. King and A. Philip Randolph announce plans for picketing the Republican and Democratic National Conventions, and later in the summer there will be marches in Chicago and Los Angeles calling for "Freedom Now."

July 31. Elijah Muhammad, head of the Nation of Islam, popularly referred to as the Black Muslims, calls for the creation of a black state. Founded in Detroit in the 1930s and headquartered in Chicago, the NOI is the chief critic within the black community of integration and nonviolence.

August 7. Twenty black and white students stage a kneel-in demonstration in white churches in Atlanta.

August-September. The Emergency Relief Committee for Fayette and Haywood Counties was formed in Chicago to support black residents of the two Tennessee counties who were suffering reprisals for attempting to vote. Such support for civil rights activities in the South helped build home-grown civil rights movements in many Northern cities.

October 19. Dr. King is arrested at a sit-in at Rich's Department Store in Atlanta. Although the charge is dropped, he is subsequently transferred to the Reidsville State Prison for violation of his probation in a traffic case. At the behest of Martin Luther King, Sr., John and Robert Kennedy successfully press for his release.

December 11. Several thousand blacks hold two mass prayer meetings and march on Atlanta's business district to protest segregation and discrimination.

December 30. Two U.S. courts issue temporary injunctions to prevent some 700 black sharecroppers from being evicted from farms in Haywood and Fayette counties, reportedly because they had registered to vote.

January 30. A third child, Dexter Scott, is born to Dr. and Mrs. King in Atlanta.

February 6. In support of the sit-ins, CORE starts a jail-in movement in Rock Hill, South Carolina, when students refuse to pay fines and request jail sentences. SNCC urges a southwide "Jail, No Bail" campaign.

April. In the largest peace demonstration in a generation, SANE mobilizes 25,000 across the country in solidarity with a British "Ban the Bomb" march.

April 17. The CIA-supported Bay of Pigs invasion fails in its attempt to overthrow Fidel Castro's government in Cuba.

May 4. The Freedom Riders, whose goal is to integrate interstate buses, leave Washington, D.C. by Greyhound bus led by James Farmer of CORE.

May 14. A white mob burns a Freedom Rider bus outside Anniston, Alabama. Riders aboard a second bus are beaten by Klansmen in Birmingham.

May 17. Despite Attorney General Robert Kennedy's plea to activists to call off the Freedom Rides for fear that someone might be murdered, they are resumed. Coordinated by Diane Nash, ten students—eight blacks and two white—leave Nashville for Birmingham.

May 20. The Freedom Riders leave Birmingham after negotiations with Justice Department, state, and bus company officials. As they disembark in Montgomery, they are again beaten. To restore order, Attorney General Kennedy sends 400 U.S. marshals to Montgomery and obtains an injunction against the Ku Klux Klan.

May 21. Whites riot outside a church in Montgomery where Dr. King, James Farmer, and the Freedom Riders are meeting. The governor of Alabama declares martial law and sends 800 National Guardsmen to Montgomery.

May 23. Twelve Freedom Riders leave Montgomery and are imprisoned immediately upon arriving in Jackson, Mississippi, when they attempt to use white restrooms. During the following months, more than 300 protesters will be arrested in Jackson.

August 22. As the head of a SNCC voter registration drive, Bob Moses accompanies black residents of Amite County, Mississippi, to attempt to register. He is beaten by the sheriff's cousin and files assault and battery charges—probably the first time a black has brought charges against a white man in Mississippi since Reconstruction. Moses, who had been born in Harlem, came to SNCC after having received a master's degree in philosophy from Harvard.

November 1. As a result of Justice Department urging, the Interstate Commerce Commission issues a regulation prohibiting separate facilities for blacks and whites on buses and trains as well as in terminal accommodations.

November 1. SNCC field secretaries Charles Sherrod and Cordell Reagon lead a sit-in at the Albany, Georgia, bus station to test compliance with the ICC ruling. This is the first step in forming the Albany Movement.

December 11. The first two U.S. military companies arrive in South Vietnam, including 32 helicopters and 4,000 men.

December 16. Dr. King, along with 250 other demonstrators, is arrested after a prayer march to Albany City Hall. Two days later he will allow himself to be released on bail as part of a settlement with city officials that includes their compliance with the ICC ruling and the release of the other demonstrators.

December. Women Strike for Peace (WSP), founded earlier in the year, mobilizes 50,000 women in 60 cities to demonstrate against the arms race.

W. E. B. DuBois joins the Communist Part, moves to Ghana, and gives up his U.S. citizenship.

1962

February 2. Four black mothers are arrested for staging a sit-in at a Chicago elementary school, one of many demonstrations against de facto segregation, double shifts, and mobile classrooms.

February 14. President Kennedy says U.S. military advisers in Vietnam will fire if fired upon.

February 27. Dr. King is tried and convicted for leading the December march in Albany, Georgia.

June 11. Students for a Democratic Society (SDS) issues the Port Huron statement, written primarily by Tom Hayden, a member of SNCC, connecting the need to end the Cold War with the need for domestic reform.

July 27. Dr. King is arrested at a prayer vigil at the Albany City Hall. By August 1, almost 1,000 demonstrators will have been arrested in Albany protests.

August 11. Police close municipal parks and the library in Albany after integrated groups try to use them.

August 15. The Shady Grove Baptist Church in Leesburg, Georgia, is burned. Black churches are often the meeting places for civil rights workers, and in the next six weeks, eight black churches in Georgia will be destroyed by fire.

August 31. While attempting to register to vote, Fannie Lou Hamer, later a major leader of the civil rights movement, is arrested.

September 20. James Meredith makes his first attempt to enroll at the University of Mississippi. On October 1, he will be enrolled by Supreme Court order and escorted onto the campus by U.S. marshals. University students and adults from Oxford and nearby communities riot on the campus.

October 1. Edwin Walker, former major general in the U.S. Army who led the federal troops during the Little Rock integration crisis, is charged with inciting insurrection by calling for "volunteers" to oppose federal forces at the University of Mississippi.

October 16. Dr. King meets with President Kennedy at the White House for a one-hour conference on the state of civil rights.

October 22. President Kennedy orders a blockade of Cuba because Soviet missiles have been spotted there. On October 28, he and Khrushchev will reach an agreement to end the missile crisis that many thought would lead to nuclear war.

November 20. President Kennedy issues an executive order barring racial and religious discrimination in federally financed housing.

James Baldwin published *The Fire Next Time*, a work that captures the protest spirit of the 1960s.

Linus Pauling wins the Nobel Peace Prize.

1963

March 28. The fourth child of Dr. and Mrs. King, Bernice Albertine, is born.

April 3. Dr. King launches SCLC's Project "C" (for confrontation) to protest segregation of lunch counters and restrooms in downtown Birmingham.

April 12. Dr. King is arrested on Good Friday for defying a state court's injunction against protest marches. While confined over Easter weekend, he will write "Letter from a Birmingham Jail."

Easter Week. Pope John XXIII delivers his last encyclical, "Pacem in Terris," which sets forth the Catholic Church's position on the issues of disarmament, nuclear weapons, the United Nations, coexistence, racial equality, and human rights.

May 2–7. SCLC organizes the "children's crusade," recruiting elementary and high school students for its marches in Birmingham. Police Commissioner Eugene "Bull" Connor retaliates with police dogs, fire hoses, and mass arrests.

May 10. Dr. King and Rev. Fred Shuttlesworth announce that Birmingham's white leaders have agreed to a desegregation plan. That night King's motel is bombed, and blacks riot until dawn.

May 11. Malcolm X calls the Birmingham campaign "an exercise in futility," and of nonviolence he says, "There is no philosophy more befitting the white man's tactics for keeping his foot on the black man's neck."

May 20. The Supreme Court rules that Birmingham's segregation ordinances are unconstitutional.

May. CNVA begins the Quebec-Washington-Guantanomo Walk for Peace to link civil rights and peace issues. After spending two months in jail in the South, the marchers will continue to Miami, where the U.S. government will deny them permission to travel to Cuba.

June 11. Governor George Wallace tries to stop the court-ordered integration of the University of Alabama by "standing in the schoolhouse door" and personally refusing entrance to black students and Justice Department officials.

June 12. NAACP leader Medgar Evers is shot to death in his home in Jackson, Mississippi.

June 18. 3,000 students boycott Boston public schools in protest of de facto segregation.

August 27. W. E. B. DuBois dies in Accra, Ghana.

August 28. In the largest civil rights demonstration thus far, 250,000 people gather for the March on Washington for Jobs and Freedom Now. At the rally, Dr. King delivers his "I Have a Dream" speech on the steps of the Lincoln Memorial.

August 30. The FBI, in an internal memo, states that Dr. King was "the most dangerous Negro of the future in this Nation."

August. Catholic Workers picket the residence of the South Vietnamese observer to the United Nations in one of the first demonstrations against the Vietnam War.

September. Dr. King's book, *Strength to Love*, is published.

September 15. Four black girls die in the bombing of the Sixteenth Street Baptist Church in Birmingham.

October 7. FBI chief J. Edgar Hoover requests permission from Attorney General Robert Kennedy to install wiretaps in SCLC's New York office and in Dr. King's Atlanta home.

October 22. Some 225,000 students boycott Chicago public schools in a
Freedom Day demonstration demanding desegregated "quality
education." Many of the boycotting students attend Freedom
Schools in black churches and study black history.

November 2. South Vietnam's president Ngo Dinh Diem is assassinated; the United States had earlier withdrawn support for him.

November 22. President Kennedy is assassinated in Dallas, Texas.

December 22. In ill health, Paul Robeson returns to the United States
after an absence of five years and retires from public life.

U.S. troops in Vietnam total over 15,000 by the end of the year; aid to
South Vietnam is over $500 million.

1964

February 3. Some 464,000 black and Puerto Rican students boycott
New York City public schools. Their demand, as in Chicago, is
for "quality education."

April 26. The Mississippi Freedom Democratic Party (MFDP) is
founded in Jackson, and its development is a major project during Freedom Summer. The MFDP says it should represent the
state at the Democratic Convention in August because the majority of black voters have been unlawfully prevented from register-
ing with the regular Democratic Party. The challenge is not
successful, but the national Democratic Party will declare that at
the next convention, the Mississippi delegation should be integrated.

May-June. Dr. King joins other SCLC workers in demonstrations for
the integration of public accommodations in St. Augustine, Florida.

June. Dr. King's book, *Why We Can't Wait*, is published.

Summer. The Mississippi Summer Project is primarily a voter registration campaign, but it is also designed to focus national attention
on Mississippi's repressive racial relations. Black and white students from SNCC, CORE, SCLC, and NAACP work on the project under the direction of Bob Moses of SNCC.

June 10. The Senate votes to end a 75-day filibuster by Southern senators against the Civil Rights Act, which will be signed into law by
President Johnson on July 2. Dr. King will be present at the signing of the bill, which integrates public accommodations and pro-
hibits job discrimination by employers and unions.

June 21. Dr. King speaks at a civil rights rally at Chicago's Soldier Field.

July 18-23. Riots in Harlem, spawned mainly by charges of police brutality, spread to the Bedford-Stuyvesant section of Brooklyn.

August 4. Three Mississippi Summer Project workers—James Chaney,
Andrew Goodman, and Michael Schwerner—have been reported
missing on June 21. Their bodies are discovered buried under an
earthen dam near Philadelphia, Mississippi. Neshoba County

Sheriff Rainey and his deputy Cecil Price will be implicated in the murders. In the process of searching for the three, a number of black bodies are also pulled from Mississippi rivers.

August 7. The Vietnam War "officially" begins with the passage of the Tonkin Gulf resolution, giving the president power to take whatever measures are necessary "to prevent further aggression."

August 11. Congress approves the War on Poverty bill.

August. 200 radical pacifists conduct a silent vigil at the Democratic National Convention protesting U.S. policy in Vietnam.

September. Dr. King and Rev. Ralph Abernathy visit West Berlin at the invitation of Mayor Willy Brandt and then have an audience with Pope Paul VI at the Vatican.

September. At the invitation of Harry Belafonte, SNCC sends a delegation to Africa as the guests of the government of Guinea. The delegation includes James Forman, John Lewis, Bob and Dona Moses, Julian Bond, and Fannie Lou Hamer. Two of the delegation continue traveling in October and meet with Malcolm X, who has recently broken with the Nation of Islam.

November. In response to Dr. King's criticisms of Southern FBI agents' handling of civil rights cases, FBI chief J. Edgar Hoover on several public occasions calls King the "most notorious liar in the country."

November 20. Assistant FBI Director William Sullivan writes an anonymous hate letter to Dr. King and has it sent to him with excerpts from tapes made from wiretaps and bugs of King's office, home, and hotel rooms.

December 2–3. The Free Speech Movement at the University of California at Berkeley organizes a sit-in to protest the decision to ban fundraising for SNCC and CORE from campus.

December 10. Dr. King, at the age of 35, becomes the youngest recipient of the Nobel Peace Prize. He divides the $54,000 prize money among civil rights organizations.

December 14. Assistant FBI Director Sullivan notes in an internal memo that "the Bureau has not yet emerged victorious in its conflict with Martin Luther King."

December 19. At the first major antiwar demonstration, 1,500 people in New York City hear A. J. Muste, Norman Thomas, and A. Philip Randolph denounce the war.

1965

January 11. In a speech at Morehouse College, Dr. King condemns the war in Vietnam.

February 4. At the invitation of SNCC, Malcolm X addresses Selma demonstrators at Brown Chapel during the voting rights campaign. This is an indication of the growing influence of black nationalism among some groups within the civil rights movement.

February 7. President Johnson orders the first U.S. bombing of North Vietnam.

February 21. Malcolm X, the leader of the Organization of Afro–American Unity, is assassinated in Harlem.

March 7. "Bloody Sunday": a group of marchers from SCLC and SNCC, including John Lewis, are beaten while attempting to cross the Edmund Pettus Bridge on their planned march to Montgomery, Alabama, from Selma. The attackers are state highway patrolmen and sheriff's deputies.

March 8–9. The first U.S. combat troops in Vietnam land at Da Nang. Some 23,000 U.S. personnel are already in Vietnam as military advisers.

March 9. Unitarian minister James Reeb is beaten by four white segregationists in Selma and will die two days later.

March 16. Alice Herz, an 82-year-old widow who fled Nazism, sets herself afire at a busy Detroit intersection in protest against the war.

March 16. Black and white demonstrators are beaten by sheriff's deputies and police on horseback in Montgomery.

March 21–25. Dr. King leads 25,000 marchers from Selma to Montgomery. After the march, Viola Liuzzo, wife of a Detroit Teamsters Union business agent, is shot and killed while driving a carload of marchers back to Selma.

March 24. The first campus "teach-in" against the war is held at the University of Michigan in Ann Arbor.

April 17. In the first national demonstration against the war, thousands come to Washington for a march organized by SDS to call for immediate withdrawal from Vietnam. One of the speakers is Bob Moses of SNCC.

Summer. SCLC organizes SCOPE (Summer Community Organization and Political Education), a voter registration drive in over 100 Southern counties, recruiting student volunteers from the North, to press Congress to pass the voting rights bill.

June. Dr. King writes in the SCLC newsletter, "I'm not going to sit by and see the war escalate without saying something about it. It is worthless to talk about integrating if there is no world to integrate in. The war in Vietnam must be stopped."

July 2. At a civil rights rally in Petersburg, Virginia, Dr. King speaks out against the war and warns that unless the Johnson Administration finds a way to negotiate peace in Vietnam, he might mass his followers in teach-ins and peace rallies.

July 26. Dr. King leads a march of 20,000 in Chicago in the struggle to improve public schools.

July 28. President Johnson announces that there are 125,000 U.S. troops in South Vietnam and draft calls will be doubled.

August 6. President Johnson signs the Voting Rights Act, which sets up a system of Federal examiners and bans literacy tests and local poll taxes. As a result, black registered voters in eleven Southern states increase from 1.5 million to 3.5 million between August 1965 and 1970.

August 6–9. Led by Robert Moses of SNCC and pacifists Dave Dellinger and Staughton Lynd, the Assembly of Unrepresented People brings together the peace and civil rights movements. On the 9th, 360 are arrested when they march on Congress and declare peace with the Vietnamese people.

August 12. At a mass rally at SCLC's annual convention, Dr. King says that racial injustice, poverty, and the Vietnam War are all "inextricably bound together."

Roy Wilkins and Whitney Young ask King to be quiet about Vietnam for fear that he might wreck the Johnson administration support for civil rights. The administration tells King that he is not an expert on foreign affairs and knows only civil rights and should stick to that.

August 11–16. In Watts, the black ghetto of Los Angeles, an uprising sparked by rumors of police brutality and by general conditions of deprivation, leave 35 people dead. On the 17th, Dr. King tours Watts and calls rioting "the language of the unheard."

September. Dr. King confers with Arthur Goldberg, U.S. Ambassador to the United Nations, to press for a negotiated settlement to the war in Vietnam.

September. In announcing plans for his Chicago campaign, Dr. King says, "The nonviolent movement must be as much directed against the violence of poverty, which destroys the souls of people, as against the violence of segregation." He says that Chicago will be "the test case for the SCLC and for the freedom movement in the North . . . we will not be aided as much by the brutality of our opponents. Egypt still exists in Chicago but the Pharaohs are more sophisticated and subtle."

October 15–16. The largest of the nationwide events during the International Days of Protest against the war in Vietnam is the Fifth Avenue Peace Parade in New York.

November 2. Norman Morrison, secretary of a Friends Meeting in Baltimore, sets himself afire in front of the Pentagon. A week later, Catholic Worker Roger LaPorte will do the same in front of the United Nations.

December. SANE and two new organizations—the Catholic Peace Fellowship and Clergy and Laymen Concerned About Vietnam (CALCAV)—sponsor a rally of 25,000 in Washington.

1966

January 6. After months of discussion, SNCC issues a statement opposing the war in Vietnam and supporting draft resistance.

January 10. Julian Bond is denied his seat in the Georgia legislature because of his support for SNCC's opposition to the war. Dr. King speaks out in defense of Bond.

January. Dr. King and associates in SCLC meet in Chicago with the Coordinating Council of Community Organizations (CCCO) to plan the Chicago campaign "to bring about the unconditional surrender of forces dedicated to the creation and maintenance of slums."

January 27. Dr. King tours a poor Chicago neighborhood and says that those who feel that the civil rights struggle is over because there is a Civil Rights Act and a Voting Rights Act should look around Chicago, where a system of "internal colonialism" flourishes in the slums, "not unlike the exploitation of the Congo by Belgium."

March 25. The Supreme Court rules any poll tax unconstitutional.

March 25–26. The second International Days of Protest mobilize 50,000 in New York and 150,000 elsewhere in the country and abroad.

Spring. Dr. King tours Alabama to help elect black candidates. For the first time since Reconstruction, blacks vote in large numbers in the Alabama primary.

April 20. Six CNVA pacifists, including A. J. Muste, are deported from Saigon after an antiwar protest at the U.S. embassy.

May. Dr. King joins the National Committee of CALCAV.

May 16. At an antiwar rally in Washington, D.C., the Reverend William Sloane Coffin, Jr., chaplain of Yale University, reads a statement by Dr. King that says, "The pursuit of widened war has narrowed domestic welfare programs, making the poor, white and Negro, bear the heaviest burdens at the front and at home."

June 1. Dr. King attends a White House Conference on Civil Rights, in which he was not asked to speak or play any role. Because of his outspokenness on Vietnam, President Johnson opposed inviting him and is no longer speaking to him.

June 6. James Meredith is shot soon after beginning his 220-mile "March Against Fear" from Memphis, Tennessee, to Jackson, Mississippi.

June 16. At a rally in Greenwood, Mississippi, during the march that Meredith had begun, Stokely Carmichael and Willie Ricks use the term "black power." This slogan will become the focus of media attention and deepen the rift between the nonviolent philosophy of Dr. King and SCLC and the growing black nationalism and militancy of SNCC.

June 29. U.S. planes begin bombing Hanoi.

July 1–4. The CORE national convention votes to adopt a resolution endorsing the concept of "black power."

July 4–9. The NAACP disassociates itself from the "black power" doctrine, contending that it is little more than a counterproductive slogan with overtones of hostility toward whites.

July 10. 30,000 Chicagoans hear Dr. King urge them to stop patronizing banks and savings and loans that discriminate against them, to boycott businesses that do not hire minorities, and to use their vote to elect a more responsive mayor.

July 12–15. Three nights of rioting sweep Chicago's West Side in the wake of a police decision to shut off fire hydrants that had been opened illegally. Dr. King and his aids attempt to stop the violence, but two people are killed and 56 injured.

July 16. Dr. King meets with leaders of the gangs involved in the disturbances and urges them to renew the commitment to nonviolent civil disobedience they had made to him earlier.

August 5. Dr. King leads a march of 600 blacks and whites through the all-white neighborhood of Marquette Park to protest segregated housing. Counterdemonstrators with Confederate flags and Nazi insignia throw bricks and bottles, one of which hits Dr. King.

August. Coretta Scott King addresses an antiwar rally in California. She is active with the Women's International League for Peace and Freedom and has strongly encouraged her husband to speak out against the war in Vietnam.

August 26. Dr. King, Mayor Daley, and city, labor, and business leaders meet and reach the "Summit Agreement" to ease some of the obstacles to fair housing. In return, Dr. King drops plans for a march through Cicero, and soon closes the Chicago campaign.

September. SCLC establishes Operation Breadbasket in Chicago, which will eventually evolve into operation PUSH. Jesse Jackson heads the program to gain jobs for the disadvantaged through boycotts and selective buying.

October. The Black Panther Party is founded in Oakland, California by Bobby Seale and Huey Newton. It will develop a ten-point program for self-determination in black communities and work to prevent police harassment and brutality toward blacks.

November 8. Edward Brooke from Massachusetts is elected the first black U.S. senator in 85 years.

November 21. The National Organization for Women is founded.

Late December-early January. The first U.S. delegation to North Vietnam—four women, including civil rights activist Diane Nash—is invited by the Vietnam Women's Union and meets with Ho Chi Minh.

By December 31, 385,000 U.S. troops are stationed in South Vietnam in addition to 60,000 offshore and 33,000 in Thailand.

1967

January. Dr. King writes *Where Do We Go from Here?*

March 1. Adam Clayton Powell is denied his seat in Congress because of charges that he misused government funds. Overwhelmingly reelected in 1968, he will be seated, but fined $25,000 and stripped of his 22 years' seniority.

March 25. With Dr. Benjamin Spock, Dr. King leads an antiwar march in Chicago. At the rally following it, he says, "We must spread the propaganda of peace. We must combine the fervor of the civil rights movement with the peace movement."

March 30. The directors of SCLC unanimously condemn the war as "morally and politically unjust" and pledge to "do everything in our power" to end it. They say they can not "tell Americans to practice nonviolence at home while our nation is practicing the very essence of violence abroad."

April 4. Dr. King speaks against the war at a rally at Riverside Church in New York City. The event is sponsored by Clergy and Laymen Concerned About Vietnam; on April 11, he will become co-chair of the organization.

April 15. Dr. King, along with Dr. Benjamin Spock, Harry Belafonte, Pete Seeger, Stokely Carmichael, and Floyd McKissick, lead a march of 200,000 to the United Nations in an antiwar rally sponsored by the Spring Mobilization Committee, of which James Bevel of SCLC is the executive director.

April 19. J. Edgar Hoover sends a memo to President Johnson's personal secretary saying, "Based on King's recent activities and public utterances, it is clear he is an instrument in the hands of subversive forces seeking to undermine our nation."

April. The NAACP passes a resolution saying, "To attempt to merge the civil rights movement with the peace movement, or to assume that one is dependent upon the other, is, in our judgment, a serious tactical mistake."

Early May. Dr. King announces plans for Vietnam Summer, a campaign patterned after the Mississippi Summer Project to "defeat Lyndon Johnson and his war."

June. Heavyweight champion Muhammed Ali is convicted for refusing to be inducted into the Army after having been denied conscientious objector status. Boxing authorities immediately strip him of his title.

Spring. More than a dozen SNCC workers who had been drafted have decided to refuse induction, and Cleveland Sellers is indicted by a federal grand jury for his refusal.

June. Army doctor Howard Levy is tried for refusing to train Green Berets, based on the Nuremberg Doctrine of individual complicity for war crimes.

June 5. The Supreme Court upholds the conviction of Dr. King and seven colleagues for demonstrating in Birmingham. In late October they will serve five-day jail terms—the 19th time that Dr. King has been behind bars.

July 12–17. Twenty-three people die and 725 are injured in protests against racism in Newark, New Jersey. During the next week, 43 people will die and 324 will be injured in Detroit's worst outbreak of violence in the century.

248

August 25–28. The National Welfare Rights Organization (NWRO) holds its founding convention in Washington, D.C. Its executive director, George Wiley, had been associate national director of CORE.

September. The National Conference for New Politics unsuccessfully attempts to build an effective electoral force combining the black rage that erupted in the summer's riots with white radical militancy.

October 2. Thurgood Marshall is sworn in as the first black U.S. Supreme Court Justice.

October 16–22. The first nationwide draft card turn-in takes place during "Stop the Draft" week; 1,500 cards are returned to the government.

October 21–22. The National Mobilization Committee to End the War in Vietnam brings 100,000 to Washington for the "March on the Pentagon to Confront the Warmakers"; 700 will be arrested.

November. Senator Eugene McCarthy of Minnesota announces his decision to run as a peace candidate against President Johnson.

November 7. Carl Stokes is elected the first black mayor of Cleveland, Ohio, and Richard Hatcher, the first black mayor of Gary, Indiana.

November 11–12. Over 500 trade unionists meet in Chicago for the National Labor Leadership Assembly for Peace and break with AFL-CIO president George Meany's pro-war position. Dr. King, one of the speakers, says, "Military adventures must stultify domestic progress to insure the certainty of military success. This is the reason the poor, and particularly Negroes, have a double stake in peace and international harmony."

November 27. Dr. King announces the formation by SCLC of the Poor People's Campaign, with the aim of representing the problems of poor blacks and whites.

Vietnam Veterans Against the War (VVAW) is founded.

By December, 475,000 U.S. troops are in South Vietnam, and all of North Vietnam is being bombed.

1968

January 15. Coretta Scott King participates in the Jeannette Rankin Brigade, led by and named for the U.S. Congresswoman who voted against U.S. entry into both World Wars.

January 30. North Vietnam launches the Tet offensive, attacking Saigon and 30 provincial capitals in a show of strength that convinces many that the United States will not easily win the war.

February 5–6. Dr. King participates in CALCAV's second Washington mobilization, which includes meetings with senators and a prayer vigil at Arlington Cemetery.

February 29. The Kerner Commission report on civil disorders is released and identifies the major cause of rioting as the existence of two separate societies—"one black, one white, separate and unequal."

March 4. The FBI launches its counterintelligence program, COINTELPRO, against what it calls "black nationalist hate groups," including the SCLC.

March 16. U.S. troops massacre 500 unarmed villagers in My Lai. In the fall of 1969, Lt. William Calley will be charged for the crime.

March 28. Dr. King leads 6,000 protesters on a march through downtown Memphis in support of the striking garbage collectors. The march becomes disorderly—stores are looted and a 16-year-old is killed—and there is some concern that there are provocateurs among the marchers.

March 31. President Johnson curbs the bombing of North Vietnam and announces he will not seek reelection.

April 3. Dr. King delivers his last speech, "I've Been to the Mountaintop," at the Memphis Masonic Temple.

April 4. While talking to Ralph Abernathy, Jesse Jackson, and Ben Branch, Dr. King is assassinated by James Earl Ray as he stands on the balcony of his second-floor room in the Lorraine Motel in Memphis. Ray escapes a police dragnet and flees the country; he will be extradited from London. As the news of Dr. King's assassination spreads, there will be riots in 125 cities across the United States.

April 23. Students at Columbia University occupy five buildings to protest university ties to the Pentagon and plans to tear down property in an adjacent black neighborhood to build a gym.

April 27. During the third International Day of Protest, Coretta Scott King speaks at a rally in Central Park in her late husband's place.

May 10. Peace talks begin in Paris between the United States and North Vietnam.

May 13. With Ralph Abernathy, whom King had chosen as his successor, heading the SCLC, the Poor People's march and rally is held in Washington, D.C., and construction starts on Resurrection City.

May 17. Sparking a series of raids on draft boards, nine Catholic peace activists, including Daniel and Philip Berrigan, use homemade napalm to burn draft files in Catonsville, Maryland.

June 5. Presidential candidate Robert Kennedy is shot in Los Angeles and will die the next day.

July 11. The American Indian Movement is founded.

August 28. Hundreds are arrested in Chicago in what will later be called "police riots" during the Democratic National Convention.

October 31. All bombing of North Vietnam is halted.

1969

January. The Chicago 7, including Dave Dellinger, Tom Hayden, and Black Panther Bobby Seale, are indicted for conspiring to cause the "police riot" during the Democratic Convention.

July 21. A. D. King is drowned in his swimming pool.

August 15. 300,000 arrive at the Woodstock festival in upstate New York for "three days of peace and music."

October 15. Two million people across the country participate in Vietnam Moratorium Day. Rev. William Sloane Coffin reports that it was wonderful to hear New Haven's mayor "make the point for which Martin Luther King in 1967 had been so roundly denounced by other civil rights leaders and *The New York Times;* namely, that the war abroad was a war against the poor at home."

November 3. President Nixon announces his Vietnamization policy: phased withdrawal of U.S. troops coupled with increased support for South Vietnamese forces and reduction of draft calls, both contingent on a halt of antiwar protests.

November 13–15. 350,000 come to San Francisco and half a million to Washington for demonstrations against the war.

1970

April 30. President Nixon announces the invasion of Cambodia.

May 4. Four students at Kent State are killed by National Guardsmen during a protest of the Cambodia invasion. Nearly 470 colleges go on strike or close in protest. On May 14, two students at Jackson State College in Mississippi will be killed when police open fire on their dormitory.

May 9. Coretta Scott King speaks to 100,000 at the Spring Peace March in Washington, D.C.

October 13. After two months as a fugitive, Angela Davis is arrested by the FBI in New York City, having been charged by the State of California with kidnapping, conspiracy, and murder at a shootout at the Marin County Courthouse. In February 1972, after an international defense campaign, she will be released on bail, and on June 4, 1972, found not guilty on all charges.

1971

April 24. Opening more than a week of demonstrations in Washington, Coretta Scott King and Ralph Abernathy speak at a peace rally. On April 30, VVAW members throw their war medals on the Capital steps. The climax of the Mayday demonstrations is the arrest on May 3 of some 14,000 people; all the arrests will be declared unconstitutional.

June 13. Revealing the history of U.S. involvement in Indochina, *The New York Times* begins publishing the classified Pentagon Papers.

August 3. George Jackson, a prison rights leader and author of *Soledad Brother*, is shot in the back by prison guards at San Quentin.

1972

January. U.S troop strength in Vietnam is now 69,000.

March 22. The U.S. Senate sends the Equal Rights Amendment to the states for ratification.

March 30. The United States renews bombing raids over North Vietnam, after a suspension of almost three years.

July. At the Democratic National Convention, George McGovern is nominated for president and will campaign for immediate and complete withdrawal of U.S. troops.

December 18. President Nixon authorizes the Christmas bombing of Hanoi.

1973

January 27. The United States and North Vietnam sign a peace treaty ending direct U.S. intervention in Vietnam, but the United States will continue to fund the Saigon dictatorship.

June. A Senate committee, headed by Sam Irvin, begins to investigate allegations of the administration's Watergate coverup.

October 16. Henry Kissinger wins the Nobel Peace Prize for his role in the Paris peace treaty. North Vietnamese negotiator Le Duc Tho refuses to share it with him until peace is established in his country.

1974

June 30. Alberta King is shot to death during a service at the Ebenezer Baptist Church by the mentally deranged Marcus Chenault.

July 27. The House Judiciary Committee votes to impeach President Nixon. He will resign on August 9.

1975

April 30. The last 1,000 Americans leave South Vietnam, ending over two decades of U.S. military involvement. The war cost the United States 56,666 lives; it lasts 14 years cost $141 billion. Over 1,250,000 Vietnamese died.

May 11. Thousands of antiwar activists gather in Central Park to celebrate the end of the war.

August 1. Martin Luther King, Sr., retires as pastor of the Ebenezer Baptist Church.

Fall. Martin Luther King, Sr., is the first black to address a joint session of the Alabama state legislature.

1976

January 23. After a long illness, Paul Robeson dies in Philadelphia.

Alone among major black leaders, A. Philip Randolph attends his funeral in Harlem.

February. The Wilmington Ten, eight of whom are high school students active in a school boycott, enter prison on framed-up charges of arson. The leader of the group is Rev. Ben Chavis, a field organizer for the United Church of Christ Commission for Racial Justice. After the "witnesses" recant and admit they had been bribed, the Ten will finally be released from prison.

Summer. Martin Luther King, Sr., delivers the closing benediction at the Democratic National Convention in New York City.

1977

January 27. President Carter unconditionally pardons almost all Vietnam War draft resisters.

1978

May 26. 15,000 demonstrate in New York City in support of the first United Nations Special Session on Disarmament.

June 28. The Supreme Court votes not to allow a firm quota system in affirmative action programs intended to remedy past job discrimination.

September 6. The House Select Committee on Assassinations opens hearings into the assassinations of President Kennedy and Martin Luther King, Jr. It will conclude conspiracies were likely in both cases, but with no hard evidence.

1979

April. The Congressional Black Caucus introduces the first of its annual alternative budgets that would cut defense spending and restore funds to social programs.

1981

February 23. The State Department issues a white paper defending U.S. intervention in El Salvador.

June 18. Congress approves a 25-year extension of the Voting Rights Act.

October 2. President Reagan announces a five-point plan for strengthening defense, including building B-1 bombers, MX missiles, and the neutron bomb.

1982

June 12. One million people rally in Central Park in support of the United Nations Second Special Session on Disarmament.

August 17. Enten Eller becomes the first draft resister since the Vietnam War to be convicted.

November. The Nuclear Freeze, a proposal for a U.S.-Soviet ban on testing, production, and deployment of nuclear weapons, appears on ballots across the country.

November 13. The memorial to Vietnam veterans is dedicated in Washington, D.C.

1983

April 12. Harold Washington is elected mayor of Chicago. The number of black mayors in the United States has grown from 29 in 1968 to 109 at the end of 1982.

August 27. A coalition of civil rights, peace, and labor groups brings together 250,000 people for the 20th anniversary March on Washington for Jobs, Peace and Freedom.

September 1. President Reagan orders 2,000 Marines into the waters just off Beirut, Lebanon.

October 31. International scientists meet to discuss "nuclear winter" and other consequences of a nuclear war.

November 14. The first U.S. cruise missile is deployed at Greenham Common, England. As a result, the Soviet Union will withdraw from Geneva talks on intermediate-range missiles.

November 2. Congress votes to make Martin Luther King, Jr.'s birthday a national holiday.

1984

May 7. Vietnam veterans win an out-of-court settlement with seven chemical companies that produced the cancer-causing Agent Orange defoliant used in Vietnam.

November 11. Martin Luther King, Sr., dies of a heart attack in Atlanta.

December. A broad coalition of anti-apartheid and peace activists and trade unionists begin regular demonstrations outside South African consulates and embassies around the country. In the spring of 1985, students on several campuses will call for their schools to divest themselves of stock in businesses that have ties to South Africa.

1985

March. Sanctuary workers Jack Elder and Stacey Lynn Merkt are convicted on federal charges of "conspiracy to smuggle illegal aliens." Since it began in 1982, the sanctuary movement in support of political exiles from Central America has grown to 50,000 participants in over 200 churches nationwide.

April 19–22. 75,000 in Washington, 60,000 in San Francisco, and thousands of others in Los Angeles, Seattle, Denver, and Houston call for an end to intervention in Central America and elsewhere, a reordering of federal priorities to meet human needs, a reversal of the arms race, and an end to racism at home and support of apartheid in South Africa.

July 13. The 17-hour Anglo-American concert, "Live Aid," raises an estimated $70 million for the starving people of Africa.

August 6. The Soviet Union begins a six-month unilateral nuclear test moratorium, inviting the United States to join them.

November 19–20. Soviet leader Gorbachev meets with President Reagan at a summit conference in Geneva.

1986

January 20. The first observation of Martin Luther King, Jr.'s birthday as a national holiday.

Select Bibliography

Writings of Dr. Martin Luther King, Jr.

Chaos or Community? London: Hodder & Stoughton, 1968. Orig. pub. as *Where Do We Go From Here: Chaos or Community?*

A Martin Luther King Treasury. Photos by Roland Mitchell. Yonkers, NY: Educational Heritage, 1964.

Strength to Love. New York: Harper & Row, 1963.

Stride Toward Freedom: The Montgomery Story. New York: Harper & Row, 1968.

The Trumpet of Conscience. New York: Harper & Row, 1967.

Why We Can't Wait. New York: Harper & Row, 1964.

Biographies and Other Analysis

Ansbro, John J. *Martin Luther King, Jr.: The Making of a Mind.*

Bennett, Lerone, Jr. *What Manner of Man; A Biography of Martin Luther King, Jr.* With an intro. by Benjamin E. Mays. Chicago: Johnson Pub. Co., 1964.

Boyd, Malcolm. *You Can't Kill the Dream. Reflections.* Photos comp. by Bruce Roberts. Richmond, Va.: John Knox Press, 1968.

Davis, Lenwood G. *I Have a Dream; The Life and Times of Martin Luther King, Jr.* Westport, Conn.: Greenwood Press, Inc., 1973.

Garrow, David J. *The FBI and Martin Luther King, Jr.: From "Solo" to Memphis.* New York: W. W. Norton, 1981.

Hanigan, James P. *Martin Luther King, Jr. and the Foundations of Nonviolence.* Lanham, Md.: University Press of America, 1964.

King, Coretta. *My Life with Martin Luther King, Jr.* New York: Holt, Rinehard and Winston, 1969.

King, Martin Luther King, Sr., with Clayton Riley. *Daddy King: An Autobiography.* New York: William Morrow and Company, 1980.

Lewis, David L. *King. A Critical Biography.* New York: Praeger, 1970.

Lokos, Lionel. *House Divided: The Life and Legacy of Martin Luther King.* New Rochelle, NY: Arlington House, 1968.

Lincoln, Eric., ed. *Martin Luther King, Jr.: A Profile.* Rev. ed. New York: Hill and Wang, 1984.

McKissack, Patricia. *Martin Luther King, Jr.: A Man to Remember.* Chicago: Children's Press, 1984.

Miller, William Robert. *Martin Luther King, Jr.: His Life, Martyrdom, and Meaning for the World.* New York: Weybright and Talley, 1968.

Oates, Stephen B. *Let the Trumpet Sound. The Life of Martin Luther King, Jr.* New York: Harper & Row, 1982.

Reddick, Lawrence Dunbar. *Crusader Without Violence.* New York: Harper, 1959.

Smith, Ervin. *The Ethics of Martin Luther King, Jr.* New York: E. Mellen Press, 1981.

Smith, Kenneth L. and Ira G. Zepp, Jr. *Search for the Beloved Community: The Thinking of Martin Luther King, Jr.* Valley Forge, Pa.: Judson Press, 1974.

Walton, Hanes. *The Political Philosophy of Martin Luther King, Jr.* With an Intro. by Samuel DuBois Cook. Westport, Conn.: Greenwood Pub. Corp., 1971.

Wofford, Harris. *Of Kennedys and Kings: Making Sense of the Sixties.* New York: Farrar, Straus & Giroux, 1980.

Periodic Literature

Fairclough, Adam. "Martin Luther King, American Preacher," *Esquire* 100 (December 1983): 306–308, 311–312.

Wise, David. "The Campaign to Destroy Martin Luther King," *New York Review of Books* 13 (November 11, 1976): 38–41.

Warren, Robert Penn. "A Dearth of Heroes," *American Heritage* 23 (October 1972): 4–7, 95–99.